Building
Resemblance

BUILDING RESEMBLANCE

❧ ❧ ❧ ❧ ❧

*Analogical Imagery in
the Early French Renaissance*

❧ ❧ ❧ ❧ ❧

MICHAEL RANDALL

THE JOHNS HOPKINS UNIVERSITY PRESS
Baltimore and London

© 1996 The Johns Hopkins University Press
All rights reserved. Published 1996
Printed in the United States of America
on acid-free recycled paper
05 04 03 02 01 00 99 98 97 96   5 4 3 2 1

The Johns Hopkins University Press
2715 North Charles Street
Baltimore, Maryland 21218-4319
The Johns Hopkins Press Ltd., London

ISBN 0-8018-5298-6

Library of Congress Cataloging-in-Publication Data
will be found at the end of this book.

A catalog record for this book is available from
the British Library.

Frontispiece: From a Book of Hours made for Mary
of Burgundy (Austrian National Library, Cod. 1857,
fol. 14v.)

For Alice

Contents

✢   ✢   ✢

Acknowledgments

❖   ❖   ❖

This work was very much a communal effort. I owe much to all who read the manuscript in whole or in part and who proferred advice. I would like to thank François Rigolot, who directed this project as a Ph.D. dissertation at Princeton University. I want also to thank Ullrich Langer, François Cornilliat, and Jelle Koopmans for giving generously of their time and expertise by reading large portions of the manuscript. I have depended on the advice of other readers, such as Gérard Defaux, Simone Perrier, Jan Miernowski, and Karl Uitti, who have also read parts of the manuscript over the years.

I would like to acknowledge the various institutions that have helped bring this study to publication. First of all, I am very pleased to acknowledge Brandeis University for its support. I would also like to thank Emory University for having accorded me a Faculty Development Award, which helped finance some of the basic research. Portions of chapter 2 have appeared in "Reversed Analogy in Jean Molinet's *Chappellet des dames,*" *Literary Nominalism and the Theory of Rereading: A New Research Paradigm,* edited by Richard Utz (Mellen Press, 1995), and portions of chapter 3 have appeared in an article entitled "L'Etymologie rhétorique dans *Le Chappellet des dames* de Jean Molinet," in *Le Moyen Français* 34 (1994): 135–44. I thank both of these publishers for the right to use this material here. In the chapters dealing with Rabelais, I have used Donald Frame's translation, *The Complete Works of François Rabelais* (University of California Press, 1991), as the basis for my own adaptation.

Without the help and encouragement of friends, this book would never have seen the light of day. Thanks then to Anthony Di Battista, Josué Harari, Louis Miller, Isabelle Lorenz, and the many others who have provided the necessary Pantagruelian support during its writing. I owe a special debt of gratitude to Alice Jarrard, who played a crucial role, both editorially and psychologically, during the writing of this study. All mistakes and oversights are my own. A final word of thanks to my copy editor, Diane Hammond, to Julie McCarthy, senior production editor, and to Eric Halpern, former editor in chief at the Johns Hopkins University Press.

Introduction

❧   ❧   ❧

Resemblance has been the key term in much contemporary understanding of the sixteenth century. Human beings in the sixteenth century are understood to have construed their world through a system of likeness; the world itself could be read like an enormous book whose words were comprehensible to those properly trained in its language. The signature of the divine was hidden in the folds of contingent existence—in plants, in the palm of the hand, in words, and in stones. Undoubtedly, the occult philosophy of Henry Cornelius Agrippa, the alchemy of Paracelsus, and the Neoplatonism of Marsilio Ficino all relied, in different ways, on the the ability of the human mind to understand the relationship of likeness that existed between Heaven and Earth.

There was a worm, nonetheless, in this shiny paradigm: difference curled its way between Heaven and Earth, eating away the connection of absolute and contingent. Just as resemblance made it possible to understand the relationship of Heaven and Earth, difference often made it virtually impossible for a human being to understand the heavens. The apple (*malum*) was simply bad (*malum*), and any effort to connect the apple to badness through the similarity of its linguistic representation was doomed to failure.

Resemblance and difference were in constant flux in literary texts from the late fifteenth century through the mid-sixteenth century in France and in Burgundy. The paradigm of similarity, as described by Michel Foucault in *Les Mots et les choses*, did hover in the background of many literary texts from the period: the invisible and absolute yet secret structure of the universe lay behind the appearance of the visible and contingent.[1] Resemblance between the visible and the invisible connected the contingent to the absolute: the word resembled the thing it represented, the imperfect human being resembled the perfect divine of which he or she was a part,

I

and the stone or plant resembled the element or occult force that gave it medicinal or magical powers.

Yet, as other critics such as Jean Paris show, the modernity of the Renaissance, or at least of Rabelais, was due to the ability to distinguish between the contingent and the absolute.[2] The visible and contingent just as often as not proved itself not only the means toward understanding but also the end. Literary works show that even if the cultural imaginary of the sixteenth century, or at least a good part of it, was dominated by the paradigm of resemblance, the epistemology expressed implicitly in many of the texts of the period is based on a paradigm of difference. The confusing and often bewildering mix of resemblance and difference in literature of the early Renaissance makes for some of the most colorful and sometimes outlandish imagery in French literature. The construction of these images is sometimes as confusing and bewildering as the image itself.

The corpus of this study is composed of the verse and prose works of three writers whose careers span the final years of the "waning of the Middle Ages" and the early years of the Renaissance: Jean Molinet, the official historiographer at the court of Burgundy from 1475 until 1507; Jean Lemaire de Belges, who followed Molinet as historiographer at the court of Burgundy from 1507 until 1512; and François Rabelais, the author of *Pantagruel* (1532), *Gargantua* (1534), the *Tiers Livre* (1546), and the *Quart Livre* (1552).[3]

Rabelais is, of course, easily recognized as a leading figure in the French Renaissance. Molinet and Lemaire, much less well known, are often characterized as *rhétoriqueur* poets, a title often given to those writers working in the courts of Burgundy and France at the end of the fifteenth and the beginning of the sixteenth centuries.[4] The term *grand rhétoriqueur*, a product of the nineteenth century, serves as a convenient label for such poets as Molinet, Lemaire, Meschinot, Cretin, and Robertet, poets who traditionally have been considered minor.[5] The problem with this term, however, other than its decidedly pejorative flavor, is that it makes for a group of sometimes very disparate writers. This study proposes to abandon the term *rhétoriqueur* as it is commonly applied to this group of writers and to study Molinet and Lemaire as writers who reacted differently to their common heritage. Although the question of complicated rhyme schemes and elaborate word games is alluded to, as it must be in a study devoted to these writers, it is superseded by an analysis of analogical imagery used to connect the imperfect to the perfect and the contingent to the absolute.

The primary question that this study asks concerns the literary representation of resemblance in analogical images. To what extent do these writers represent a world in which resemblance holds the world together? Analogical images that claim to reveal the universal or the divine through an imperfect or contingent sign appear with great regularity in the works of Molinet, Lemaire, and Rabelais. And yet often these images take on odd shapes and sometimes even seem to reverse the ordering of imperfect and perfect, so that the "prose du monde" becomes either self-referential, pointing not at some invisible and ideal but rather at itself as form, or political, and pointing to some earthly monarch.

The development of analogical imagery studied in this book is divided into three periods, corresponding to the literary careers of Molinet, Lemaire, and Rabelais. The works of these authors demonstrate how the notion of resemblance was very fluid in the late fifteenth and early sixteenth centuries and how the often uneasy balance between resemblance and difference in this period helped create literary images that continue to intrigue and confound readers even today.

The prose and poetry of Jean Molinet is characterized by a highly tensive poetics of likeness and difference. In much of Molinet's poetics, the human mind cannot identify any likeness between the divine and the imperfect through reason, and yet images that appear to connect the imperfect to the perfect through analogical resemblance do appear throughout Molinet's poems and prose. Often, however, these images take on unusual and highly complex shapes. In poems like the *Chappellet des dames* (1478), the poet creates connections between imperfect and perfect, between contingent and absolute, in order to attain a likeness between things or persons in the real world and some hidden but perfect ideal or property. Yet these works end up revealing far less about the invisible perfect they are supposed to expose than they do about the very visible and highly imperfect term of the comparison. Works like the *Chappellet des dames* are grounded in the paradigm of difference even when they are motivated by a desire for resemblance.

The only real likeness in Molinet's poetics is an internal and incomprehensible one. To attain any likeness between contingent and absolute, the human being in Molinet's literary world must turn inward to create an interior likeness between human and God, as happens in *Le Roman de la Rose moralisé* (1500). In this work, which spiritualizes the carnal love of the *Romance of the Rose*, the Lover attempts to overcome his difference from the perfect divine through an act of affective contemplation. Love rather than reason becomes the way to God. Yet this likeness ends up being as problematic as the conventional likeness of the *Chappellet des dames,* since it is incomprehensible. Images depicting likeness in this work cannot finally refer to that which they claim to represent, because the author clearly places understanding of the divine beyond human reason. The images in the *Roman de la Rose moralisé,* like those in the *Chappellet des dames,* end up turning in on themselves, becoming ornate decorations that proliferate like flamboyant tracery across the face of a fifteenth-century transept.[6]

Molinet's troubled images can be understood in relation to the epistemological context of the late fifteenth century. The late Middle Ages was marked by a critique of scholastic realism which insisted on the singularity of knowledge. Where the scholastic realism of Thomas Aquinas had created a synthesis of faith and reason that allowed the devout Christian to understand through reason what he knew through faith, the fourteenth and fifteenth centuries were marked by a critique that emphasized the individual and intuitive nature of knowledge of the divine.[7] William of Ockham's nominalist critique of realist metaphysics insisted on the singularity of knowledge: at the base of all abstract knowledge lay a singular and intuitive understanding of an individual phenomenon. Things were either singular or they were not, and all the great universals that had held the universe together in realist metaphysics became purely mental structures.[8] The nominalists effectively conventionalized the connections that had held the universe together like tendons to bones in realist metaphysics.[9] The various elements of the world did not participate in some great chain of being that connected the smallest bit of dust to that which is most high and holy. All understanding was based on the singular, and since human reason was imperfect, it could never have a one-to-one understanding of the perfection of God. Human reason was simply incapable of understanding the divine.

Parallel to this nominalistic critique of scholastic realism, the late Middle Ages was also marked by a notable development of the mystical theology that had long played an important part in medieval thought but that had been held in abeyance by scholasticism. In Germany and the Low Countries in the fourteenth and fifteenth centuries, an essentialist and theocentric form of mysticism developed that was heavily influenced by Meister Eckhart.[10] In France, another form of mysticism developed, which was eclectic in theological orientation. It emphasized the power of the will and of love in effecting the return to God. It was also much less essentialistic in its view of mystical union and believed that a human being did not lose his or her essential being in that of the divinity.[11] Perhaps the most famous of these French mystics was Jean Gerson, who was the chancellor of the University of Paris from 1395 until his death in 1429. Gerson's mystical theology represents a curious synthesis of nominalist epistemology and mystical return to God. Gerson emphasizes the limits of human understanding of the divine and turns to the mystical tradition in order to effect a return to God. This combination represents, as the historian of religion Heiko Oberman explains, a "mystical marriage" of nominalism and affective theology.[12]

The poetry and prose of Jean Molinet reflect the often confusing epistemology of his time. Poems like the *Chappellet des dames*, which features a comparison of Mary of Burgundy and the Virgin Mary, effectively conventionalize the analogical connections between the perfect divine and imperfect human. Instead of having the minor term of the analogy explain the glory of the major term, this analogy reverses the ordering of perfect and imperfect and makes the perfect term explain the minor. The analogical symbol in poems like this becomes a purely conventional sign that can be manipulated at will. Although it depends on the notion of participation and resemblance in order to have meaning, it is also grounded in difference and singularity. The contingency of human existence allows the poet to play with and create odd images that seem to reflect a metaphysical system of resemblance when in fact they bear witness to the demise of analogical understanding. This poem is marked by a series of analogical symbols that ultimately do not connect the contingent sign to the divine and absolute. Rather, just the opposite happens, and the absolute and divine is used to illuminate and glorify the contingent and imperfect.

Molinet's *Roman de la Rose moralisé*, which offers a spiritual interpretation of the carnal love of the *Romance of the Rose*, turns inward to an internal and arational experience of Jesus Christ through affective contemplation, much like that described by Jean Gerson. The *Roman de la Rose moralisé* is marked by a contrast between an often humorous critique of those human beings who believe they can have a rational understanding of the design of God's universe through external resemblances and a very serious use of affective contemplation to come to the spiritualized rose, Jesus Christ. Reason is satanized in this work when it is used to understand the divine, whereas the arational and penitential contemplation of Christ's stigmata allows the Spiritual Lover to come to Christ. The paradigm of resemblance is at the heart of this work, since it consists of an extensive effort to show how the carnal love of the *Romance of the Rose* in fact is the likeness or resemblance of spiritual love. However, images that claim to depict a resemblance between the carnal and the spiritual become highly improbable in this context; they claim to create a resemblance between the carnal love of the *Romance of the Rose* and a higher Christian form of love, yet they as often reveal the difference between the perfect and the imperfect in their flamboyant and sinuous shapes.

The second movement of analogical imagery studied here is exemplified in the poetry and prose of Jean Lemaire de Belges. In Lemaire's poetry and prose, the human mind is able to understand the universal through the particular, and the ontology criticized by the late-medieval critique of scholastic realism can be construed as once again being fully operative. In poems like the *Couronne margaritique* (1505), an encomiastic portrait of Margaret of Austria, the Foucaultian paradigm of resemblance is fully evident. In works like this, the human mind can trace the invisible resemblances between contingent and absolute through physical phenomena in the world. Lemaire's poetics is obviously heavily influenced by the Neoplatonism of writers like Marsilio Ficino and by the occult philosophy of writers such as Henry Cornelius Agrippa.[13] Although Lemaire might use Molinet's *Chappellet des dames* as a model for his *Couronne margaritique*, his poetic imagery exults in the observable connections between contingent and absolute visible in the physical world. Things really do resemble their ideal forms in the *Couronne margaritique*. Where the analogical symbol in Molinet's poetics turns in on itself, becoming a private and often confusing image, Lemaire's images open up the contingent and singular world to the general and the Ideal. Geometric forms, perfect numbers, and astrology provide Lemaire's reader with a means to attain the ultimate knowledge of a true hidden meaning through the image itself. The imagery, for which Lemaire is well known, features plastic detail and an exuberance unknown in Molinet's *Chappellet des dames*.

The third movement traced in this book studies the "gargantuan" imagery of François Rabelais. The balance between resemblance and difference in Rabelais's diverse and often contradictory works is made up of an unstable mix of contingency and plenitude. Rabelais's books harbor a proliferation of bizarre images that both promise and deny a higher meaning. Over time, the imagery of Rabelais's works undergoes a change that parallels much of the debate about allegorical meaning during the sixteenth century. In his early books, *Gargantua* (1534) and *Pantagruel* (1532),

Rabelais's imagery often holds out the promise of a rationally comprehensible hidden meaning. These works bring, at least in theory, the contingent and absolute into a revealing and fulfilling relationship. In these works, the imperfect image can reveal, theoretically, the reality of the transcendant. Yet throughout his works, and especially in his later novels, the contingent reality of words works against any possible higher meaning that might be revealed through the word's resemblance with a transcendent referent. By the time Rabelais finished the *Quart Livre* (1552), his imagery had become much darker and less comical. Parallel with this shift in imagery, the notion of a higher meaning had also become far less promising, as the Pantagruelians became progressively less enchanted with the totalizing theories of the peoples they met on their voyage.

Rabelais's itinerary can be read in light of the polemical debates of the sixteenth century. The early books, when a universal law, or *ius gentium,* is said to overcome the individual differences of things so that all peoples everywhere would understand the meaning of various colors, can be read as representative of a certain humanistic optimism. The new learning of the humanists held out the promise that the fortuitousness of things could be overcome in a plenitude of meaning and being. The language of the Egyptian hieroglyph stands as a theoretical paradigm for the new learning. By going back to the original language, the real meaning of things would become transparent and the fortuitousness of things would disappear. The later books, however, reflect the demise of the new learning and of the hopes of the new religion as Europe sank deeper and deeper into the intractable positions that would result in the wars of religion. Anyone in the *Quart Livre* who believed that he could understand the design of the universe and God's meaning was roundly criticized. In the 1550s evangelical moderates like Rabelais were increasingly caught between the extremists on both sides of the religious spectrum, and the *Quart Livre* can be read as an acerbic call for moderation in the face of increasingly virulent claims of truth.

This background sketch of various theological and social issues does not mean that the literary works by Molinet, Lemaire, and Rabelais can be read only as representative of these issues. These matters are brought into the analysis so that the literary appropriation of analogical symbols and concepts can be understood within a certain context. Nor is this theoretical context meant to be purely deterministic. The works of these authors can be studied in many different ways, and there is sufficient slippage within any individual work to allow for a counterreading. This analysis is offered simply as a means of understanding a general direction within individual works.

Theological and philosophical texts are included because of a simple premise that underlies this book as a whole: that each writer's method of understanding the universe directly affects his production of literary images. Just as Rabelais's use of allegorical imagery cannot be understood without studying his own understanding of an *altior sensus*, Molinet's often confusing allegorical imagery should not be dismissed as merely bad or immoral (as it often has been) without first understanding the context in which it was written.[14] The essays of theologians from the period offer proof of how these problems might have been construed by the authors. These theological texts are read for what they can explain about the literary texts, and their analysis should be understood within the limits of this literary discussion. Theological analysis per se is beyond the scope of both this study and the competency of the author.

The term *analogical imagery* is used in two different but related ways in this study. It refers first of all, in a fairly loose fashion, to types of imagery that connect the contingent and visible existence of human beings to an absolute yet hidden existence of divine dimensions through the process of resemblance. As such, this term includes analogy in a more precise theological sense as well as allegory, etymology, and, to a lesser extent, alchemy and astrology. All of these methods of expressing a higher truth or invisible structure governing the universe occur in the works of the three authors studied, and they are all sensitive to the play of like and unlike. In allegories, analogies, and etymologies, the imperfect world of earthly creation is used to understand the perfect world of the divine. The degree to which the image bridges the gap between visible and invisible is largely determined by the balance of resemblance and difference respected by each author.

The importance of allegory to medieval culture is hard to exaggerate. Throughout works such as Dante's *Commedia* and Guillaume de Lorris and Jean de Meung's *Romance of the Rose*, allegory allowed the medieval mind to depict a spiritual or abstract reality through a sign. Thomas Aquinas's scholastic theology makes specific mention of allegory, explaining that the spiritual meaning of a sacred text was a natural extension of the literal level of meaning.[15] Dante explicitly identifies fourfold exegetical allegory as being crucial to the understanding of his *Commedia*: the reader was not simply to stop at the literal level but was to continue on to the higher or spiritual meaning.[16] What happens, however, when that kind of meaning is defined as beyond understanding? This is the case in works like Rabelais's *Quart Livre*, in which the contingency of human existence becomes a keystone of understanding. In this work, the humanly generated sign cannot refer to a divine referent, since human beings are considered unable to understand the divine. And yet allegorical structures continue to exist in works like this, often enticing the reader into a search for a higher meaning only to have that hope dashed as the allegory itself collapses. Those creatures in the *Quart Livre* who believe that they can understand the divine and provide images of what God looks like are routinely mocked. The tension between a desire for a higher meaning and an epistemological context that makes such a meaning impossible gives a particular and sometimes odd twist to works like the *Quart Livre*.

Analogy in its limited theological sense was a crucial element in the realist theology of Aquinas and his fifteenth-century followers, such as Thomas de Vio, Cardinal Cajetan, because it allowed the human mind to understand, through imperfect comparison, the perfection of the divine.[17] It provided a median way between equivocity, or total difference, and univocity, or complete resemblance. The two terms of an analogy, especially the sort of analogy developed by Cajetan at the end of the fifteenth century, participated to unequal degrees in the same quality. Analogy of this sort was extremely sensitive to the notion of resemblance because it depended on partial likeness: the terms of the comparison resembled each other in part but not completely. When resemblance between the terms was not considered feasible, analogy lost its ability to connect discreet and different elements. Without even partial likeness, analogy could not reveal the perfection of the divine to the imperfect human since there was nothing connecting them. Without some common middle term, the analogy could not even be ordered, and the term that should have been used to reveal the truth of the other could become that which was revealed. The reversed and collapsing analogies found in Molinet and Rabelais offer further proof of the demise of the analogical paradigm. Yet the fact that these figures continue to flourish in their works also bears witness to the continued domination of the paradigm of resemblance in the fifteenth and sixteenth centuries.

Etymology is perhaps less obvious to modern readers as a means of illustrating how the idea of resemblance functioned in the fifteenth and sixteenth centuries. It was, however, an important element in the arsenal of medieval and Renaissance writers, because a word's power, or *vis*, was established traditionally through its resemblance to its referent.[18] The properties of a word were thought to arise from the appearance of the thing to which it referred. The word or name revealed to the perspicacious reader the truth of its referent through the resemblance of word and thing. Yet throughout the works of poets and religious writers from the Middle Ages and the Renaissance, the arbitrary nature of language is exploited to rhetorical ends. Although the desire for the origin of a word might motivate etymological images, often these images depend on the difference between word and thing. Paranomasia, or linguistic resemblance, overpowers and dominates any real or ontological resemblance between word and thing. Difference rather than resemblance ends up being the decisive factor in literary and homiletic appropriations of etymology.

This book depends on the previous scholarship of writers who have tended to establish the Neoplatonic and Hermetic leanings of the sixteenth century as well those who have more recently brought to light the influence of singularity and contingency. George Mallary Masters in *Rabelaisian Dialectic and the Platonic-Hermetic Tradition* and A. J. Krailsheimer in *Rabelais and the Franciscans* eloquently evoke the influence of the Hermetic tradition of the Neoplatonists and the Scotist tradition of the Franciscans.[19] More recently, critics such as Ullrich Langer and Antoine Compagnon have offered a rectification of the overly Neoplatonic viewpoint of many studies of the sixteenth century.[20] Langer's *Divine and Poetic Freedom in the Renaissance: Nominalist Theology and Literature in France and Italy* shows how the problem of freedom and will in the fictional world of Renaissance literature can be understood in relation to nominalist theology. Compagnon's *Nous, Michel de Montaigne* analyzes the development of Montaigne's *Essays* from a "realist" plural to a "nominalist" singular.

Two other recent works also examine how the notion of linguistic contingency played a dominant role in the French Renaissance. François Cornilliat's "*Or ne mens*": *couleurs de l'éloge et du blâme chez les "grands rhétoriqueurs"* analyzes the rhetoric of the *équivoque* in the literature of the end of the fifteenth and early sixteenth centuries.[21] Cornilliat's book explores some of the same terrain analyzed here and sometimes arrives at different conclusions, especially concerning Jean Lemaire de Belges. It is hoped that our books complement each other and lead to a more nuanced and complete understanding of the often ignored poetry of writers such as Molinet and Lemaire. Marie-Luce Demonet's *Les Voix du signe: nature et origine du langage à la renaissance (1480–1580)* magisterially shows how "the arbitrary nature of the sign not only dominates but is a constant in the linguistic thought of the Renaissance."[22]

The work of Paul Zumthor, Claude Thiry, Cynthia J. Brown, and Pierre Jodogne has been of great assistance in those sections of this study dealing with Molinet and Lemaire.[23] For the section dealing with Rabelais, the rich and erudite scholarship of critics such as Michael Screech, Gérard Defaux, and Edwin Duval has been extremely useful, as it will be in any work devoted to the literature of the sixteenth century.[24] Defaux's *Pantagruel et les sophistes* has been an especially rewarding source for understanding the often tangled relationship of Rabelais and his medieval precursors. Scholars such as Terence Cave, François Rigolot, and Michel Jeanneret have been immensely helpful in explaining the notion of a *plus hault sens* in the sixteenth century.[25] Cave's *Cornucopian Text* and Rigolot's "Cratylisme et Pantagruélisme: Rabelais et le statut du signe" were particularly important in helping to set the parameters of this study. Tom Conley's work on the relationship of flamboyant gothic architecture and early sixteenth-century writing has also been of great help in explaining stylistic developments in the writing of the period.[26]

Although this study tries to situate literary texts in a specific cultural moment, it is not a historical study; the questions examined here have more to do with the production of meaning than with history. The meaning produced by analogies, allegories, and etymologies depends on an institutional context, and the writers studied in this book write within and against that institutional code. The writings of Gerson, Cajetan, Ficino, et alia are provided as examples of the institutional meaning that is appropriated to literary ends by Molinet, Lemaire, and Rabelais. This study does not intend to treat the literary as a social document that merely relates the Weltanschauung of the early Renaissance. The theological texts are used to help read the literary. Although the worldview expressed in the literary can be understood without these extratextual sources, I believe that the analogies, allegories, and etymologies in the poetry and prose of Molinet, Lemaire, and Rabelais need to be deciphered at the institutional level of meaning before they can be understood as literary products.

This book, finally, is an attempt to read texts written during an era when human understanding of the world was changing rapidly. Our postmodernity and its critique of Enlightenment reason in some ways resembles the fifteenth and sixteenth centuries, when the subjective self was still an occulted force within the disintegrating analogical system. Before there was a rational self that needed to have its unconscious liberated by

Freud, the poets working at the courts of Burgundy and France at the end of the fifteenth century were creating ghostly and refracted selves. Separated from us by three and one-half centuries of the Cartesian analytical tradition, the writers of the early sixteenth century are in many ways closer to us than those of more recent times. Perhaps we of the late twentieth century are particularly able to appreciate the conflicted imagery found in the works of Molinet, Lemaire, and Rabelais as we confront a rapidly evolving world in which paradigms from the past haunt our imagination and new realities gather with sometimes frightening speed.

CHAPTER ONE

The Flamboyant Allegory
of Jean Molinet's
Roman de la Rose moralisé

⚜   ⚜   ⚜

As Erwin Panofsky notes, the late Middle Ages was marked by a nominalist and mystical critique of the synthetic power of reason that had characterized the scholastic theology of the thirteenth century.[1] This critique destroyed the "scholastic cathedral" of the thirteenth century, described by Panofsky, since it threw knowledge back on an intuitive and psychological experience of the world. Panofsky describes the late gothic hall church as the late medieval architectural equivalent of the high gothic cathedral.[2] As the cathedral represents the fusion of faith and reason in high scholasticism, the hall church encloses a "wildly pictorial and apparently boundless interior," which corresponds to the intuitive and subjective understanding of the late medieval critique of scholastic realism.

Panofsky's architectural analysis can be used to illustrate a similar development in literature. Literary works such as Jean Molinet's *Roman de la Rose moralisé*, written in the late fifteenth century, represent flamboyant equivalents of thirteenth-century allegorical "cathedrals" such as the *Romance of the Rose*. Molinet's work strives to function like its famous allegorical predecessor, yet due to its epistemological context, it falls short of the structural coherence of the work by Guillaume de Lorris and Jean de Meung. The *Roman de la Rose moralisé* becomes an enormously ornate and often confusing work that reflects an epistemological context in which a higher or spiritual meaning can be produced only in a highly subjective and intuitive fashion. Yet, like many of the flamboyant gothic churches of the fourteenth and fifteenth centuries, its highly complex and often "wildly pictorial" appearance fascinates the modern eye that tries to follow the meandering and sinuous curves of its decorative surface.

A key element in William of Ockham's nominalist critique of thirteenth-century realism was the notion of singularity.[3] For Ockham and other nominalists, all knowledge of the abstract had to be based on an initial intuitive understanding of the singular.[4] This insistence on a singular and intuitive cognition effectively brought to an end any abstract metaphysical understanding of the divine. If all abstract understanding is grounded in an intuitive understanding of a singular, this means that all the metaphysical systems were grounded in an initial intuitive understanding of the divine. Intuitive understanding of this kind, however, was reserved exclusively for the beatified, such as Saint Paul. For the imperfect human being traveling through life, the *viator*, all understanding of the divine had to be understood as conventional. All the "real" connections that realist theologians claimed held between the various parts of the universal whole simply became conventional links in a purely human understanding. These connections did not really hold. They simply existed because they helped human beings understand the universe. The scope of theological inquiry would be severely curtailed following Ockham's critique of realist universals. Within the *via moderna*, the school of Ockham and his followers, the sphere of faith widened, while that of "rational" religion shrank.[5]

Ockham's critique of realist scholasticism also "gave free rein to the deep current of mysticism which had irrigated Latin Christendom since Saint Augustine but had been stemmed by the success of scholasticism."[6] By limiting the role of human reason in understanding the divine, Ockham opened the floodgates of late medieval mystical spirituality, which insisted, as mystics always had, on the unknowableness of God.[7] Where the scholastic realist could create a rationally comprehensible metaphysical system that could explain what the devout Christian knew through faith, the mystic turned inward to experience what he knew through faith. The mystic experienced the divine in a moment of ecstatic rapture that allowed him to overcome his imperfect nature. The hiddenness of the divine could be overcome only through an individual and inward experience, which remained inexpressible.[8] Although very different in nature and purpose, the personal and intuitive character of nominalism and mysticism placed a fracture in the great "cathedral" of scholastic realism.[9]

Jean Molinet's *Roman de la Rose moralisé* provides a picture of singular understanding. Throughout this work, human beings who try to describe the divine through their reason are mocked and satanized. At the same time that the knowledge provided by these individuals is rejected, Molinet develops a very involved use of affective contemplation that allows the spiritual lover to come to God through the power of love. The spiritual lover turns inside and creates an immense space there that contrasts with the limited range of human understanding outside. The mystical theology of Jean Gerson, which both emphasizes the limits of human understanding and develops a return to God through affective contemplation, provides a theoretical illustration of Molinet's literary practice in the *Roman de la Rose moralisé*. This is not to say that Molinet was directly affected by Gerson's theology; rather, Gerson's theological essays are used here simply to illustrate what happens in Molinet's literary work. The advantage of turning to Gerson is that he explains these issues explicitly, where they appear only implicitly in Molinet, even though the final effect is even more noticeable in the literary work.

Although not as well known as earlier theologians such as Saint Thomas Aquinas or William of Ockham, Gerson was a key figure in late-medieval intellectual history. The fifteenth century has even been called the "siècle de Gerson."[10] He is perhaps best known today for having sided with Christine de Pisan in the *Querelle de la Rose*, which pitted him alongside Christine against Jean de Montreuil, Gontier, and Pierre Col.[11] Although Gerson sided with Christine, his reasons for attacking the *Romance of the Rose* had less to do with the misogyny of Jean de Meung than with the immorality of the work. Gerson advised that the *Rose* be thrown on the fire and avoided like the plague since it was like the flame of the candle to the moth.[12] Gerson, along with Pierre d'Ailly, his predecessor as chancellor of the University of Paris, was also one of the most important theological conciliarists who attempted to reconcile the schism that divided the Catholic Church at the end of fourteenth and the beginning of the fifteenth centuries.

Gerson's mystical theology can be understood as part of a long tradition that turns away from the arid logical discussions that came to characterize much nominalist discourse while also maintaining a basically nominalist epistemology. As historians such as Renaudet note, in the fourteenth and fifteenth centuries, the Ockhamist critique of speculative theology developed into different movements.[13] Besides the nominalism of those theologians who continued to develop the logical distinctions of Ockham and Buridan, there was also a spiritual or affective form of nominalism that was independent of, if not consciously opposed to, dialectical philosophy.[14] Both of these developments remained true to the Ockham-

ist principle that imperfect human beings could not have a rational understanding of the perfect divine.[15] God and human are essentially in no way
alike, and since understanding is based on a principle of likeness, no real
understanding of the divine can be had through human reason. The logicians emphasized how only a conventional understanding could be had,
and the spiritualists turned to the affective part of the soul, which does
not depend on faulty human reason in order to have an understanding of
the divine.

It was as part of this spiritual development of the late-medieval critique of the intellectual and intellective excesses of scholasticism that Jean
Gerson developed his mystical theology in the early fifteenth century.
Throughout his essays, especially during the early part of his career, Gerson emphasizes the limits of human understanding and the need for
human beings to limit the scope of their rational scrutiny of God's design.
At the same time, Gerson turns increasingly to the affective part of the
soul to effect a return to God. Gerson's mystical theology has been called
a form of "affective transcendentalism" that was capable of spanning the
gulf left between God and reason by a purely Ockhamist epistemology
and understanding of faith.[16]

A common theme in many of Gerson's essays is the need to recognize
the limits of human understanding. He explains in *De sensu litterali Sacrae
Scripturae* (1414) that the first cause of error is ignorance about the extent
of human understanding.[17] Gerson emphasizes that the arrogance of such
misunderstanding helped lead, in fact, to the heresies that plagued Europe
at the time—and that Gerson was instrumental in combating.[18] As chancellor of the University of Paris, Gerson was all too aware of the increasingly sophisticated and vain speculations of both the Scotist *formalizantes*
and the nominalist logicians. In *Contra curiositatem studentium* (1402),
Gerson criticizes the excesses of theologians and scholars who do not recognize the limits of human reason. The vain speculation of the theologians, he says, opens the door to every sort of error and heresy.[19]

This essay's theme, "paenitemini et credite evangelio" (repent and believe in the Gospel), was taken from the Gospel of Saint Mark and would
become the epitaph on Gerson's tombstone; it stood as an eloquent yet
simple answer to the overly ambitious speculation of scholastic theologians and scholars. The simple wisdom of the penitent Christian is far
more valid for Gerson than the vain knowledge of the overly curious the-
ologian. Gerson can perhaps be understood as turning back to the mystical tradition as a response to the vain speculation he attacks in *Contra*

curiositatem studentium. He begins his *De mystica theologia speculativa,* written in the winter of 1402–3, and which would become the first part of the *De mystica theologia* of 1408, with the same passage from Saint Mark that he cites in *Contra curiositatem studentium*: "Repent and believe in the Gospel."[20] He also refers directly back to the *curiosa singularitas* that he condemns in the earlier essay, saying that he feared being guilty of the same sort of sin in his own explanation of mystical theology.[21] In both of these essays, Gerson comes back time and again to the importance of recognizing the limits of human understanding. Devout penitence is always superior to vain speculation, and an internal and subjective experience of God is always superior to any misleading rational understanding. The penitent and mystical search for the good (*bonam*) is superior to the search for the truth (*veram*), which is the aim of the scholastic philosopher.[22]

With a rational understanding of God greatly reduced, Gerson moves away from what he calls symbolic or speculative theology to the internal way of the mystic tradition. Love rather than reason becomes the motor propelling this return. Where speculative theology could lead only to error, the power of love could lead the most simpleminded idiot to God. Instead of trying to reach God through rational understanding, the spiritual lover is drawn to him through loving desire. In *La Montaigne de contemplation* (1400), Gerson describes the process in terms of ordinary human love, of the kind that draws one individual to another.

Gerson first describes worldly love either as a longing for money, honor, and dignity or as carnal desire. The person who is caught up in this desire can think of nothing else, "telement qu'elle en pert toute raison et en devient comme folle ou yvre ou forsenée." (so much so that he loses all reason and becomes as if mad or drunk or frenzied).[23] Gerson then uses this carnal love as a model to explain spiritual love.[24] The movement in both spiritual and worldly love is the same. The person who is caught up in worldly love (*amour mondaine*) languishes from desire for what he loves madly. His whole being is so devoted to this single object of desire that everything else ceases to exist. This obsessive love becomes a paradigm for spiritual love. The spiritual lover, like the carnal lover with regard to a human object of affection, forgets the world and everything else since he is so devoted to the object of his spiritual devotion. The world is only a dream or a fable in relation to God and his glory. The only difference between the obsession of the carnal lover and that of the spiritual lover is the nature of the object of desire.

This does not mean to say that Gerson ignores the intellect in his mystical theology. It plays, in fact, a key role in his affective contemplation, even if the way to God passes through the affect rather than through the intellect. Gerson divides the soul into three levels, making sure to explain that these distinctions are purely nominal and that they do not really exist.[25] Each of these three levels has corresponding intellective and affective powers. Gerson places on the affective side of the soul, from top to bottom, synderesis, rational desire, and animal desire. On the intellective side the powers that corresponded to the affective powers are pure intelligence, reason, and sensibility. The idea is to use the affective side of the soul, which was less damaged in the fall from grace, to accede to the divine and then to transfer that intelligence to the intellect. Synderesis, the highest affective power, is the natural inclination of the soul to good. The contemplative individual is able to use the affect to rise to the divine, which is beyond the reach of reason. But one is able to bring the experience into the highest part of the intellect (pure intelligence), which is superior to reason. The affective side of the soul simply has the advantage of not having to use damaged reason in its move toward the divine.[26]

Gerson's mystical theology features a moderate view of mystical union. In *De mystica theologia,* the insurmountable difference between perfect divine and imperfect human prevents affective contemplation from coming to complete fruition.[27] The principle of likeness might draw the affective mystic to God, but the ultimate difference between divine perfection and human imperfection prevents them from ever joining in an essential mystical union. The Gersonian mystic does not become one with God, as the Flemish mystic John of Ruysbroeck believed; he or she simply enacts the mystical union in his or her mind and becomes one with God in the same way two lover's hearts and minds are conjoined. In *De mystica theologia,* Gerson specifically singles out John of Ruysbroeck's *The Adornment of the Spiritual Marriage* for expressing a blasphemous commingling of perfect and imperfect.[28] Gerson explains that this would imply that the contemplative human being would join essentially with the divine in mystical union, which is impossible within the context of separation of human and divine that is operative in his mystical theology. Gerson avoids "this mistake" (*hunc errorem*) by explaining that the conjoining of divine and secular happens only in the mind as an act of the will. He criticizes analogies that would imply that the imperfect contemplative human being might become one with the divine the same way that a drop of water might become one with a jar of strong wine.[29] The spiritual lover does not physically join with the object of desire; the lover simply does this the same way an obsessive lover joins with the object of desire in his or her thoughts.

Despite this essential gap between human and divine, Gerson describes the unbounded force of the desire that draws the spiritual lover to the love object of his affection in graphic terms, saying that the movement from desiring subject to unattainable object is like a horse that leaps from its corral.[30] When the contemplative human turns the mind's eye to the perfection of God in mystical rapture, he or she is drawn to that perfection with almost uncontrollable force. The attraction is not dependent on intellect, even though it occurs in the mind. The power of love overpowers the distance between human and God that reason could not overcome. Love rather than reason brings the creature back to the creator. By contemplating the perfection of God, the human being's mind boils over and leaps beyond its normal boundaries. Despite the force of this attraction, the two never achieve essential union, as Gerson's critique of John of Ruysbroeck indicates. Gerson's description of affective contemplation underlines both the force of such spiritual longing and the separation of God and human.[31]

Gerson calls the experiential coming to God through ecstatic rapture anagogical. Henri de Lubac explains that there were two kinds of mystical anagogy in the Middle Ages: doctrinal anagogy, which completed the fourfold exegetical allegory; and spiritual anagogy, which represents a completely arational experience that denies allegorical understanding altogether and introduces a person directly to the mystical life.[32] In *De mystica theologia*, Gerson defines mystical theology as an anagogical motion that draws the individual up to God through ardent and pure love.[33] Affective contemplation is used, since human reason is incapable of understanding the perfection of the divine. Gerson turns inward to the affect, since he cannot understand the reality of God through the external signs of what he calls symbolic or speculative theology. This turning inward away from the way of speculative theology might bring him to God, but it creates a problem for him: How is he to speak of that experience that he places beyond understanding and expression?

Gerson's language when talking about anagogical experience is curiously oblique. He uses the Gospel story about the fishermen on the Sea of Galilee to explain the movement of the contemplative individual to God through anagogy. In the story, Jesus Christ comes across Zebedee and his sons fishing on the sea and calls out to them. The men then return to shore. Gerson explains the meaning of each character and object in the story: the sea is sensuality, the shore is eternity, the winds are passions, the fish or reptiles are sensual desire and phantasms, the fisherman is the spirit, the boat is natural reason, the nets are worldly cares, Zebedee is the fluidity of time, the mercenaries are worldly philosophers, and the voice is Jesus Christ. He uses this explanation as a schema for the contemplative experience. The contemplative individual is to abandon the misleading and perilous boat of natural reason and turn to the eternity of Jesus Christ through the power of love.[34]

This anagogical explanation is indicative of the problem that Gerson creates for himself with his development of affective contemplation. On the one hand, he explains that he will turn away from symbolic theology in order to have an experiential understanding of the divine through the affect. On the other hand, he needs to have recourse to language to talk about the experience. By moving inward rather than outward to escape the erroneous ways of what he calls symbolic theology, Gerson leaves himself unarmed as far as symbolic representation is concerned. The anagogical description remains exterior to the actual experience. Gerson cannot say what he or any other individual actually sees during the act of affective contemplation, so he is reduced to describing the movement toward the divine from the outside. His anagogical description of the movement of the devout Christian to Jesus Christ follows the process but does not say what happens during the process itself. His language floats as it loses its deictic function and becomes more poetic, pointing at itself as form rather than at its impossible referent. The contemplative individual might answer the call of Jesus Christ and come to eternity, but that experience is and always will be incomprehensible. The point of affective contemplation is to rise above the imperfect human image or sign, which inevitably brings the individual back to the fallen human condition. The circular nature of this problem would seem inescapable.

The problem is similar to one Gerson describes in relation to the act of contemplation itself. In *De mystica theologia*, he is very careful to explain that one of the great dangers in affective contemplation is taking visions or phantasms that originate in the human mind for a real anagogical experience.[35] He describes three levels of contemplation that correspond to the three levels of understanding in the soul (already mentioned): cogitation, meditation, and contemplation. Cogitation is associated with sensuality, meditation with the intellect, and contemplation with the pure intelligence of the divine. It is important, he explains, not to allow images that are associated with the senses or with the human intellect to interfere with a truly divine infusion.[36] Images, signs, or visions that come from the senses or the human intellect will not always lead to the divine. His aim is to rise above these images in order to concentrate on the affective contemplation of God and thus to experience that which cannot be understood or described. Access to the divine can be had only through an arational ecstatic rapture, which is beyond human comprehension and depiction. By staying at the level of humanly grounded signs and symbols, it is impossible to move beyond vain cogitation and error-laden intellect. Spiritual anagogy, which surpasses these inferior forms of understanding and enters, as Lubac explains, *hic et nunc* in the world of the divine, needs to liberate itself from language but inevitably falls back into it.[37]

The topography of Gerson's mystical theology outlined here is simplified for the sake of clarity. In general, it is characterized by a limiting of the speculative capacities of human reason. Human beings simply should not try to understand what their own rational limitations prevent them from understanding. The speculative excesses of metaphysical inquiry would be the butt of Gerson's critique even in the last period of his life. In *De modis significandi* (1426), he explains that metaphysicians who take the imaginings of their own minds for reality are like madmen who take their own dreams for reality.[38] The turning inward to affective contemplation also involves a turning away from images or visions that come from the human psyche. The idea is to rise above the level of human cogitation and intellect and be drawn into the contemplative awareness of God. Finally, Gerson's description of the experience of the divine through contemplation as anagogical leads him to place that experience beyond expression. Human language can describe the coming to the divine in only the most oblique way. The actual experience remains beyond understanding and expression.

Although Gerson's mystical theology is not concerned with literary questions, many of the problems and issues confronted by his turning away from external understanding and expression are replicated in a purely literary form in Molinet's *Roman de la Rose moralisé*. It is hoped that this short sketch of Gerson's mystical theology can help explain the often confusing and much maligned imagery found in the *Roman de la Rose moralisé*, since it too is grounded in a similar epistemological context. In both Gerson's mystical theology and Molinet's *Roman de la Rose moralisé*, the human being turns to the affect in order to avoid the pitfalls of human reason. The contrast between the paucity of human understanding of the divine through reason and the force of the interior and incomprehensible power of love would be even stronger in Molinet than in Gerson. Molinet would also be guilty of the sort of pictorial excess that Gerson criticizes; however, Gerson's example can perhaps help to explain why the flamboyant imagery of the *Roman de la Rose moralisé* appears so aberrant to modern readers.

Although the exact date when Molinet composed the *Roman de la Rose moralisé* is unknown, a manuscript in the Royal Library at the Hague suggests that Molinet wrote it sometime in the final years of the fifteenth century.[39] First published in 1500, it is an odd work. Molinet, at the command of Philip of Clèves, Lord of Ravestain, divided the *Romance of the Rose* into 107 chapters in prose and added a *moralité* at the end of each one.[40] These *moralités* offer a spiritual interpretation of the tale of love by Guillaume de Lorris and Jean de Meung. In recent times, the *Roman de la Rose moralisé* has most often been described as an allegory, and a bad one at that: Pierre-Yves Badel calls it "aberrant," and Rosemond Tuve calls it "immoral."[41] If the *Roman de la Rose moralisé* is an allegory, it is a strange one, one that cannot enunciate the higher or hidden truth it purports to expose.

Molinet explains in the prologue to the *Roman de la Rose moralisé* that he was reluctant to comply with his *seigneur*'s order to "deversify and moralize" the *Romance of the Rose*.[42] He says that he feared what the *mauvaises langues* would say about such an undertaking.[43] Whether Molinet is simply repeating the topos of the unwilling author or is sincerely reluctant to comply with the duke's command, his initial reluctance to undertake the project is indicative of the problematic nature of the *Roman de la Rose moralisé*. In a certain sense, Molinet is guilty of bad faith in his gloss of Guillaume de Lorris and Jean de Meung. An unwilling but loyal servant, Molinet applies his *engin,* or intelligence, to the task, but the trepidation expressed in the prologue vitiates the *Roman de la Rose moralisé* from one end to the other. What Molinet says he is going to do is very different from what transpires in the work itself. In the prologue, there is a strange shift in register that reveals Molinet's conflicted status as both public *indiciaire* and as private individual with concerns and ideas that are not necessarily those of his patrons at court. He begins the prologue with an address to his *seigneur,* which is decidedly military in tone:

> Ne suffist a vostre treshaulte seigneurie prosperant en fleur de jeunesse militer soubz le triumphant estandart de mars le grant dieu des batailles dont vous avez veu les exploitz plus que nul prince de vostre eage: se avecques ce

comme embrase dardant desir esprins damoureuses estincelles ne desirez estre champion des dames ensuyvant le tresplaisant guidon de venus deesse damours. Dont jasoit ce que les arcz/ les dartz/ les lances/ et les arnoys de l'amoureuse artillerie soyent de plus tendre trempeure que ceulx de guerre que lon forge a milan.[44]

[It is not sufficient for your most high lordship in the flower of youth to fight under the triumphant banner of Mars, the great god of battle, whose exploits you have seen more of than any prince your age, if lit by ardent desire and taken with amorous spark, you desire to be the champion of ladies following the very pleasant lead of Venus, goddess of love, whose bows, arrows, lances, and harnesses of amorous artillery are said to be of more tender temper than those military arms forged in Milan.]

The references to "jeunesse militer," "estandart de mars le grant dieu des batailles," and "le tresplaisant guidon de venus deesse damours" all point to a purely secular and carnal love. It has been suggested that the aim of the *Roman de la Rose moralisé* was to help the addressee become a "champion des dames."[45] However, this military and secular tone is soon dropped, and Molinet reveals that his real purpose is to convert the corporeal love of the *Rose* into a more spiritual kind of love:

Et affin que je ne perde le froment de ma labeur et que la farine qui en sera molue puisse avoir fleur salutaire jay intencion se dieu men donne la grace de tourner et convertir soubz mes rudes meules le vicieux au vertueux/ le corporel en spirituel/ la mondanité en divinité/ et souverainement de le moraliser.[46]

[And so as not to lose the fruit of my labor and so that the wheat which will be milled from it might have salutory flower, I mean, if God permits, to convert with my rough millstone the depraved into the virtuous, the corporeal into the spiritual, the worldly into the divine, and supremely to moralize it.]

By the end of the first chapter it is obvious that neither Philip nor any other member of the court of Burgundy can be the real addressee of the *Roman de la Rose moralisé*, at least not in their secular capacities. Instead of a noble attempting to become a "champion des dames," the hero of Molinet's retelling of the *Rose* is a contemplative monk attempting to reach Jesus Christ. The "vergier de deduit" (garden of delight) is converted into a "saint cloistre de religion" (holy cloister of religion). The birds that inhabit the garden are identified as "les devotz religieux/ possessans/ mendians/ reformez/ riglez chanoines/ et nommez enseignans lisans et chantans les louenge de dieu et des glorieux saintz" (the devout religious—rich, mendicant, reformed, regular, and appointed canons—teaching, reading, singing the praises of god and of his glorious saints).

The profession of loyalty that the lover must make to "dieu damours" (god of love) becomes "la profession que fait le jeune religieux a son superior" (the profession that the young religious makes to his superior).[47]

The problematic nature of the *Roman de la Rose moralisé*, hinted at in the prologue, becomes much clearer here. The public work might be directed toward the worldly concerns of the Burgundian court, but the private work is much more concerned with issues related to the spiritual concerns of a devout Christian. It would be very difficult for a member of the court of Burgundy to follow the moral lesson of the *Roman de la Rose moralisé*, unless, of course, he or she desired to leave the active life of the court for the contemplative life of the convent. It is quite possible, of course, that Molinet was playing with a literary conceit and pretending to create a more religious work than he really was. The character of his "moralisation," nonetheless, is much more religious than the opening lines of the prologue would lead a casual reader to believe.

The divergent objectives of the *Roman de la Rose moralisé*, alluded to in the prologue's switch from military to monastic registers, are also revealed in Molinet's only allusion to Gerson. In the very last *moralisation* of the work, the one in which the Rose is gathered, he mentions that Gerson had criticized the *Rose* during the "Querelle de la Rose" and had sided with Christine de Pisan in attacking the *Rose* as immoral.[48] He pointedly says that Gerson had not understood the real meaning of the *Rose* and had only stopped at the hard outer shell of the work, never reaching its rich inner meaning. This overt critique is couched, nonetheless, in terms that implicitly show the respect that Molinet had for the defunct chancellor of the University of Paris. The critique begins with an explanation that Gerson undertook his critique of the *Rose* only under duress, "a la requeste faveur daucunes notables dames (at the particular request of certain notable ladies). Molinet also explains that Gerson never really bothered to apply the "subtillité de son engin" (subtlety of his intelligence) to the *Rose* and preferred to concentrate on "matières ardues et de plus haulte speculacion" (difficult matters and of higher speculation). Although Gerson is criticized for not having understood the real meaning of the *Rose*, the terms Molinet uses to express his criticism are those of someone who would seem to agree rather than disagree with the author of the "Contre le roman de la Rose." The terms that Molinet uses to express his admonishment perhaps show the real nature of the *Roman de la Rose moralisé*.

Publicly, the *Roman de la Rose moralisé* is a court ornament or decoration, which must exhibit the *Rose* in a positive manner, like one of the tapestries that were so popular at the court of Burgundy. The characters from the *Rose* appear much as they were in the original, only in slightly different dress. Privately, the *Roman de la Rose moralisé* is the story of an intense, inward spiritual journey. Although criticized by Molinet within the context of the official and public version, Gerson plays an important role in the private journey of the Spiritual Lover. In truth, the *Roman de la Rose moralisé* has much more to do with a mystical theology similar to Gerson's than it has to do with the thirteenth-century text it purports to deal with. In the prologue, Molinet sets up a hierarchy of love very similar to the three levels described by Gerson (f. 4v.). He will also mention at one point that his aim is to use the carnal love of the *Rose* in the same way that the love depicted in the *Song of Songs* is used to come to Christ (f. 23r.). It is possible, of course, that Molinet was affected more generally by the mystical theology that was highly prevalent in northern France and Flanders during the fifteenth century. Gerson's example is used simply to explain theoretically the implicit practice of Molinet's text.

The limits of human understanding provide some of the most humorous scenes in the *Roman de la Rose moralisé*. In these passages the temerity of those human beings who are convinced that they can understand the design of God's universe through reason becomes the target of Molinet's sometimes caustic humor. Two sections in particular treat this question thematically. In chapters 81 and 84, Molinet treats the problem of human understanding of the divine in relation to astrology and predestination. He ends chapter 84 by addressing both astrology and predestination as one issue relating to a faulty and blasphemous understanding of the divine. The other section concerns the debate between Reason and the Lover from the *Rose* and occurs in chapters 17 and 22 through 35. In both of these sections, human reason is unequivocally depicted as incapable of piercing the mysteries of the divine. These sections are far from being the only ones that concern the question of human understanding of the divine, but their thematic treatment of the question makes them especially noteworthy in this study.

In chapter 81, Molinet begins his critique of human understanding of the divine by criticizing the astrological predictions of court "prognostiqueurs," who were very common in the courts of Europe at the time. Molinet glosses the woman who tries to pry secrets from her husband in the *Rose* as "le prenosticqueur qui savance de juger des particulieres fortunes de lhomme" (the prognosticator who proposes to judge the particular fortunes of man). This chapter also contains an "invective contre celle supersticion" (invective against that superstition). Molinet makes a distinction between the study of the stars and the planets and their interpretation:

> Ceste femme qui ainsi sefforce de tyrer le secret de son mary pour le desprimer est la presumptueuse ame pecheresse/ comme lon diroit dung prenosticqueur a qui ne suffit scavoir la saincte doctrine des venerables docteurs de saincte eglise pour congnoistre dieu son createur et espoux se soubz les appentis de astrologie comme font les astronomiens modernes ne sentremeslent djuger lheur et malheur/ la courte vie et la longue durée/ non seulemens des royaulmes et contrées/ mais des particuliers princes et petits personnaiges. Je ne dis mye que icelle science ne soit honneste/ licite/ naturelle et vraye quant a la cognicion des opposicions/ stacions/ cours/ et eclipses du soleil de la lune et des estoilles/ mais celle que les mathemaciens ensuyuent en prenosticquant des choses advenir/ tant des nativitéz des hommes comme de leurs meurs ou autrement est une espece de ydolatrie/ chose vaine/ prohibée et supersticieuse. (f. 109r.)

> [This woman, who tries to force the secret from her husband in order to demoralize him, is the presumptuous sinful soul. Just as one would say about a prognosticator for whom it is not enough to know the holy doctrine of the venerable doctors of the holy church in order to know his creator and husband if not through the appendices of astrology. She is like the modern astronomers who mix themselves up with judging the luck and misfortune, the short life and long duration, not only of kingdoms and countries, but also of particular princes and less important people. I do not mean to say that this science is not honest, lawful, natural, and true regarding the understanding of the oppositions, stations, path, and eclipses of the sun, the moon, and the stars, but that the science of the mathematicians who foretell things to come, births of men and their customs or otherwise, is a kind of idolatry, a vainful thing, prohibited and superstitious.]

This passage shows that the problem with astrology has less to do with meaning in the stars than it does with human beings trying to understand that meaning. Human reason is entirely competent when it is simply a question of following the positions, stations, and eclipses of the stars and planets, but it is not able to predict things that are to happen in the future.[49] For Molinet it is only when astrologers, or "prognostiqueurs," begin to make predictions about "choses advenir" (things to come) that the study of the stars becomes "une espece de ydolatrie/ chose vaine/ prohibée et supersticieuse" (a kind of idolatry or vain, forbidden, and superstitious thing). Molinet admits that there might be some truth in the stars and planets but is not willing to let the human mind understand any meaning in these stellar phenomena.

One of the most humorous episodes in the *Roman de la Rose moralisé* occurs in Molinet's invective against astrology.[50] The narrator explains that he cannot understand how an astrologer can possibly know the "fortunes des hommes" when they can't even understand what is happening in their own lives: "comment cuydent scavoir prenosticqueurs les fortunes des hommes par linfluence du ciel qui leur est loingtain quant ilz ne parcoyvent mye tout ce que lon fait a leur hostel qui leur est si prochain" (just as prognosticators think that they know the fortunes of men by the influence of the sky, which is far away, when they cannot see everything that is done in their home which is near) (f. 109v.). To illustrate this point, he gives the example of a French king who was badly counseled by his astrologer. Wanting to go hunting with his entourage, the king asks the *prenosticqueur*, or court astrologer, if the weather will be fine "selon la disposicion des planettes" (according to the arrangement of the planets). The astrologer assures him that on his word he had not seen an "aussi belle journee" (so beautiful a day) for ten years.

On the astrologer's counsel, the king assembles a hunting party of barons, squires, lords, gentlemen, and innumerable hunting dogs and sets out for the forest. On the way to the hunt, the king and his party meet a miller and his ass; the miller warns the king that it will rain and that he should go back to the castle. The king, preferring the assurances of his astrologer, ignores the miller's warnings and goes hunting. Within half an hour of passing the miller, the king and his party are drenched by the worst storm of the year. Back at the castle, the king calls for the astrologer and the miller. When he asks the astrologer how he could have made such a mistake, the wretched man answers that, in his rush, he had looked at the wrong page of his book. The king then asks the miller what he knows of the "planettes" (planets) and the "estoilles" (stars). The miller says he knows nothing of "plas netz" (empty plates) beyond those left on his table after dinner and nothing of "autres toilles" (canvasses) besides the canvas wings on his mill. If he knows nothing of the planets and the stars, the king asks him, how could he possibly know anything about the weather? The miller says that he knew by experience that when flies gathered around his ass's ears it was going to rain and that he had never seen so many flies as when the king and his party rode by on their way to the hunt. The king immediately fires the astrologer and hires the miller and his ass.

In this passage, Molinet reduces the concept of resemblance to mere homonymic likeness. Likeness does not provide knowledge of the weather; rather, experience does. Resemblance between the stars and contingent reality is shown to be linguistic and not ontological. The astrologer's error was not to understand what the miller knew intuitively—that knowledge is empirical and that any understanding of God's design is doomed to error. Molinet's story about the astrologer and the miller could easily be read as a figural rendition of Nicholas Oresme's critique of astrology in his *Livre de divinacions*, in which Oresme claims that a common field hand or sailor is more competent in predicting the weather than any *prenosticqueur* who depends on an understanding beyond his cognitive capabilities.[51] Intuitive understanding of a material and contingent phenomenon is superior to an abstract understanding of an abstract or absolute phenomenon. Human knowledge in the *Roman de la Rose moralisé*, as in Oresme, is constrained to the material and contingent while the speculative excesses of astrology are roundly rejected as misleading and prone to error.[52]

The same separation of secular and divine that makes astrology so problematic for Molinet also influences his depiction of predestination and free will. In this matter, Molinet once again takes a skeptical viewpoint of human understanding of the divine. He illustrates his position on predestination by telling a story. The narrator recounts how the bridge of Nôtre Dame is washed away in a great flood. A young girl is swept to her death, and after she is pulled from the river her family stands around bemoaning her fate. A young Franciscan friar (*cordelier*), Maistre Jehan Barthelemieu, happens by and is asked to offer his condolences to the family. When an old busybody tells him that the poor girl has finally met with "la poure destinée quelle devoit avoir" (the unhappy destiny that she had to have), the *cordelier* hits her on the head. The old woman complains that the monk has greatly wounded her. The friar's reply expresses, with Molinet's usual bite, a starkly skeptical view of human understanding:

Cest vray dist le cordelier. Il devoit ainsi advenir selon vostre mauldicte opinion/ Mais se ceste jeune fille dont dieux ait lame ne se fust point partie de lhostel de son pere et vous fussiez demourée en vostre maison et moy en mon convent ce piteux cas ne fust point advenu/ et si neussiez receu ceste busse et la fille neust pas la vie perdue. Mais entre vous vieilles aggreigées chanues tant rides et crespies estes au jourdhuy boutées en ceste fole et maulvaise fantasie et supersticieuse erreur quant vous jugez des malheureuses fortunes et dictes que il devoit ainsi advenir. Il semble que vueillez necessairement asservir la puissance divine aux mirables actes qui surviennent au monde/ dont vous mesmes estes la principale cause. Et en procedant plus oultre en matiere de predestinacion ce venerable pere fist illec sur le Champ une collacion tant fructueuse eloquente et bien aornée de langaige que parens et amys de la deffuncte ensemble le peuple de ce quartier qui bien lentendit en fut est de ceste heure grandement edifié.[53]

[That is true, said the friar. It had to happen in this way according to your cursed opinion. Yet, if this young girl whose soul is now with God had not left the house of her father, and if you had stayed in your house, and I had stayed in my monastery, this woeful case would not have happened. And you would not have received this blow on the head and the girl would not have lost her life. Yet you old, wrinkled, rough-skinned harridans are today thrown into this mad and evil fantasy and superstitious error when you judge unhappy fortune, and say that it had to happen in this way. It seems that you want necessarily to subjugate divine power for prodigious acts that happen in the world and of which you are yourselves the principal cause. And proceeding more along the same lines regarding predestination, this venerable father made straight off a sermon so fruitful and eloquent and well adorned with language that the family and friends of the dead girl together with the people from the neighborhood who heard it were all greatly edified.]

The friar repeats what the miller told the king in the previous story: that human beings are incapable of understanding God's will and should not be so presumptuous as to believe they can. When they do, they guarantee erroneous results and risk committing the sin of idolatry as they set themselves on the same level as God. Cut off from God by the Fall, the human being, the *viator*, is responsible for his or her actions. Human beings cannot save themselves by understanding the will of God or the secrets of the planets, but their virtuous actions enable them to attain the saving grace of God. The emphasis is clearly placed on the inability of human beings to know God's truth and the necessity of exercising one's own will.[54]

At the end of these sections, Molinet ties the issues of astrology and predestination together and sums up his views succinctly:

Tout leu et bien considéré ce que dit est se nous voulons sans investiguer les secretz de dieu des estoilles ou des planettes congnoistre aucunement ceulx qui dignes sont destre escriptz au livre de vie qui sont predestinéz et en train destre saulvéz selon la tradicion des theologiens sont ceulx qui servent craingent/ honnorent et glorifient leur createur/ ceulx qui veulent ouyr parler de luy. . . . et ceulx qui paciemment portent les adversitez du monde/ les maladies du corps et les necessitez des choses. Les vrayes ensaignes et les certaines marcques pour entrer et parvenir. *Ad sancta sanctorum sunt multe tribulationes iustorum.*[55]

[Having read and considered everything that has been said, if we want, without inquiring into the secrets of God in the stars and planets, to know those who are worthy, those who are being written in the book of life, according to the tradition of the theologians, those who are predestined and in the process of being saved are those who serve, fear, honor, and glorify their creator, those who want to hear him spoken of . . . and those who patiently bear the adversities of the world, the diseases of the body, and necessities of things. These are the true signs and sure marks of entering and succeeding. *Ad sanctorum sunt multe tribulatione justorum.*]

The trials and tribulations of the just are the only certain marks of salvation. There is no way for human beings to understand God's design, and the only ones who will be saved are those who "servent, craingent, honorent et glorifient leur createur." Human reason is shown to be lacking irredeemably in these passages, and all those who attempt to interpret God's will end up mocked like the *prenosticqueur* or abused like the old woman who believed in predestination. In the *Roman de la Rose moralisé*, as in Gerson's essays, human beings should not be so presumptuous as to try to understand the reason, cause, or the just will of God. They should simply do what they can and leave speculation about God's design to astrologers, scholastic theologians, and other misguided souls.

The inability of human reason to penetrate the perfection of the divine, implicitly at the heart of the passages concerning the miller and the friar, is made explicit in Molinet's treatment of Jean de Meung's Debate between the Lover and Lady Reason.[56] With reason's ability to understand the divine so severely curtailed in the *Roman de la Rose moralisé*, it is perhaps not surprising to find love being proposed as the alternative way back to God. Molinet's treatment of the Debate between Lady Reason and the Lover brings love and reason into a direct confrontation, which the former wins in no uncertain terms. Molinet's gloss demarcates the limits of reason and the power of love in reaching the Godhead.

In Jean de Meung's original text, Lady Reason tries to dissuade the Lover from following the advice that God of Love has given him. In Molinet's retelling, Lady Reason becomes Behemoth and Satan when she attempts to turn the Spiritual Lover away from God of Love's counsel. Reason is satanized because she, like Lucifer, thought that she was the equal of God. Her subtle temptations and seditious warning turn the Lover away from God:

> Survient pour le parbouter oultre et le confondre plus que nul autre/ ung personnaige nompas raison combien quil en soit ou ait este participant/ mais est nomme en grec Behemoth qui vault autant a dire que lucifer ou lennemy du Genre humain jadis cree au ciel de lincrée creature. Car nature ne scaroit telle oeuvre faire. Il porte couronne en chief comme roy des enfans dorgueil/ il a les yeulx surtilans comme chandelles. Il est escript de luy. *Videban sathanam quasi fulgur de celo cadentem.* Il est descendu de sa haulte tour en ceste valee

de misere pour tribouler les loyaulx amoureux. Cest celluy qui par subtiles temptacions et sedicieuses cautelles prohibe et deffend de non aymer son createur le bouton eternel.[57]

[Then arrives unexpectedly to shove and confound him more than any other, a character who is not reason, no matter how much he did or still does participate in reason, but who is named in Greek, Behemoth, which means to say Lucifer, or enemy of the human race, created in the sky in the past by the uncreated creator. Since nature would not know how to make such a work. He wears a crown of children of pride on his head like a king, he has eyes that glimmer like candles. It is written of him: *Videban sathanam quasi fulgur de celo cadentem.* He descended from his high tower into this valley of misery to agitate the loyal lovers. It is he who by subtle temptations and seditious cunning prohibits and prevents from loving his creator, the eternal bud.]

The satanization of Lady Reason in this passage clearly underlines the restricted nature of human reason in the *Roman de la Rose moralisé.* The intellect is incapable of leading the Lover to "le bouton eternel": in order to reach the divine, love rather than intellect is the preferred way.

The limits of reason are made even clearer when Lady Reason restricts herself to matters of human morality. Although Lady Reason is satanized when she attempts to lead the Lover away from the way of God of Love, when she confines herself to matters of human morality, reason is considered an adequate source of knowledge. When Lady Reason speaks of avarice and ordinary mortal love in chapter 25, Molinet does not even bother to gloss Jean de Meung's text. The *moralité* at the end of this chapter reads: "Le chapitre precedent est fondé totallement en doctrine morale qui riens ne derogue a lamour divine qui est ma principale intention et ne parcois histoire digne destre figuree: par quoy je le laisse dautelle condicion que je le trouve" (The preceding chapter is totally founded on moral doctrine, which does not depart from the law of divine love, which is my principal intention. And I do not see any story worth being figured. Therefore, I leave it in the self-same condition that I found it) (f. 38v.).

The fact that Molinet does not deem it necessary to "figure" Reason's discourse when she talks of "doctrine morale" and not of "amour divine" emphasizes the distinction between the secular and the divine and the place of reason in the hierarchy of being. Lady Reason's admonitions are acceptable in matters of moral doctrine having nothing to do with divine love and do not represent a transgression of the perfect divine by imperfect human reason. It is only when Lady Reason tries to turn the Lover away from the God of Love's amorous instructions that she becomes Behemoth. Reason is never questioned within the human realm; it is only when it is applied to the divine that reason is rejected as insufficient.

The carnal love of Guillaume de Lorris and Jean de Meung is not transformed into a more rational form of understanding in Molinet's retelling. It becomes, in fact, the paradigm for the movement of the Spiritual Lover toward God. Molinet uses carnal love as his model to explain the coming of the Spiritual Lover to God the same way Gerson does in *La Montaigne de contemplation*. The paradigmatic relationship of gloss and original is very important because it shows how the *Roman de la Rose moralisé* does not contradict the love of the *Rose*. It merely changes the nature of the object desired from carnal to spiritual in the same way that Gerson describes in *De mystica theologia* and in *La Montagne de contemplation*. The way of love, exemplified in the instructions that God of Love gives the Lover in the *Rose*, is juxtaposed graphically with the rational discourse of Lady Reason. In the *Roman de la Rose moralisé*, love can lead the Spiritual Lover where reason cannot—to his spiritual beloved, Jesus Christ.

The paucity of human understanding of the divine through reason contrasts with the range of understanding offered through an internal affective contemplation similar to that described by Gerson. Just as affective contemplation allows Gerson to circumvent imperfect human reason and come to the divine, it also fulfills this function in the *Roman de la Rose moralisé*. The perfect divine is out of reach of the astrologer, of the old lady who tries to understand God's design, and of Lady Reason, so the Spiritual Lover must find some other way of joining his beloved. Contemplation is what provides this *regressus ad deum*. The all-important Dame Oiseuse from the *Rose* is glossed as Dame Contemplacion, who is described as "tant eslevee et ententive a considerer les choses eternelles et celestielles" (so elevated and understanding in considering eternal and celestial things). She lets the Spiritual Lover into the garden, which is transformed into a religious order in the *Roman de la Rose moralisé* (f. 10r.). On a purely narrative level, contemplation plays a uniquely important role, since without Dame Contemplacion the rest of the story could not take place. Without Dame Contemplacion, the Spiritual Lover would never be able to effectuate the conversion of carnal to spiritual.

Contemplation is not only important for the narration of the *Roman de la Rose moralisé*, it is also at the epistemological center of this work. On several occasions, Molinet describes scenes in which affective contemplation is used to bring the secular and the divine together. In chapter 10, Molinet glosses the arrows that Doulx Regard shoots at the lover in the *Rose* as the stigmata of Christ, which the Spiritual Lover is to contemplate until his mind boils over in rapturous exaltation:

Lhistoire precedente qui bien y veult mediter nous est figuré et enseignement de la vie contemplative/ car ainsi comme le fol amant temporel est enamouré de la belle dame vermeille comme rose pour la grant beaulté quil voit en elle/ pour son simple maintien et contenance pour la courtoisie quelle luy donne/ pour la compaignie et entretenance quelle luy preste et pour le beau semblant quelle luy monstre qui sont les cinq flesches barbées adressant au cueur dont il est tant fort navré que il en pert entendement et sens se gary nest par la plaisant rose sa souveraine medicine. *Semblablement lamant espirituel eslevé en contemplacion regardant de loeil de son entendement les cinq playes vermeilles et lexcellente beaulte du bouton eternel/* congnoissant sa simplesse/ son unite/ son humble maintien et la pureté de son innocence/ considerant sa largesse charitable qui sestent sur toutes creatures/ pensant comment il est en la compaignie danges/ archanges/ glorieux saintz et sainctes/ . . . . *Et ainsi lamant qui ce medite et pense a le cueur navré damour espirituel. Non pas au chief/ es bras/ ne es piedz mais seulement au cueur:* comme il est escript es cantiques. *Vulnerasticor meum in uno oculorum tuorum.*(f. 17v.–18r.; emphasis mine)

[The preceding story, for whoever wants to meditate on it, figures and offers a lesson about contemplative life. Thus, just as the mad temporal lover is enamored of the beautiful lady, vermillion as a rose—for the great beauty he sees in her, for her simple bearing and purity, for the courtesy which she gives him, for the company and conversation which she offers him, and for the welcome which she shows him—these are the five arrows aimed at his heart, which is so deeply grieved that he would lose all understanding and sense if he were not cured by the pleasing rose, his supreme medicine. *Likewise, the spiritual lover, elevated in contemplation and looking through the eye of his understanding at the five vermillion wounds and the excellent beauty of the eternal bud,* knowing its simplicity, its unity, its humble bearing, and the purity of its innocence, considering its charitable liberality, which extends to all creatures, thinking how he is in the company of angels, archangels, glorious saints. . . . *And thus the lover who meditates on and thinks about this has his heart wounded by spiritual love. Not in the head, nor in the arms, nor in the feet, but only in the heart* as it is written in the Song: *Vulnerasticor meum in uno oculorum tuorum.*]

Affective contemplation becomes a natural counterpart to the limitation of reason indicated in the episodes about the astrologer, predestination, and Lady Reason. Human reason cannot understand God, and the human being needs to turn to the affective part of the soul to effect his or her return to God. Affective contemplation brings the Spiritual Lover to God in the eye of his understanding. The Spiritual Lover fixates on the object of his devotion exactly as the carnal lover fixates on the object of his desire. The movement from subject to object is purely libidinal.

The contrast between the limits of the astrologer's understanding and the range of human understanding through arational affective contemplation is exceptional. Where the astrologer was chastised for trying to understand the secrets of nature, this very same sort of understanding is described as possible through contemplation. By contemplating the stigmata of Christ the devout person can rise from within to the heights of the divine. In one of the most daring comparisons in the entire work, the narrator likens the revealing of a woman's body during an act of carnal love to the mystical contemplation of Christ's body:

> Ce corps est le precieux corps de nostre redemptur. Ceste macelle est la glorieuse face qui se amonstre aux vrays contemplatifs qui des yeulx de leur entendement le regardent par grant compassion. Ilz considerent les busses quil a receuz en ces macelles/ les batures de ses bras les poinctures de ses mains/ louverture de son coste et aultres bontez incomprehensibles ou ils prengnent plaisir inextimable. Et avec ce pour magnifier ses admirables ouvres leur est permis de regarder soubz la ceinturelle cest lespece du firmament qui ce bas monde circuit et embrasse. La sont les secretz de nature/ la sont les admirables corps celestialz qui par leurs influances besongnent sur les humains et engendrent merveilleux monstres qui se presentent a noz yeulx. Soubz ceste ceinturelle sont les plaisans motelettes ou les vrays amans se doyvent arrester par contemplacion sans descendre en la valee. . . . Sur ces mottellettes dignes de recommendacion se doivent recreer le vrays amoureux sans descendre en ceste miserable valee mondaine plaine dordure puante de vieulx pechez et de viles corruptions. (f. 24v.)

> [This body is the precious body of our redeemer. This visage is the glorious face that shows itself to the true contemplative individuals, who with the eyes of their understanding look at him with great compassion. They consider the bruises that he received on his face, the wounds of his arms, the wounds of his hands, the opening of his side, and other incomprehensible kindnesses in which they take inestimable pleasure. And with this to magnify his admirable works it is permitted to them to see beneath the belt; it is that part of the firmament that circles and embraces this lowly world. There are the secrets of nature, there are the admirable celestial bodies that by their influences affect humans and engender the marvelous sights that present themselves to our eyes. Under this belt are the pleasant hills where true lovers must linger in contemplation without descending into the valley. . . . On these hilltops worthy of recommendation, true lovers must entertain themselves without descending to this miserable worldly valley full of stinking filth and old sins of vile corruption.]

The contemplative person can see in the contemplation of Christ's body the same celestial bodies that the astrologer was not able to describe. Although these physical phenomena are transformed into a mystical version of Christ's body, they still represent a considerably different range of understanding than that offered to the astrologer. By concentrating on the stigmata of Christ, the contemplative individual can rise above the imperfection of human reason, which remains at the level of the corrupt and vile valley of human existence.

The difficulty with this experience, of course, is that it is indescribable. Molinet never says what these celestial bodies look like, and the image that he uses to attain that understanding is a conventional one of scenes from the Passion of Christ. The narrator explains that the "glorious mysteries of triumphant glory, of the life of the contemplative, the knowledge of the ardent love of admirable and perdurable essence and several subtle and invisible things cannot be brought to our notice without perceptible, human, and visible things, especially to people of simple understanding" (24r.). Yet how is he to express that experience if all human and visible things necessarily fall back into the realm of the imperfect existence of human reality?

The perfection of the singular and interior experience of the divine is beyond human expression, which necessarily has recourse to images related to human existence. The remarkable and sometimes confusing imagery of the *Roman de la Rose moralisé* can be understood as a result of this dilemma. The actual experience of the divine is beyond words, and yet Molinet must connect the carnal love of the *Rose* to the spiritual love of his gloss. When Molinet describes the rose itself in terms of affective contemplation, the transfer from carnal to spiritual can be understood as functioning, if only in a limited way. In these scenes, Molinet indicates that the act of affective contemplation is happening, yet he never describes the experience itself, since it is beyond description. He has recourse to a description of the effect that the experience has on the body of the contemplative individual, describing his tears, sighs, and feelings of great longing. His language is oblique, as happened in Gerson's description of the anagogical experience in *De mystica theologia*. Although Molinet says that the contemplative individual might have access to a view of the celestial bodies, he never describes them. They remain out of view and beyond description.

The greatest part of the *Roman de la Rose moralisé*, however, is made up of comparisons of passages from the *Romance of the Rose* with higher or spiritual meaning. When Molinet limits himself to using a passage from the *Rose* to teach a moral lesson, there is no transgression of the limits of human understanding; the *Roman de la Rose moralisé* can be read as a form of tropology, using the spiritualization of the *Romance of the Rose* as a moral lesson. These images can appear confused and arbitrary. The real problem occurs when Molinet gives a spiritual meaning to a character or object from the *Rose* by likening it to a divine individual such as Jesus Christ or the Holy Spirit. In these cases, the difference between perfect and imperfect makes the likenesses take on often troubling and confusing contours.

It is not that Molinet does not succeed in giving a spiritual meaning to the *Rose*'s carnal love. His recounting of the Spiritual Lover's quest of the spiritualized rose holds together from beginning to end. The construction of the allegory is, however, highly complex and sometimes contradictory. For example, Malebouche, the evil character from the *Rose,* is given two contradictory glosses. First, in chapter 19 he is glossed as Murmure, which would seem in keeping with the drift of the *Rose* itself, since Malebouche is responsible for spreading rumors about the lover (f. 30r.). However, in chapter 37, Malebouche is glossed as synderesis, which is at the very apex of mystical contemplation (53v.). Normally, synderesis should be able to help the Spiritual Lover come to the spiritualized rose, but here it becomes a negative force working against the Holy Spirit. The same sort of thing happens to Jesus Christ, who is used at various times as the spiritual equivalent of the rose, of Samson, of Vulcan, of Bel Accueil, of the Sun, and of Cadmus, the founder of Thebes (ff. 16v., 61r., 61v., 89v., 97v., 123r., 137r.). The less Molinet can actually connect the two terms of his comparison, the more elaborate they seem to become. There is no symmetry here and no architectural wholeness of being. The image is caught in the bind of needing to say that which it cannot say.

Like the stars and the clean plates in the miller and the astrologer episode, the image and its referent often have nothing in common. To compensate for the inadequacy of the similitude, Molinet simply increases the number of terms used to describe the spiritual meaning. It is sometimes as if the *Roman de la Rose moralisé* suffers from an acute case of *horror vacuii*. When a simple image might do, Molinet offers either several or one of such detailed complexity that the reader can lose track of what exactly is being figured. The *moralité* in chapter 4 exemplifies the complexity of this imagery. In this chapter, Molinet glosses God of Love as the Holy Spirit. The *moralité* begins "Par le dieu damours qui depart les amourettes a sa plaisance ou bon luy semble nous est signifié le saint esperit" (By God of Love who shoots his arrows at his pleasure wherever he pleases is signified for us the Holy Spirit) (f. 12r.). The *moralité* gives a point-by-point symbolic interpretation of each of God of Love's physical attributes in the *Rose* itself. The colors of God of Love's robe of flowers and the animals surrounding him are all given specific, if not highly abstract, meanings:

> Par ce quil estoit vestu dune robbe de flourettes dont les couleurs/ yndes/ jaulnes ou blanches subtilement assises causoient ymages doyseaulx/lyons/ leopars et autres bestes qui selon la difference de leurs proprietez estoient aucunes pitoyables cremeteuses mansuetez/ forces ou subtiles nous sont designees les vertus dons et gratuitez du saint esperit infuz es creatures embrasees de son amour. Dont les aucunes ont don de sapience en amant. Don dentendement en congnoissant/ don de conseil en enseignant/ don de force en soubstenant/ don de science en conservant: don de pitie en condoulant/ et don de cremeur en reverendant. Par les roussignolz et autres oyseaulx dont il estoit chargie/ lesquelz voletans autour de son chief abatoient les fueilles de son chappeau de roses nous sont notifiees ses infusions et graces que nous soubdainement devons recueillir/ les logier/ et encasser au parfond coffre de noz devotes pensees. Par doulx regard son escuier qui tenoit deux arcs de diverses facons ensemble dix fleches destranges sortes nous est figure inspiracion divine. (f. 12r.)

> [His robe of flowers whose subtly arranged colors (Indian yellow and whites) created images of birds, lions, leopards, and other beasts that, according to the difference of their properties, were either fearful and milkily tame, or strong, or subtle. These images designate for us the virtues, gifts, and exemptions of the Holy Spirit, which are infused in creatures enflamed by his love. Some of which have the gift of wisdom in love, some the gift of understanding in knowledge, some the gift of counsel in teaching, some the gift of strength in assistance, some the gift of science in saving, some the gift of pity in consoling, and some the gift of fear in reverence. By the nightingales and other birds flying about his head, which knocked the leaves from his hat of roses, are signified to us the infusion of grace that we suddenly need to gather, house, and place in the deep coffer of our devout thoughts. By Doulx Regard, his squire who held the two bows of different design with the ten strange arrows, is figured for us divine inspiration.]

Images such as this one proliferate in the *Roman de la Rose moralisé*, covering the surface of the work and cutting off both the underlying allegory and often obscuring the meaning of the image. Instead of simply giving a spiritual equivalent of God of Love, the image refers back to itself as a product of the imagination, as a highly artificial creation. Its complexity provides an indication of the problematic nature of a higher meaning in this work.

The rational incomprehensibility of the divine remains a constant throughout the *Roman de la Rose moralisé* even after scenes of affective contemplation describe the Spiritual Lover as coming to Christ. Any description of the divine remains beyond the pale in the *Roman de la Rose moralisé*. In the last chapter, Christ is described as the "incomprehensible rose" (f. 152r.). And the beauty of the Virgin Mary is described as "ineffable/ incomprehensible et inenarrable/" (ineffable, incomprehensible, and unrelatable) (f. 107v.). Incomprehensible to human intelligence, the perfection of these divine figures can be known only by the imperfect Spiritual Lover through affective contemplation. The images used to describe the divine or to equate the carnal love of the *Rose* with its spiritual counterpart are tainted by imperfection and turn in on themselves, becoming decorative and phantasmagorical. The images purporting to depict the spiritual meaning of the *Rose* cannot refer to that which they claim to represent, since only inexpressible affective contemplation can allow the human being access to the divine.

The images in the *moralités* are neither purely deictic nor purely poetic; they point toward the divine, but they cannot represent it. They can become self-referential in their exuberance, as happens in the image of the Holy Spirit. They can become highly illogical, such as the multiple uses of Jesus Christ as the spiritual equivalent of the various characters from the *Rose*. They can take on odd shapes, as many of the descriptions do, or they can take on a life of their own, like the *moralités* concerning the astrologer and the flooded bridge. They can shock and bewilder, like the moralization that uses the image of a woman showing her body to her lover to figure the contemplation of the body of Jesus Christ. All of these images move toward the final resolution of the story, but they cannot be construed as actually describing a truly higher meaning. They remain outside the interior space in which the true spiritual experience takes place.

The pictorial splendor of the *Roman de la Rose moralisé* brings to mind the flamboyant architecture of the hall church that Panofsky cites as an example of the late medieval critique of scholastic realism.[58] The *Roman de la Rose moralisé* exhibits a vast interior space through its allusions to affective contemplation. The affective individual is able to lift himself well above the limits of human understanding gained through rational interpretation of outside phenomena. And yet that interiority remains a blank space, one that cannot be depicted or described. The *moralités* giving the spiritual equivalent of the *Rose*'s carnal love are like the intricate tracery on a flamboyant gothic church. They, like flamboyant architecture that loses the order and symmetry of the high gothic, become highly decorative. The spiritual gloss of the *Rose* is not what provides real understanding of the divine: that can be had only through affective contemplation. The image attracts the eye but soon loses it, leading off in varied directions, which betray the symmetry of its model. The difference between the perfection of the ostensible referent and the imperfection of the symbol used to depict it skews the images and makes them into highly complicated and flamboyant forms that cover the surface of the page.

CHAPTER TWO

Molinet's Reversed Analogies

⚜   ⚜   ⚜

The flamboyant allegories of Molinet's *Roman de la Rose moralisé* pale beside his analogies in *Le Chappellet des dames* (1478) and the *Chroniques* (1486).[1] Molinet's literary appropriation of analogy, like virtually all metaphysical analogies during the Middle Ages, brings the perfection of the divine into a participatory relationship with the imperfection of the earthly. However, Molinet reverses the analogical relationship of perfect and imperfect, so that the perfect reveals the imperfect. Instead of the imperfect earthly term of the analogy revealing the perfection of the divine, the perfect term reveals the less perfect reality of the earthly term. Some of the oddest and most complicated imagery in the ornate canon of the fifteenth century results from Molinet's appropriation of analogy.

Molinet's conflicted use of analogy illustrates the conflicted state of fifteenth-century understanding and expression. On the one hand, analogical understanding was viewed as completely consistent and was defended by Thomistic apologists such as Thomas de Vio, Cardinal Cajetan, who synthesized and commented on Aquinas's analogical theories in the *Analogy of Names* (1498). On the other hand, a basic tenet of nominalist philosophy common in many of the universities of the time was the singularity of human existence. Things simply could not participate in an analogical relationship. Underlying this epistemological conflict was the question: How much does a human being resemble God and share in his perfection? Although the positions of the Thomists and the nominalists were not always all that different, their differences would have far-reaching consequences on the early modern conception of the universe. They can also be understood as being reflected in poems such as the *Chappellet des dames*.

By the end of the sixteenth century, the analogical way of understanding the universe would be more or less replaced by a more analytical understanding in scientific circles.[2] In theological circles, Protestants would take a decidedly less optimistic view of analogical understanding, and the Jesuits would openly contradict the Dominican interpretation of Aquinas.[3] Yet throughout the fifteenth and sixteenth centuries, questions about analogy are raised in the works of writers such as Rabelais, Montaigne, Ficino, and Calvin. Perhaps because of its demise, analogy inspired as much commentary in these centuries as it ever did in the Middle Ages.

Many of the bizarre images produced during the fifteenth and sixteenth centuries can be read as the products of the conflict between the desire for analogical representation and the impossibility of such a representation. The wondrous images that characterize the works of Rabelais, Montaigne, and Du Bartas are, at least in part, manifestations of the tension between the developing epistemology of the modern analytical age and the dying analogical system that still lurks behind nearly all depictions of the transcendental throughout the sixteenth century. Molinet's works illuminate the analogical imagery of these later and better-known works because they show the analogical paradigm in a slightly earlier period. At this time, the analogical paradigm, while still active and determinant at the level of the imaginary, was already deeply eroded in practice.

Analogy is virtually as old as Western thought. In Greek, it means proportion and was translated by the Latins as *proportio,* or "relationship of parts between themselves and with their whole."[4] Essentially, analogy establishes how one element relates proportionally to another. This method allowed Plato to explain the relationship of human beings and the transcendent. In the "Allegory of the Cave" in the *Republic,* Plato explains that the shadows cast on the walls are to the statues and figures of animals carried through the cave what these objects are to reality.[5] They are the median, or third term, that allows Plato's analogy to function. Plato's analogy provided a means of understanding the Ideal. At the heart of Plato's analogy lies the concept of participation; the terms of the analogy participate to different degrees in the same third element while remaining ontologically different.

For Aristotle, the relationship of the terms of an analogy is logical, in the same way a syllogism establishes the relation between its members. Aristotle's analogy does not depend on the terms participating in a common third element, because his analogy is based on proportional likeness but not on participation. The two elements share a common measure even if they do not participate in some common term. For example, a bird's wing bears a proportional likeness to a fish's fin; both help the animal move through its environment.[6] However, the bird's wing and the fish's fin do not participate in any common third term. For Aristotle, the relationship between the parts of an analogy is logical rather than cosmological.

The Aristotelian leanings of the High Middle Ages are unmistakable, but as Etienne Gilson writes, "Aristotelianism might finally lighten Neoplatonism or correct it, but it will never succeed in eliminating it."[7] It is not so ironic, then, that the participation so important in Plato should become one of the most fundamental parts of the theology of Saint Thomas Aquinas, one of the foremost Aristotelians of the Middle Ages. Participation is crucial to Aquinas because his analogy deals not only with logical distinctions but also, and more important, with being. The *analogia entis*, or analogy of being, is a way of explaining the relationship of actual beings whose existence was at the same time united and discrete. It allows Aquinas to show how the "one" of the universe, which is God, is connected with the multiplicity of existence. Human beings and God participate in the same qualities but to different degrees. Aquinas uses this idea to help prove the existence of God when he explains that God represents the ultimate perfection and that all things participate to various degrees in that perfection.[8] God's goodness is total, while everything else's imperfect participation is considered partial.[9] The relationship of the good man to the better man gives an idea of the hierarchy of being that leads to God. The good man partakes to a lesser degree than the better man of the perfect goodness of God. The fact that the terms *participatio* or *participare* and their derivatives are found throughout Aquinas's works gives an idea of how deeply this concept penetrates the theology of the Angelic Doctor.[10]

Although Aquinas never wrote a treatise called "De analogia," the question of analogy is present in many of his theological works.[11] Analogy is crucial because it allows Aquinas to avoid a purely univocal or equivocal understanding of the relationship of human and God. Aquinas believes that human and God share or participate in some qualities but that they do not share or participate in them entirely.[12] There is some resemblance between them, so their relationship is not completely equivocal. And yet, human and God are essentially different, so their relationship cannot in any way be considered univocal. Their relationship is curiously both univocal and equivocal at the same time.

The large number of interpretations of Aquinas's theory of analogy attests to the difficulty of describing exactly what analogy means for the Angelic Doctor. For the purposes of this study, it will suffice to understand the most general outlines of Aquinas's use of analogy and especially its appropriation in the fifteenth century by Thomas de Vio, Cardinal Cajetan. The differences between Cajetan's interpretation of Aquinas and that of Francisco Suarez, at the end of the sixteenth century, are profound and far-reaching and have been treated in depth by modern scholars.[13] Since Cajetan's *Analogy of Names* was written in 1498, his interpretation will be considered as defining a contemporaneous Thomistic view. This work also thematizes the use of "participation" in a way that helps explain the curious analogical shapes of Molinet's literary creations.

In the *Analogy of Names*, Cajetan schematizes three types of analogy that appear in Aquinas and then eliminates all but the last one. The three types of analogy identified by Cajetan are (1) unequal analogy, (2) analogy of attribution, and (3) analogy of proportionality.[14] Cajetan then illustrates how these three kinds of analogy can and cannot be used for understanding the relation between God and creature. The first kind of analogy, by inequality, is rejected by Cajetan because the analogates (the different terms of the comparison) are considered equal only formally through a common name.[15] The second kind of analogy, of attribution, depends on extrinsic relationships.[16] Cajetan gives the example of the word *healthy*. An animal is healthy intrinsically, whereas urine, medicine, and other similar things are called healthy not because of any health inherent to them but, extrinsically, insofar as they signify health, cause it, or have some relation to it. The animal participates in the quality *healthy* directly, whereas the urine and medicine are associated with health only indirectly, by signifying or causing it. This form of analogy is also rejected by Cajetan because it involves no real ontological participation.[17]

The only true form of analogy for Cajetan is the third type, analogy of proportionality. Cajetan explains that Aquinas refers to this variety as analogy "according to be" and according to intention.[18] Here, the analogates are considered equal neither in the perfection expressed by the common name nor in the "to be" of this perfection, yet they agree proportionally both in the perfection expressed by that name and in its "to be."[19] This means that there is both ontological and conceptual analogy, implying that the terms are neither univocal nor equivocal. Both analogates participate to varying degrees in a common element (analogon). In this way, *goodness* can be described as an analogon common to both God and creature. The goodness that exists imperfectly in the creature exists perfectly in God. Their difference in relationship to the analogon reflects the participatory likeness on which analogy of proportionality depends.

A crucial element in analogy of proportionality is the order in which the analogates (1) are known and (2) exist ontologically.[20] Although the goodness of God preceded the lesser goodness of the creature, it is the imperfect goodness of the creature that is known first. This ordering of the analogates into *prius* and *posterius* must therefore respect the sequence of what is known first, even if ontologically the order is the opposite. This is so because of the participatory nature of the analogates' relation to the analogon. The relationship between the creature and goodness and God and goodness is not the same. It is not univocal. Because God and the imperfect analogate participate to different degrees in the same analogon, they must maintain a rigid ordering in their expression. The imperfect analogate (the earthly term of the comparison) must be known first, even if its existence is ulterior to that of God. To propose that the divine term of the comparison can be known first would destroy the entire ontological foundation of this sort of analogy.

Placing the ontologically posterior term first in the analogy is crucial for Cajetan, who goes to great lengths to emphasize this point. The perfect goodness of God can only be known analogically, through the initial comprehension of the imperfect goodness of his creature. The ordering cannot be changed, because, if it were, this would imply that God is participating in the imperfection of his creature, which is both illogical and blasphemous. The ontologically prior analogate, God, cannot be given first in the analogy because this would imply that God resembles his creature in the same way that a painted subject resembles his portrait. Aquinas explains this situation succinctly: "And thus the creature has what is God's, and therefore is rightly said to be like God. But it cannot be said in this way that God has what belongs to His creature: wherefore neither is it fitting to say that God is like His creature, as neither do we say that a man is like his portrait, although we declare that his portrait is like him."[21]

Aquinas's use of the metaphor of the painting and its subject to explain the notion of prior and posterior is extremely important in the analysis of Molinet's appropriation of analogy. Although the painting is seen first, it is preceded ontologically by its subject, and only the latter can be said to resemble the former. To say that the subject is like the painting reverses the underlying ontological relationship of prior and posterior and destroys the notion of participatory analogy altogether. It is at this point that the nominalistic critique of realism comes to bear.

Although William of Ockham also never wrote a treatise on analogy, his understanding of the universe implies that analogy is impossible.[22] As discussed here in chapter 1, reality is singular for Ockham.[23] This means that two phenomena cannot participate in a common third term; if they did, they would by definition be that third term. Participation of any sort becomes improbable if not impossible in this context. Ockham, in fact, reduces anything susceptible of being analogical to univocity or equivocation.[24] For Ockham, things are either singular or they are not.

As far as knowledge of the divine is concerned, Ockham's theory of univocity is decidedly different from Aquinas's analogy, although it is structurally similar. Where Aquinas sees analogy as providing a way between univocity and equivocation, Ockham understands knowledge as being uniquely univocal in nature. He identifies three types of univocity that can be used to establish understanding: (1) perfect (like to like), (2) imperfect (somewhat like to somewhat like), and (3) conceptual (unlike to unlike).[25] Although structurally similar to Aquinas's conception of analogy, which provides a middle way between univocity and equivocity, Ockham's theory of univocity features one major difference, a difference with far-reaching repercussions. Ockham rejects the first two types of univocity as being relevant to an understanding of the divine, because human and God are in no way alike. Only the third kind of univocity is appropriate, because it allows two dissimilar terms to be brought together.[26] Although this sounds much like Cajetan's description of Aquinas's analogy of proportionality, there is a profound difference between Cajetan's analogy and Ockham's conventional univocity: there is no ontological participation in conceptual univocity.[27] The two terms of the concept do not share a common third term.

In Ockham's nominalism, an understanding of God can exist only as a concept abstracted from an imperfect creature. As such, it refers to God through convention, as a mental sign.[28] Ockham's understanding of the divine depends on God's creature construing his or her maker through a conventional sign. An individual cannot understand the goodness of God through a commonly shared analogon between God and a good person. There is no real but hidden structure holding the universe together, except, of course, for God's all powerful will, and real univocal resemblance between imperfect creature and perfect creator is rendered impossible. The only kind of resemblance possible is a conventional one, and human beings cannot be said to participate in the perfection of God, since God and human are in no way alike.

Although Ockham's concept of conceptual univocity did not bring an end to analogical thinking in the late Middle Ages, as Cajetan's later defense of Aquinas makes clear, it did trouble the analogical edifice on which so much literary imagery depended. Literary images in the late Middle Ages and throughout the Renaissance continued to depend on the analogical relationship of perfect and imperfect, but often those images reflected the troubled nature of the analogical edifice itself. This is the case, at least, of Molinet's *Chappellet des dames* and *Chroniques,* in which the analogical paradigm plays a dominant role in the poet's imagination at the same time that the analogical edifice is cracked and fissured. These cracks show that, although the relationship of resemblance between imperfect creature and perfect creature continues to dominate the cultural imaginary, this relationship is vitiated by the concept of difference. In these works, the desire for resemblance between perfect and imperfect motivates the literary image at the same time that the concept of difference allows the poet to manipulate his image in sometimes curious and often troubling ways.

Molinet's *Chappellet des dames* was written in 1478 for a secular patron, Mary of Burgundy, but it features an analogy of the Virgin Mary and Mary of Burgundy that is eerily reminiscent of Cajetan's theological definition of analogy. The divine or invisible reality of the Virgin seems to be the paradigm for the earthly and visible reality of Mary of Burgundy. By understanding how the imperfect and the perfect are proportionally related, the feeble human mind could have some inkling of what the divine might be like. The analogates are quickly reversed, however, making the visible and imperfect reality of Mary of Burgundy the paradigm for the invisible and perfect reality of the Virgin. The ontological ordering of prior and posterior is reversed, and the portrait of Mary, used to depict the invisible, takes on the allure of the visible. As it loses its referential footing, the portrait becomes exemplary of the flamboyant art criticized by Focillon and other modern critics as parasitical "excroissances" that obscure the surface of the underlying medieval tradition, of which they mark the "baroque" and degenerated end.[29] Molinet's flamboyant excess is not without its own particular beauty and fascination; however, it is necessary to understand these reversed images in the context of late fifteenth-century analogical practice.

Written as an encomiastic portrait of Mary of Burgundy, the *Chappel-*

let des dames resembles much of the poetics of late fifteenth-century Burgundy. It presents a grandiose picture of a politically powerful person at the court of Burgundy and subsumes the poet's voice in that of an anonymous narrator. The poem begins with the protagonist, L'Acteur, having an allegorical dream in which he is transported to the top of "une grosse montaine."[30] In a garden at the top of this mountain, the Acteur meets Dame Vertus and her attendants. She weaves a garland of flowers, a *chappellet*, for the Acteur, who is unable to understand its meaning. Dame Experience, one of Dame Vertus's attendants, offers to explain the meaning of the garland to the Acteur. At the end of Dame Experience's explanation, which employs the etymological identification of a *vis,* or power, with a person's name, the narrator makes an analogy between the Mary identified with the garland and Mary of Burgundy. The Mary that has just been etymologized is clearly identified as the Virgin Mary.

The relationship established between the two Marys in this analogy can be understood as revealing Molinet's complex understanding of analogy. It can be read as showing how the analogy of proportionality found in Thomas Aquinas continues to exist as a cultural paradigm but is also, at the same time, occluded in the general demise of analogical understanding as manifested in the nominalist critique of Ockham. At the end of Dame Experience's explanation of the garland, Dame Vertus tells the Acteur to return "au quartier dont tu es party" (to where you came from) and to present the necklace to "l'imaige de la glorieuse dame la plus propre et la mieux figuree qu tu sçairas trouver au monde" (the most fitting and exact image of the glorious lady you find on earth) (122). When he returns home, the Acteur begins to look for painted or sculpted images of the Virgin Mary in churches. However, all of the "imaiges" that he finds are inadequate because they are all "mal amesurees, tant en taille comme en painture" (badly wrought in stone and in paint) (123). It is only when he thinks about Mary of Burgundy that he finds an adequate "imaige" of the Virgin. Molinet's noble patroness is a good, but imperfect, equivalent of the Virgin Mary on earth:

> Et lors je pensay bieucop ou je porroie assir mon chappellet et me sembla que ma redoubtee dame, Madame Marie de Bourgogne, ducesse d'Austrice, secluse la virginité, estoit la propre et vive imaige de la roÿne supernelle, tant pour les loables vertus qui en elle florissent que par le mistere de nostre salut qui en elle est appropriet. (123)

> [And then I thought where I could place my garland and it seemed to me that my formidable lady, Dame Mary of Burgundy, Duchess of Austria, except for

her virginity, was the most exact living image of the eternal queen, as much for the praiseworthy virtues that flourish in her as by the mystery of our salvation that she possesses.]

Molinet's comparison of Mary of Burgundy with the Virgin Mary represents an exemplary use of Thomistic analogy of proportionality, for Molinet's reader understands the perfect virtue of the Virgin Mary by comparison with the less perfect virtue of Mary of Burgundy. In order for this comparison to work, Mary of Burgundy must participate in the perfect virtue that is manifested in the Virgin. The relationship between the Virgin Mary and Mary of Burgundy is neither entirely equivocal nor univocal, it is analogical, as Aquinas defined the term. Mary of Burgundy is similar to the Virgin Mary by the "loables vertus qui en elle florissent," but she is also different in her imperfection "secluse la virginité." The imperfect participates in the perfect, and Mary of Burgundy resembles the Virgin Mary as a portrait resembles its subject.

Once he has set up this "analogy of proportionality," Molinet then develops a comparison that reverses the sequence of analogates and destroys the notion of participation. He justifies his comparison of the Virgin Mary and Mary of Burgundy by proclaiming that the divine resembles the secular:

Et ne se doit nul esmerveiller, si je fais comparaison de la marrine a la filloeule, de la dame a la chambriere, de l'innocente a la pecheresse et de la vierge a la continente; car nostre seigneur et createur est souvent figure a sa creature, comme au lyon et au serpent, qui sont bestes ravisans, horribles et irraisonnables. (123)

[And no one should be surprised if I make a comparison of the godmother to the goddaughter, of the lady to the chambermaid, of the innocent to the sinner, and of the virgin to the chaste, since our lord is often figured by his creatures such as the lion or the serpent, which are horrible, irrational, and plundering beasts.]

The notion of participation is roundly rejected in this passage, and difference dominates instead of similarity. Molinet underlines the difference between the two terms of his comparison. The "innocente" does not participate in the sin of the "pecheresse," and Jesus Christ certainly does not participate in the horrible or unreasonable qualities of the lion and the snake.[31] By emphasizing the equivocity of the terms of his comparison, Molinet illuminates their ontological separation. This is not an analogical relationship, because there is no proportional participation involved. If there is any resemblance between the terms compared, it is entirely conceptual, and no one term can be considered ontologically prior or posterior to the other. Because neither term participates in some analogous quality, there is nothing to establish the ordering of the terms.

Throughout the rest of his comparison, Molinet destroys any notion of ontological ordering of the analogates. In the *Chappellet des dames*, the divine explains the earthly, rather than the other way around. The entire analogical structure, however, depends on this ontological ordering, without which such comparisons would make no sense. Without the need to respect the ordering of *prius* and *posterius*, Molinet's analogical imagery explodes into a chaotic mix of earthly and secular. In this reversed world, where the invisible is used to depict the visible, the story of the Virgin Mary and Jesus Christ is used to explain the history of the House of Burgundy. For several pages, Molinet uses the biblical story of Christ and the Holy Family to illustrate the illustrious nature of the House of Burgundy. The images in this section proliferate across the page like the tracery on a flamboyant gothic church. Like such flamboyant tracery, Molinet's analogical imagery has no structural support or function. It is purely decorative and is exemplary of the sort of figurative excess reviled by critics such as Huizinga and Focillon.

The panorama of this comparison is monumental. First, Adam and Eve's expulsion from the Garden of Eden is used as the paradigm for the Burgundian people's distress at the death of their monarch. Just as humanity is saved by the coming of the Virgin Mary and her son, so too the people of Burgundy were saved by their own Mary and her son:

> Ainsy dont comme liniaige humain fut englouti au perfond limbe pour le mors des premiers parens, tellement que le prince des tenebres tenoit tout le monde en possession, jusques ad ce que Dieu eust fait saluer la vierge et envoyé son fils en terre, le pouvre poeuple de la maison de Bourgongne estoit pareillement trebuchiet au limbe de doeul par la mort de son redoubté pere et a esté tourmenté de ses ennemis, jusques ad ce que le souverain des roix, c'est a savoir l'empereur, a fait saluer Marie, tres humble pucelle, et que, de son arche imperial, il a envoiet son fils en ce val miserable, par lequel elle a conchut le noble fruict qui sera cause de nostre redemption ou reparation.[32]

> [Thus just as the human lineage was swallowed into deepest limbo for the bite (*mors*) of the first parents, so much so that the prince of shadows held all the world in his possession, until God had hailed the virgin and sent his son to Earth, the people of the House of Burgundy were likewise thrown into the limbo of grief by the death (*mort*) of their redoubtable father and were tormented by their enemies, until the sovereign of kings, meaning the emperor, had hailed Mary, the most humble maiden and, from his imperial ark, sent

his son to this vale of misery, by whom she conceived the noble fruit that will be the cause of our redemption or repair.]

The comparison between the divine and the House of Burgundy appears at least eleven times in the poem, so that what had begun as a purely orthodox comparison of an imperfect earthly analogate with a perfect divine one, based on a proportionately shared analogon, becomes a massively overwrought portrait that overwhelms the borders of the initial analogy.

The following list gives only a small idea of the exuberance of the comparison of the divine with the secular in the *Chappellet des dames*. The column on the left describes the divine term of the comparison, and the column on the right gives its earthly equivalent:

—The expulsion from Eden and salvation through the Virgin Mary and Jesus Christ	—The despair of the Burgundian people and their salvation through Mary of Burgundy and her son
—The Virgin Mary and Joseph go to Bethlehem ("maison du pain")	—Mary of Burgundy and the council go to Bruges ("maison d'affluence")
—The Trinity	—Frederick, Maximilian, and Philip
—The Angels	—The Lords of the chapel
—The Christ Child in the manger between the cattle and an ass	—Labor and merchandise
—Octavian seeing the holy mother and child in a "cercle d'or"	—The Emperor reading news of the birth in a letter sealed with a golden signet
—Twelve years of peace	—Twelve months of peace
—Circumcision	—Baptism performed by M. Ferry de Glugny
—The three kings who come to worship the infant Jesus	—Three powerful persons: Mme. Marguerite, M. de Ravestain, M. de Sainct Pol
—The old man Simeon	—The people of Flanders.

Like a baroque decoration that spreads itself out and over its frame, Molinet's analogy spreads out beyond its initial premise. It spills across the limits of the form so that the minor term that was supposed to explain the major becomes the center of attention. Mary of Burgundy does not point toward the Virgin, but the Virgin points to Mary of Burgundy.

In the final section of the poem, the analogical reversal begun with the comparison between the "dame" and the "chambriere" finishes in a self-referential flourish. Although this passage seems to return to the Thomistic analogy of the section's early verses, it in fact erases the comparative relationship of the two Marys and becomes completely descriptive of one of the terms:

> Ainsy doncques appert par figure et similitude que nostre vertueuse princesse Marie est la vive face, protraction et imaige de la seulle emperis du ciel, non point celle que sainct Luc vault pourtraire, mais celle que le paintre immortel et souverain imagineur a volu tailler et former a son digne imaige et samblance: c'est nostre dame, nostre princesse, c'est nostre Marie, c'est nostre maistresse, a laquelle, en l'honneur de la roÿne du ciel, je presente ce vertueux chappellet. (125–26)

> [Thus therefore it appears that by figure and likeness our virtuous Princess Mary is the only living face, portrait, and image of the only empress of the heavens, not that Mary which Saint Luke wanted to portray but she who the immortal and sovereign image-maker wanted to cut and form from his own deserving image and resemblance: it is our lady, our princess, it is our Marie, it is our mistress to whom, in honor of the queen of the heavens, I present this virtuous garland.]

The "decadence" of the analogical system that has characterized the poem can be interpreted as giving way in this passage to a new but still occulted system of reference. The "c'est nostre dame, nostre princesse, c'est nostre Marie" is the fold between two ways of understanding. The analogical system, weakened by the nominalistic critique of ontological participation, gives way to a more analytic referential system. Over the course of the poem, Mary of Burgundy goes from an imperfect, earthly analogate of the Virgin Mary to a portrait whose features bear witness to a symbolic but structurally useless analogy with the Virgin Mary and, finally, to a nascent subjective presence that can be analyzed without any recourse to a comparative "other" that authorizes its presence.

The final stanzas offer a fitting resolution to the confused analogical structure of the poem. At the end of the section in which the narrator declares that it is to "nostre Marie, c'est nostre maistresse" that he is presenting the garland of flowers, there are three stanzas that destroy the poem's referential premise so that the poetic image produced to make the analogy function finally absorbs the analogy itself. In these stanzas, especially the first one, it becomes nearly impossible to say to whom the Hail Mary is being said:

> En disant Ave Maria,
> D'une voulenté non marrie,
> A celle qui bon mary a,
> Imaige a la vierge Marie,

Mon bel chappellet se marie;
Tres noble et bonne Marie ay je;
N'y a jusques en Samarie,
De fleurs aussy beau mariage. (126)

[While saying Hail Mary / With a will extraordinary / To she who is well
married / Image of the Virgin Mary / My garland does marry; / Such a noble
and good Mary I have; / And such flowers in marriage, / Cannot be found
from here to Samary.]

To whom is the Hail Mary being addressed? To the Virgin Mary? To
Mary of Burgundy? Or to no one at all? The trompe l'œil of this stanza
is exemplary of the troubled status of referential language in this poem.
The poem is obviously addressed to Mary of Burgundy, but how is she to
be referred to? The analogical model provides a philosophical justification for the poem and allows the poet to talk about Mary of Burgundy in
near divine terms. However, the reversal of the analogical paradigm indicates that this model of reference is no longer completely valid. The nominalist emphasis on the singular helps break down the analogical model
but does not provide an adequate discourse to deal with an analytical
mode of reference. In this stanza, it is obvious that there is no discourse
adequate to describe the emergent power of the political individual without recourse to an analogy with the divine. Yet that model is no longer
completely adequate, and it proves illogical and blasphemous when applied to an earthly figure. It can refer only to the divine and not to the
earthly.

The narrator says his Hail Mary to neither the Virgin nor to Mary of
Burgundy. His discourse falls outside the purview of analogical reference,
yet it does not establish clearly whom he is talking about in some other
system of reference. The Hail Mary is neither here nor there; it refers to
no one, because it relies on the referent being the Virgin Mary, although
the referent has been established as Mary of Burgundy. The poet cannot
refer to Mary of Burgundy in these terms, and the analogical paradigm of
the poem shifts the referent from the earthly to the divine. This analytical
mode of reference is beyond the poem's epistemological reach, yet the
subjectivity of the royal presence is manifest. The poem is not capable of
expressing the subjectivity of the individual, even though this subjectivity
is implicated in the nominalist concept of singularity. The analogical
model dominates the poem, even as an eviscerated form whose utility is
doubtful. The old ways of thinking have resulted logically in the appearance of this subjective presence, yet the discourse capable of dealing with

this presence has not yet evolved. Later, in the sixteenth and seventeenth centuries, such a discourse would be developed by the emergent scientific rationalism. At the end of the fifteenth century, however, this subjective presence is occulted in minor poems such as those of Molinet, hidden in the death throes of the analogical system that it someday would replace.

The evolution of the poem from hermeneutic analogy to panegyric image is much too careful to ascribe the eventual portrait to mere carelessness. The fact that Molinet uses almost exactly the same procedure in the *Chroniques* lends credence to the idea that this baroque portrait is grounded in the conscious use of a traditional form of analogy to decidedly nontheological ends. The move from analogy of proportionality to the final trompe l'œil Hail Mary is entirely consistent with Molinet's use of other forms of revealing a *plus hault sens*. He begins with a theoretical form that depends on certain metaphysical presuppositions and then internalizes those presuppositions so that the hierarchical structure inherent in that metaphysics is conventionalized. The analogy of Mary of Burgundy with the Virgin Mary depends on a specific ontological relationship that makes the two terms of the comparison proportionally similar but distinct. By destroying the proportional similarity of the two terms, Molinet also breaks down the necessary sequence of the analogates.

Once that sequence is no longer respected, Molinet can then compare the two terms as conceptually univocal elements. The subject and the portrait can be compared as images without worrying whether there is any ontological resemblance involved. Within the context of this conceptual univocity, a void is created that is filled with images. The *horror vacuii,* for which the final years of the Middle Ages are famous, is perhaps due to this lack of ontological order. At the beginning of the analogy, Mary of Burgundy was simply a subsidiary element used in understanding the perfect virtue of the Virgin Mary; by the end, Mary of Burgundy has become the sole subject of the portrait.

If the *Chappellet des dames* were the only example of this sort of inverted analogy, it could easily be dismissed as sloppy writing or as being overdetermined by political expediency. There is no doubt that Molinet's position as official historiographer had much to do with the shaping of the analogical portrait of Mary of Burgundy in the *Chappellet des dames*, yet many examples of these reversed images occur throughout Molinet's poetry and prose. The same tension between an analogical theory that reveals the nature of the perfect divine through proportional participation in a common quality and a practical emptying of analogy's ontological basis is also manifest in the "Paradis terrestre" in chapter 125 of the *Chroniques*, which Molinet wrote to commemorate the meeting of the emperor Frederick, his son Maximilian, and his grandson Philip in Brussels in 1486.[33] As in *Le Chappellet des dames*, Molinet here creates an analogy between the Holy Trinity and the House of Burgundy that reverses the ontological ordering of prior and posterior. The "Paradis terrestre," like the *Chappelet des dames*, is astride an "epistemological rupture," which helps explain their flamboyant nature.[34] Analogical understanding authorizes the comparison of the earthly and divine terms. Yet a nominalistic critique of analogy allows the poet to deconstruct the analogical paradigm and use it as a purely rhetorical form.

The "Paradis terrestre" is initially promised as an imperfect equivalent of the heavenly paradise so that simple people might have an understanding of the divine. Molinet says that he is going to "monstrer visiblement ung petit Paradis Terrestre par lequel figurativement ilz [the simple people] aront ung cognoissance d'ung seul Dieu tout puissant regnant en trois personnes" (show visibly a small Earthly Paradise by which they will figuratively have an understanding of a single all-powerful God reigning in three persons).[35] The premise is clear. The invisible and incomprehensible reality of the divine will be understood, in part, through an analogy with an earthly example.

Molinet repeats this idea four pages later, when he says: "Il loist jetter nostre regard en bas et enquerir quelque chief d'œuvre exquis en qui l'ymage deificque soit au vif fort bien empraintée . . . affin de veoir, de perchevoir, d'apprendre et de comprendre quelque beau paradis terrestre" (It is permitted to cast our gaze downward and to look for some exquisite masterpiece in which the deific image is well imprinted in life . . . in order to see, to perceive, to learn, and to understand some beautiful earthly paradise).[36] He then looks for such a place on Earth and, after rejecting both England and France, finally finds what he is looking for in Burgundy:

> Tournons doncques nostre face en orient . . . sur le saint throsne imperial, nous trouverons les personages qui nous donront similitude de la redemption humaine; non pas que je voeulle deiffiier les princes, mais, pour ediffiier le simple peuple qui à dur croit les saintes escriptures, je feray comparaison de l'invisible au visible, de l'éternel au temporel, et du facteur à la facture: car les hommes sont plus propres à ce faire que ne sont lyons ou bestes sauvages.
> (534–35)

> [Let us turn then our face toward the east . . . [to] the holy imperial throne. We will find there characters who will give us a likeness of human redemp-

tion. Not that I want to deify princes, but in order to edify the simple people who firmly believe the Holy Scripture, I will make a comparison of the invisible to the visible, of the eternal to the temporal, of the creator to the created, since human beings are more apt to do this than are the lions or wild beasts.]

Here, Molinet begins to reverse the analogical process he has established as his theoretical model. He says that he will compare the invisible to the visible, the eternal to the temporal, and the creator to the created. Molinet, in effect, does exactly what Aquinas said should not be done in an analogy: he compares the subject to the portrait. The subject resembles his portrait, and not the other way around. Using this inverted analogical model, Molinet makes the Holy Trinity his paradigm for the House of Burgundy. God the Father becomes the earthly equivalent of the emperor Frederick, Jesus Christ becomes the equivalent of Maximilian, and the Holy Spirit becomes the equivalent of Archduke Philip (536). The parallel drawn between Jesus Christ and Maximilian would seem particularly blasphemous:

Il [Maximilian] est à grant triumphe descendu en nostre val . . . pour remunerer les bons et reprouver les malvais. . . . Et, quant le roy sera assis au throne de sa majesté pour diffinir sentence criminelle et tous peser à la balance, les bons seront appellez à sa dextre, auxquelz il dira: "*Venite, benedicti patris mei!* Pour ce que vous m'avez receu, repeu, visité, secouru et asisté en mes concquestes, vous arez part à mon royaume." Puis il dira aux crueulx satrappes, pervers tirans et hideux satelites, qui seront au costé senestre: "Pour ce que vous m'avez tormenté, despité . . . departez vous arière de ma face, car vous serez brulez en feu de malediction . . . et les bons seront eslevez au throne d'honneur et en gloire de mon beau paradis terrestre, patron, figure et exemplaire de celeste court triumphante." (539)

[He (Maximilian) triumphantly descended to our valley . . . to remunerate the good and to condemn the bad. . . . And, when the king shall be seated on the throne of his majesty to establish criminal sentences and to weigh all peoples on his scales, the good shall be called to his right, to whom he will say: "*Venite, benedicte patris mei.* Because you have received me and replenished me, visited me, saved me, and helped me in my conquests, you shall have part of my kingdom." Then he will say to the cruel despots, twisted tyrants, and hideous henchmen, who will be on his left: "Because you have tormented and vexed me, . . . remove yourselves from my view, you shall be burnt by the fire of malediction . . . and the good shall be raised to the throne of honor and in the glory of my earthly paradise, the model figure and example of the triumphant celestial court."]

Here, Jesus Christ becomes the prior analogate both ontologically and hermeneutically to Maximilian. He also becomes equal proportionately to Maximilian. There is perfect participation for both analogates; both Jesus Christ and Maximilian participate equally in the same quality. According to Aquinas, there needed to be both intrinsic and extrinsic participation for both analogates. Here there is a univocal relationship between Jesus Christ and Maximilian of Austria. What applies to Jesus Christ applies equally to Maximilian. The final line reasserts the difference between divine and human by having Maximilian proclaim that his realm is the "paradis terrestre, patron, figure et exemplaire de celeste court triumphante," but this would seem too little and too late to undo the effect already created by his "Venite, benedicte patris mei." The last sentence reasserts the Thomistic structure of the analogy, but the image depicted breaks down that structure and depends on a purely conceptual relationship between the terms of the comparison. Just as in the *Chappellet des dames*, the literary image depends on a conceptual univocity of the type described by Ockham. The frame that makes the image possible is Thomistic, at least in the sense that the imperfect analogate is supposed to reveal the truth of the perfect.

Because Molinet does not observe the sequence of *prius* and *posterius*, his images not only become conceptually univocal, they also become extremely ornate. In the image used to represent the earthly analogates, Molinet mentions the seven planets, the seven virtues, the seven electors, the seven burning lamps, the seven stars, and the seven candelabras—in the middle of which is found the "filz de l'homme"(537).The Antichrist and his numerological equivalent, 666, are also included, without forgetting the damned, those in Hell, and the archangels. Although Molinet concludes his analogical portrait by declaring that his earthly paradise is the "patron, figure et exemplaire," as mentioned above, it is clear that it is the heavenly paradise that is the model for the earthly one.[37] The analogical form remains, but it has been divested of its epistemological function.

Without this function, the analogy becomes misshapen, as the image of the House of Burgundy moves to the center of the portrait. No longer a paradigm, by the end of chapter 125 the image of the House of Burgundy is a full-blown panegyric that uses the divine image to illuminate its own shape and relief. If analogy as defined by Saint Thomas Aquinas were used to explain Molinet's portrait of the House of Burgundy, it would be necessary to say that the divine term participates imperfectly in the absolute perfection of the earthly term. The Holy Trinity explains the triune character of the House of Burgundy in the *Chroniques*, just as the Virgin Mary explains Mary of Burgundy in the *Chappellet des dames*. And, just as in the *Chappellet des dames*, Molinet frames his reversed analogical portrait in a Thomistic analogy of proportionality. The beginning of the analogy promises to reveal the secrets of the heavens by finding an earthly image in which "l'ymaige deificque soit au vif fort bien empraintée," as does the end, when Molinet says that his earthly paradise is the "patron, figure et exemplaire."[38] Yet the portrait itself uses the heavenly as a model for the earthly.

Molinet's use of analogy is a historically specific phenomenon that can perhaps best be understood in light of contemporary fifteenth-century intellectual developments. Whether or not Molinet manipulates analogy according to Ockhamistic or Thomistic precepts, and whether he manipulates them implicitly or explicitly, is impossible to say. This analysis simply demonstrates that modes of understanding and expression were in full evolution at the end of the fifteenth century. The *prose du monde,* instead of revealing a higher or hidden meaning, is used as a rhetorical tool. This earthly trace of a higher reality is not the same as other forms of writing. It retains the luster that its former epistemological function accorded it. A spiritual glow or aura is reflected on the object it is used to describe, even if that object is in no way holy or divine. The metaphysical discourse of analogy sanctions Molinet's comparisons of the Virgin Mary and Mary of Burgundy, and the nominalist discourse of conceptual univocity allows Molinet's portraits in the *Chappellet des dames* and in the *Chroniques* to flourish in the curiously baroque fashion that we know.

These portraits are indicative of a shifting *episteme*. Northern France in the late fifteenth century was neither completely analogical nor completely antianalogical, in the sense that Foucault uses the word. The means of access to a hidden world were still found within the discourse of the late Middles Ages, yet these means are heavily contested.

CHAPTER THREE

"Etymologies tant ineptes"

❖   ❖   ❖

As the previous chapter has shown, the analogical paradigm that characterized so much of the medieval and Renaissance world depended on a closely woven relationship of likeness and difference. Likeness allowed two elements to be drawn into a relationship of resemblance, and difference allowed these elements to retain their proper identity. Too much likeness makes the world disappear in a miasma of univocal sameness; too much difference reduces the world to unsurmountable equivocity.

In the fifteenth and sixteenth centuries, the tension between sameness and difference was a crucial element in etymological understanding. Etymologies traditionally exploited the idea that words necessarily corresponded to the properties of things. A word's *vis*, or force, was established by means of resemblance between the word and its referent. In the etymologies of the fifteenth and sixteenth centuries, there was a shift toward difference as the analogical paradigm began to disintegrate. Although the old system of resemblance continued to authorize and frame the use of etymology, a newer conception of meaning, based on difference, motivated a purely rhetorical use of conventional language. This new use of language depended on the very fact that words were different from the things they signified.

The tensive poetics of likeness and difference reaches a high point in the work of François Rabelais, in which figures constantly invite the reader to look for an *altior sensus* that would reveal itself through allegories, analogies, and etymologies. Rabelais's mix of like and unlike is uniquely his but is not without precedents in either the literature or the theology of the fifteenth and sixteenth centuries. In this chapter, examples of linguistic resemblance are examined in the works of Molinet and two minor fifteenth-century theologians to show how the evolving tension between resemblance and difference, as exemplified in literary and homiletic etymologies, was a determining factor in the creation of figurative imagery during the years when the Middle Ages was giving way to the Renaissance.

Etymological practice in the fifteenth and sixteenth centuries was grounded in a long medieval tradition. Until the end of the fourteenth century, etymology was considered a science and was a constant element in literary and theological works.[1] Isidore of Seville's seventh-century *Etymologiae*, often considered one of the most important and influential texts of the Middle Ages, describes how the force, or *vis*, of a name is found by identifying the originary moment at which it was separated from its referent.[2] In the thirteenth century, Thomas Aquinas would repeat in the *Summa theologiae,* the medieval maxim that words must correspond with the properties of things.[3] In a more literary context, Philip of Thaon's *Comput,* written circa 1150, established an ontological resemblance between the referents of the words *lundi* (Monday) and *lumière* (light) because of the morphological resemblance of the words themselves.[4]

Medieval naïveté regarding etymology must not be overestimated, however, since there is much proof that writers and theologians were aware of language's conventional nature. Isidore's *Etymologiae*, besides mentioning Adamic origins for words, also describes language origins that were established *secundum placitum*, or by convention.[5] Aquinas might allude to the natural connection between word and thing in the *Summa*, but he emphasizes the conventionality of names in his commentary of Aristotle's *On Interpretation*.[6] If Philip of Thaon uses morphological resemblance to connect *lundi* and *lumière,* he also places his work under the guise of a conventional exercise when he states early in the *Comput* that every priest should have a *comput* in order to keep track of feast days.[7] All of these examples show that the medieval world was as conscious of the individuality and difference of linguistic representation as it was of its universality and resemblance.

The balance between resemblance and difference tips in favor of the latter in William of Ockham's fourteenth-century nominalistic critique of realism, which conventionalized written and spoken language.[8] Although Ockham's nominalism did not "definitively bury" etymology, as has been suggested, it did go far in problematizing the notion of linguistic resemblance in the later Middle Ages.[9] Instead of establishing a word's meaning through its referent, Ockham understood a word's meaning as the product of the human intellect. Because the relationship between referent and human language was no longer considered crucial, meaning could no longer be established through morphological resemblance. In the fifteenth century, Gerson explained that signification is an *operatio intellectus*, an operation of the intellect.[10] For Gerson, signification became a purely mental process instead of the product of the metaphysical resemblance of linguistic and ontological.

Although the shift from resemblance to difference is explicit and easily identifiable in the theoretical writings of writers like Ockham, it is more occulted in literary and homiletic uses of etymology in the fifteenth and sixteenth centuries. In these examples, etymologies bear witness to the troubled state of analogical understanding in the years immediately preceding the emergence of an analytico-referential paradigm that would mark the discourse of the modern era.[11] Throughout these works, writers justify or authorize etymologies according to the word's resemblance with its referent and then exploit this justification to rhetorical ends using methods that deny any meaningful connection between word and reference. Signification becomes less a question of resemblance between word and referent as the analogical paradigm fades and difference fractures the authority of "la morne figure du Même."[12]

In Molinet's *Chappellet des dames*, an etymologization of the name *Marie* typifies the tension between like and unlike that characterizes the agon of the analogical paradigm. Much of the complicated imagery of this poem is the product of a tensive relationship between the revelatory capacities of etymology, based on the resemblance between words and things, and its more rhetorical capacities, based on the basic difference between words and things.[13] As explained here in chapter 2, the *Chappellet des dames* is made up of two main sections: 549 lines of prose and 298 lines of verse. The first is the etymology of the name *Marie*, the second, already discussed, is an extended analogy of the Virgin Mary and Mary of Burgundy. The poem begins with the protagonist, the Acteur, falling asleep in the woods during a walk in the month of May. Lulled by the song of a bird, he is transported to the top of a high mountain where he finds a "Vergier d'Honneur" (Garden of Honor). Dame Vertus, one of the occupants of this *vergier*, weaves a garland of flowers for the Acteur. Because he is unable to understand the meaning of the flowers, Dame Experience, another inhabitant of the *vergier*, offers to explain "la totale signifiance" (the whole meaning) of the *chappellet* to the Acteur.[14]

The promise to reveal the "totale signifiance" of the *chappellet* sets the theoretical ground of the etymology. Dame Experience tells the Acteur that "il y a cinq lettres, cinq flourons, cinq vertus et cinq coulleurs, desquelles, se tu me prestes silence, tu auras par ordre et en brief la totalle signifiance"[15] (there are five letters, five flowers, five virtues, and five colors, of which, if you will remain silent, you will have, in order and in brief, the whole meaning). The resemblance of the words and their referents will allow Dame Experience to reveal the hidden meaning of the *chappellet*, for only she can see that resemblance. The letters are a form of the *prose du monde*, the signature of a hidden but similar reality, which Foucault talks about in *Les Mots et les choses*.[16] It is by reading this visible trace of an invisible reality that Dame Experience promises to reveal the "totale signifiance" of the *chappellet*.

The actual elaboration of the etymology proves quite different from the promised explanation. Instead of revealing a hidden or secret structure of the universe, the letters of the *chappellet* reveal a highly conventionalized grouping of flowers, virtues, and women.[17] Instead of being determined by a hidden but real organization of the universe, the letters are determined by the need to create a portrait of Mary of Burgundy, the poet's protector at court. The etymology, though theoretically established in the presumed similarity of word and referent, depends on the radical difference of the word and the thing it represents. Resemblance motivates the poem, but difference makes it possible. Without the potential resemblance of words and things, the etymology could not work theoretically. And without the real difference between word and thing, Molinet would not have been able to arrange the letters and figures according to the dictates of his political needs.

Dame Experience's explanation of the first flower illustrates how the entire etymology is developed:

Le nom de la premiere fleur se commence par M et est une fleur blance, propre et gente nommee marguerite . . . De ceste gratieuse flourette depend une vertus commenchant par meisme lettre, appelee Mundicité de corps et d'ame, de laquelle plusseurs sainctes et beatifies dames, habituees tant de leur fleur comme de la vertu, ont estés grandement loees, souverainement celles qui ont estés dignes de porter son nom exellent. Et premier Madame saincte Marguerite, tres humble vierge, gardant les aigneaux aval les champs . . . Marguerite de Prouvence . . . Marguerite de la Riviere.[18]

[The name of the first flower begins with M and is a clean, gentle and white flower called marguerite (daisy) . . . A virtue beginning with the same letter, called *Mundicité de corps et d'ame* (Health of body and soul) depends on this flower. Several holy and beatified ladies, as familiar with the flower as with the virtue, have been greatly praised, supremely those who have been worthy of bearing her excellent name. And the first was Madame Saint Margaret, a very humble virgin, tending the sheep in the fields . . . Margaret of Provence . . . Margaret de la Riviere.]

The etymology is grounded in the commonality of the letter *M* in various nouns. The flower marguerite, the virtue *Mundicité de corps et d'ame*, and the proper name Marguerite all share the same initial letter. Although in the case of the letter *M* there is an exact resemblance between the name of the flower and the name of the woman, this is not true in all cases; the only necessary common element between flower, virtue, and women is the initial common letter (see table). In order to provide a *totale signifiance*, these letters should be determined by a higher meaning beyond the Acteur's understanding. The actual rhetorical use of the etymology, based on contingent political needs, is made clear, however, once all the letters are put together and the identity of the etymological subject becomes apparent.

Letter	Flower	Virtue	Name
M	Marguerite	Mundicité de corps et d'ame (well-being of body and soul	Madame saincte Marguerite et alia
A	Ancolye	Amour a Dieu (Love of God)	Madame saincte Anne et alia
R	Rose	Recouvrance de grand leesse (recovery of great happiness	Madame saincte Rose de Viterbe et alia
I	Jennette	Instruction de bonnes meurs (instruction of good manners)	Jhenne, épouse (wife) de Philippe le Bel et alia
E	Englentier	Esperance de mieux avoir (hope of better things)	Dames d'Engleterre (English ladies)

The hidden meaning that results from Dame Experience's etymology is the identification of a woman named Marie; her virtues are the same as those associated with the list of flowers and exhibited in the list of women. No metaphysical truth is revealed through this *prose du monde*, and the connection between word and thing is entirely subjective and conventional. The association between the letter *A*, for example, the flower ancolye, the virtue *Amour a Dieu*, and Madame Sainte Anne is not established by resemblance. The flower's meaning results from the poet's manipulation of the arbitrarily configured "virtue" and the exempla of politically powerful women at the court of Burgundy. The flower resembles neither the virtue nor the women.

No essential likeness is revealed in these phenomena through a natural connection between word and thing. The word's *vis* is established by the creation of a meaning for the word at the level of what we could call the signified (virtue and exemplum). This association is purely nominal and is established through the arbitrary connection of signifier and signified. The desire for resemblance motivates the poem, but the actual elaboration of the etymology is determined by the portrait of Mary that Molinet is making and is grounded in the essential difference of word and referent.

In the poem, the predominance of an arbitrary or nominal resemblance over a real (in the medieval sense) or metaphysical one results in the total eclipse of the properties and virtues traditionally accorded to flowers and stones at this time. The structure of the poem, like that of medieval sermons (to be discussed later), completely subsumes the magical and medicinal properties accorded to flowers and stones in herbals and lapidaries. Instead of grounding the flowers' meaning in the properties commonly associated with them in herbals, the *Chappellet*'s flowers ground their meaning in the portrait of Mary of Burgundy that the poet is making.

Through the Middle Ages and the Renaissance, plants and herbs were held to have magical properties through the power of resemblance or sympathy.[19] In both herbals and in works of natural philosophy and alchemy, plants were described as having the power to cure ill bodies by reestablishing the elemental and occult equilibrium that had been lost due to sickness.[20] Natural philosophers like Henry Cornelius Agrippa and Paracelsus understood stones and herbs as possessing the powers or virtues of the celestial bodies with which they were connected.[21] The moon and the planets, bearing the powers of divine "intelligence," shared their occult and elemental capacities with the flowers and stones. Often the connection between flower or stone and its elemental virtue was based on resemblance. Stones, for example, that were dark and heavy were called "earthy," and those that were transparent and compacted of water, such as crystals, beryls, and pearls, were called "waterish."[22]

Within this tradition, herbals and lapidaries assigned medicinal virtues or powers to flowers and stones. Although the daisy was far from the most important flower in most herbals and alchemical treatises, it did have specific medical uses. An English herbal dating from 1525 explains that the daisy had the virtue of healing "botches."[23] A French herbal from the fifteenth century also notes the daisy's ability to cure wounds and venomous bites.[24] Gerard's *Herball*, from 1597, explains that the daisy is effective in healing sore eyes.[25] The other flowers enumerated by Molinet—ancolye (columbine), rose, jennette (broom), and englentier (wild rose)—all appear frequently in herbals throughout the Middle Ages and the Renaissance.[26] The rose, especially, had extensive symbolic importance in these works.[27] None of these definitions appears in the *Chappellet*.

Rather than describing the flowers' prophylactic or magical virtues, as found in herbals and alchemical treatises, Dame Experience assigns them values that valorize Mary of Burgundy. Instead of explaining which planet governs the occult or elemental value of each plant or giving its medicinal value, Dame Experience assigns values such as "mundicite de corps et d'ame" or "instructions de bonnes moeurs." These values are determined by the portrait that the poet makes of his poetic subject. The flowers' meanings are not associated with some metaphysical universe of which they would be the signature. They are purely arbitrary and determined by the immediate political situation of the historiographer.

The tension between the desire for a plenitude of meaning (which would be revealed through the flowers' magical properties or through the etymological *vis* of the name *Mary*) and the poetic deployment of the flowers and the name according to the whim of the poet's desire is also found in nonliterary works of the late fifteenth century. For example, Bernardino de' Busti, an Italian Franciscan monk, wrote a collection of sermons devoted to the Virgin Mary in 1493.[28] One of the sermons in Bernardino's *Mariale* is based on an etymology of the name *Maria* and follows the rhetorical structure described in the *Artes praedicandi* of the late Middle Ages.[29] First there is the theme (*thema*), a word or phrase taken from the Bible. Then the protheme (*prothema*) elaborates on the initial theme. Following the protheme, the division (*divisio*) divides the protheme into various parts. Further complications of the theme are made possible by a development (*dilatatio*).

Bernardino sets his theme by quoting from Saint Luke: "Nomina virginis Maria."[30] In the following section, corresponding with the protheme, Bernardino sets the theoretical ground of his etymology. Although he debates the nature of proper names, Bernardino gives short shrift to theories that deny a natural connection between word and thing and devotes much more time and space to defending natural language.[31] He quotes Thomas Aquinas to this effect ("nomina debent proprietatibus rerum correspondere") and says that it is a great privilege to be called Maria.[32] Once he establishs the suitability of the Virgin's name, Bernardino divides his sermon into three parts: attribution (*appropriatio*), figuration (*figuratio*), and meaning (*significatio*). This organization is even marked *divisio* in the text's margin. Each of these parts represents a "development" and provides the actual subject material of the sermons.

Structurally, Bernardino's amplification of the name *Maria* is very similar to the etymology found in Molinet's *Chappellet des dames*. In the sermon, for example, attribution relates the Virgin Mary's name to stones commonly found in medieval lapidaries.[33] The letter *M* is connected with the stone *margarita* or pearl. The qualities of the pearl—beauty, clarity, etcetera—are then associated with the Virgin. The other letters are *A* for *adamas* (diamond), *R* for *rubinus* (ruby), *J* for *jaspis* (jasper), and *A* for *allectorius* (cockstone). Figuration unites the letters of the Virgin's name with the names of women from the Hebrew Bible. *Maria* is developed into *Michol, Abigail, Rachel, Judith*, and *Abisach*. Finally, in Bernardino's scheme, meaning links the name of the Virgin Mary to five beneficial roles she plays for humankind; she is *mediatrix nostra, auxiliatrix nostra, reconciliatrix nostra, illuminatrix nostra*, and finally *advocata nostra*. These three sections (attribution, figuration, and meaning) compose nine-tenths of the sermon.

The elaboration of the letters allows Bernardino to develop his theme— the Virgin's goodness and greatness —but does not reveal a secret meaning. It is also in these three sections that the theoretical premise of the sermon, based on resemblance, comes into conflict with the principle of difference. Because the letter cannot establish a morphological minimal pair with an extralinguistic referent, its *vis* cannot be established through its resemblance with a referent. It is the lack of real resemblance between the letter and any extralinguistic referent that allows the preacher to dispose of his sermon as Bernardino does in the *divisio*. For this very reason, Thomas Waleys, the author of a late fourteenth-century *ars praedicandi*, had earlier advised preachers not to use this sort of etymological structure in organizing their sermons.[34] There is not enough resemblance between the constitutive elements of the etymology to make a claim to real meaning. Alphabetic likeness is not strong enough to establish a word's *vis* etymologically.

The conflict between the theoretical promise in Bernardino's protheme, in which he talks of the natural connection between word and thing, and the rhetorical practice of his "development" reveals the same tension found in Molinet's *Chappellet des dames*. Although Bernardino grounds his sermon in a theory of natural language, his use of the letter *A* in all three "developments" shows that his rhetorical practice depends on a conventional use of language. In the section devoted to "appropriateness," for example, the letter *A* is identified as both "adamas" and "allectorius." Waleys's comments in *De modo componendi sermones*, mentioned above, can be applied to Bernardino's etymology of *Maria*. The referential quality of the letter is shown to be arbitrary. If there were something inherent in the letter *A* then it could not be applied to both *adamas* and *allectorius,* which have different properties. In Bernardino's sermon, Aquinas's prescription is reversed: "nomina *non* debent respondere proprietatibus rerum." The relationship between word and thing has been established according to the whim of the writer.

No hidden or mystical structure of the word is revealed through Bernardino's etymology. It is purely rhetorical in nature, allowing the preacher to amplify an initial theme. The only hidden structure revealed is the sermon's rhetorical armature: theme, protheme, division, and development. The balance of resemblance and difference collapses in Bernardino's sermon, since the minimal resemblance of the different elements is not enough to prevent their proliferation into discrete and distinct units. As Waleys says, this kind of rhetorical organization, while showing the formal characteristics of etymology, does not provide adequate resemblance. The etymology's theoretical premise based on resemblance is erased by its rhetorical practice based on difference.

The problems confronted in Bernardino's sermon are exacerbated in Jean Mombaer's *Rosetum exercitiorum spiritualium,* compiled in 1494 as a collection of spiritual exercises practiced by the followers of the *Devotio Moderna.* As in Bernardino's sermon, the balance of resemblance and difference is destabilized in favor of the latter.[35] In a later edition of the *Rosetum,* published in 1510, a section devoted to the qualities of the Virgin Mary, missing in the earlier 1494 edition, appears.[36] A part of this section is an etymology that Mombaer openly admits he took from Bernardino.[37]

Mombaer schematizes Bernardino's homiletic etymology so that it resembles the spiritual exercises that compose much of the *Rosetum*:

	m		Margarita puritatis et confortationis
	a		Adamas reconciliationis amoris
per	*r*	intelligitur	Rubinus letitie et illuminationis
	i		Jaspis tutele et securitatis
	a		Allectorius bone fortune glorie et honoris

Item per quinque illustres	*m*	Michol
feminas testamenti veteris	*a*	Abigail
	r	Rachel
	i	Judith
	a	Abisack
Item ethimologizatur		Mediatrix
secundum quinque		Auxiliatrix
beneficia	quia	Restauratrix
		Illuminatrix
		Advocatrix
Item secundum quinque		Misericordia pietatis
perfectiones eius	quae sunt	Altitudo contemplationis
		Religiositas devotionis
		Innocentia puritatis
		Affluentia virtutis

Each letter is connected with a stone, a quality, or a woman, in much the same way that Bernardino describes them. Although, as Mombaer admits in his introduction of Bernardino's etymology, these stones are found in medieval lapidaries, their meanings have been remotivated to such a degree, in order to agree with the name being etymologized, that they no longer bear any resemblance to the "virtues" found in lapidaries.

The context of this etymology, in which the balance between likeness and difference clearly favors the latter, is grounded in the principle of resemblance. Mombaer begins the section of the *Rosetum* devoted to the etymologization of the Virgin's name with a subheading: "Considerations on the worthiness of the name Mary."[38] He discusses the nature of proper names in much the same way Bernardino does, offering arguments both for and against natural language. Like Bernardino, he cites Thomas Aquinas and other theological authorities in defense of natural language and explains that the perfection of the Virgin's name is evident in its relation to the morning star, "stella maris." He justifies this connection by saying that the morning star is immutable and incorruptible and that it offers guidance to sailors in the same way that the Virgin offers guidance to human beings. What is true of the star is true also of the divinity; their commonality is manifested in the morphological similarity of the words *Maria* and *Maris*.[39]

Mombaer's theoretical premise is contradicted, however, once he attempts a kabbalistic etymologization of the name *Maria*. In order to show how special the Virgin Mary is, Mombaer explains that, in the Greek of the New Testament, the mother of Christ's name always ends in the Greek equivalent of the Latin "am," while the other Marys' names end in the Greek equivalent of the Latin "a."[40] This nuance, he notes, is lost in Latin. He also explains that in the Gospel of Saint Matthew and elsewhere, the name *Mariam* (when it refers to Christ's mother) is written in Hebrew, but with the letters representing the Latin *m* reversed.[41] Normally, Mombaer says, the letter *mem* in Hebrew has an open form (*mem apertum*) at the beginning of a word and a closed form (*mem clausum*) at the end. In this case, however, the closed *mem* is found at the beginning. This, he says, is the Holy Spirit's way of revealing the mystery of Mary, whose coming was known to God but unknown to man ("Et sic apertam Deo; clausam viro").[42] He then explains the numerological equivalent of the different *mem*s, based on kabbalistic principles. The closed *mem* has a value of six hundred, and the open *mem* has a value of forty.[43] Then, remarking that the name of Mary (*hoc nomen*) is also seen with an open *mem* at the beginning and a closed *mem* at the end, he seems to lose confidence in his etymology and confesses that he cannot understand how anything of the truth could be understood in all of this ("Quid igitur veritatis subsit ego nescio").[44]

It is as if the diversity of values, both linguistic and numerological, troubles Mombaer's understanding. So long as each letter has a stable and univocal meaning, etymologization is possible. Once there are too many values assigned to each letter, depending on its position in the word, then the etymology becomes impossible to follow. He concludes this section on the value of the name *Mary* by leaving all future investigations of this nature to the studious-minded scholar and by declaring that, after all, Mary's name is full of wonder and amazement.[45]

In his schematic appropriation of Bernardino's etymology of the Latin name *Maria*, Mombaer repeats the error that he identifies in the kabbalistic etymology of *Mariam*. Mombaer wants the etymology to reveal a secret meaning, but he is blind, in Latin, to what his own linguistic incompetence made him aware of in Hebrew. He repeats Bernardino's dual attribution of qualities to the letter *A*. According to Mombaer, the letter *A* can mean *Adamas* or *Allectorius*, but it can also mean *Auxiliatrix* and *Advocatrix*. The *plus hault sens* that is revealed through resemblance, and that Mombaer mentions in his theoretical discussion about proper names, is denied by the conventionality of the language he uses in his own etymology. His inability to make the Hebrew etymology work because of the equivocal nature of the letter *mem*, at least in his own misunderstanding, reflects this problem. The tension between resemblance and difference that is necessary to etymology is destroyed when either term overpowers the other. Too much resemblance erases all difference in overwhelming univocity, while, as happens here, too much difference leads to incoherent equivocity. Although this lack of resemblance allows Mombaer to appropriate Bernardino's homiletic etymology, it also prevents him from understanding the kabbalistic etymologization of the word *Maria*.

In the sixteenth century, the tension between like and unlike will end in an explosive mix in the works of François Rabelais. Rabelais's extensive use of linguistic resemblance in place of ontological resemblance places his epistemology squarely in the nominalist fold. The relationship of "or donné par don" and "ordonne pardon," that he makes in the inscription above the door in the Abbey of Thélème, at the end of *Gargantua*, for example, is strictly linguistic. Yet lurking constantly behind these nominal connections lies the theoretical possibility that words can reveal the secret organization of the universe.[46] Rabelais also alludes to this possibility when he says that Egyptian hieroglyphics did offer linguistic plenitude.[47] He contrasts the ineptitude of contemporary sixteenth-century court emblematists who exploited the very sort of homonymic resemblance he uses in the coupling of "or donné par don" and "ordonne pardon" with the meaningful resemblance of hieroglyphics.

The ambiguity between knowledge based on linguistic likeness and knowledge based on linguistic difference, which characterizes so much of Rabelais's work, is part of the same tradition to which Molinet, Bernardino, and Mombaer belong. The tension between theory based on resemblance and practice based on difference is crucial to Molinet's etymological portrait of Mary of Burgundy as well as to Bernardino and Mombaer's works. During the "waning of the Middle Ages" and the early years of the Renaissance, resemblance was loosening its grip on difference, and meaning was becoming more a question of the intention of the writer or speaker and less a matter of the word's resemblance with its referent.

This evolution from likeness to difference was neither unique to Rabelais nor completely new in the fifteenth and sixteenth centuries. Already implicated in the medieval idea that "words should correspond with the properties of things," the play of resemblance and difference in etymology slips more and more toward difference in the works studied here, working out in a literary and homiletic context the development manifested in the nominalist critique of realism in the fourteenth century. As the works of Molinet, Bernardino, and Mombaer show, difference con-

stantly vitiates the theoretical desire for the wholeness of being that resemblance represents, showing resemblance to be fictitious and often
dangerous.

These works can be understood as products of the epistemology that
was slowly emerging from the analogical world. Resemblance still exists
as a state of desire and authorizes the use of etymology, yet it is resemblance's weakened state that allows difference to separate the word from
its referent and to introduce a new means of signification. This nascent
form of signification, which understands meaning as the product of what
we would now call the signifier, is part of the development of the old system and does not represent a radical break with the past. This new form
of understanding is observable in the agonistic struggle of analogical understanding that characterizes all the works studied in this chapter. As
these texts show, Rabelais's text, and others from the sixteenth century,
represent less a rupture with the past than a continuation of a struggle
between resemblance and difference. The modernity, or futurity, of Rabelais is obvious in the skepticism that the Pantagruelians show toward
forms of knowledge based on contingent resemblance, yet that very skepticism is a product of the analogical tradition itself.

Throughout the works studied in this and the preceding chapters, allegories, analogies, and etymologies are caught between the desire for plenitude of meaning and individual difference. The unsurmountable chasm
between secular and divine and between perfect and imperfect prevents
the contingent human sign from representing a higher or hidden meaning.
Desire for plenitude, for contact with the absolute, drives these works and
pushes the human sign into ever more convoluted shapes in the poet's effort to overcome the fallen nature of human existence.

Molinet's poetics is shackled by his peculiar understanding of the universe, but these shackles create an atmosphere that makes possible images
as strange as the Hail Mary at the end of the *Chappellet des dames*. In this
work, the conflict between resemblance and difference turns the image
away from its referent, which slips steadily from the poet's grasp. Intellectually anchored in difference, Molinet's poetics bears the trace of a
tradition, which successfully surmounts the contingency of human existence. Images such as the analogy between the Virgin Mary and Mary of
Burgundy and the etymologization of the name *Marie* bear witness to the
tradition of understanding that brought perfect and imperfect, absolute
and contingent, and divine and human into a relationship of participa-

tion. At the same time, these images, in their own flamboyant exuberance, illustrate how that tradition of resemblance was riven by difference and singularity.

Within the analogical tradition, the human being was part of the chain of being, which allowed him to understand his part in the whole. The peculiar genius of Molinet's poetics depends on the poet's inability to grasp the nature of the whole. Were this whole to become comprehensible, Molinet's twisted allegories, analogies, and etymologies would lose their force. They would straighten out and become logically coherent as the relationship of part and whole was reestablished.

In the poetics of Jean Lemaire de Belges, Molinet's successor at the court of Burgundy, this is precisely what happened. Lemaire's poetics connect the particular to the whole. Molinet's ghostly, disembodied images will be replaced by Lemaire's dazzlingly plastic images, whose material beauty will allow the poet and the reader to accede to the ideal whole. Although the poetics of resemblance manifested in Lemaire's writing will provide some of the best-known poetry of the French Renaissance, the history of sixteenth-century French literature will show that, by the end of the century, Molinet's troubled reading of the universe is the way of the future.

CHAPTER FOUR

Jean Lemaire de Belges:
A Metaphysical
Plus hault sens?

⚜   ⚜   ⚜

Jean Lemaire de Belges, who succeeded Molinet as *indiciaire* at the court of Burgundy in 1507, provides both the historical and theoretical midpoint in this study.[1] Historically, he is connected to both Molinet and Rabelais. Although it has never been conclusively proven, Molinet has even been identified as Lemaire's uncle.[2] There is little doubt that Lemaire recognized Molinet as his mentor and as a poet of significant stature.[3] In the *Plaincte du desiré*, for example, Lemaire says:

> . . . Si croy que Rhetorique
> Finablement avec eux se mourra.
> Un bien y ha qu'encor me reste, et dure,
> Mon Molinet moulant fleur et verdure,
> Dont le haut bruit iamais ne perira.[4]

> [It is believed that Rhetoric / Finally will die with them. / Yet one remains, and continues still, / My Molinet milling flower and greenery, / Whose fame shall never perish.]

Just as significantly, from a theoretical viewpoint, Lemaire often adopts Molinet's imagery. The *Couronne margaritique*, for example, takes the etymological structure of Molinet's *Le Chappellet des dames* as a model, and the *Concorde du genre humain* offers an adaptation of the *Chappellet*'s analogy between the Virgin Mary and Mary of Burgundy. The ways in which Molinet's imagery is both repeated and changed in Lemaire's poetry illustrate how the subjective and intuitive understanding that dominates Molinet's poetics develops into something quite different in Lemaire's prose and verse.

As Lemaire accords Molinet a special place in his literary world,

Rabelais will also single out Lemaire in his work.[5] When Epistemon returns from the dead after having his "couppe testée" in *Pantagruel* 20, he recounts having seen Lemaire along with François Villon in the Champs Elysées:

> Je veiz Maistre Jehan Le Mayre qui contrefaisoit du pape, et à tous ces pou-vres roys et papes de ce monde faisoit baiser ses piedz: et, en faisant du gro-bis, leur donnoit sa bénédiction, disant: "Gaingnez les pardons, coquins, gaingnez, ilz sont à bon marché. Je vous absoulz de pain et de souppe: et vous dispense de ne valoir jamais riens." Et appela Caillette et Triboulet, disant: "Messieurs les Cardinaulx, depeschez leurs bulles; à chascun un coup de pau sus les reins." Ce que fut faict incontinent.[6]
>
> [I saw Master Jean Lemaire impersonating the pope, and he had all those poor kings and popes of this world kiss his feet; and putting on the dog, he gave them his blessing, saying: "Get your pardons, scoundrels, get them, they're cheap. I absolve you *de pain et de souppe* (of bread and soups), and dispense you from ever being good at anything." And he called Caillette and Triboulet, and said: "My Lord Cardinals, dispatch their bulls: to each one a bang on the loins with a pike." Which was done straightaway.]

Rabelais alludes in this passage to Lemaire's attacks on the papacy in *Le Traicté de la différence des schismes et des conciles de l'église* and in *Le Traicté nommé la légende des Vénétiens*, where Lemaire explains that all of the schisms in the church have been caused by the pope and all the rec-onciliations have been effected by secular kings.[7]

Other links between Lemaire and Rabelais appear in Rabelais's work. For example, Raminagrobis, one of the central characters in the *Tiers Livre*, has also been identified as Lemaire, although no direct attribution is possible.[8] The Hesiodic "manoir de Areté," which houses Gaster in the *Quart Livre*, has also been interpreted as a direct borrowing from Lemaire's *La Concorde des deux langages*.[9] Like Lemaire's own borrow-ings from Molinet, Rabelais's repetition and alteration of imagery from Lemaire serves to illustrate how the Middle Ages and the Renaissance constitute one period marked by a continuing tradition of change.[10]

Perhaps even more than Molinet, Lemaire is "à cheval" the divide between what is construed as two epistemological systems.[11] His use of symbolic forms of discourse to represent a higher or hidden meaning is as conflicted as Molinet's, but where in the *Chappellet des dames* Molinet conventionalizes the metaphysical presuppositions of etymology and analogy, Lemaire tends to reestablish the possibility of a metaphysical ref-erent. Here, Erwin Panofsky's distinction between a nominalistic North and a more idealist South in Europe during this period can provide a useful point of entry. Although Panofsky's theory is broad, it does help map out certain crucial differences and similarities in Lemaire's and Molinet's works. Panofsky states that the Italian Renaissance strives for the "ideal" under the influence of Neoplatonists like Marsilio Ficino, whereas the "via moderna" of the North claims that the quality of reality belongs exclusively to the particular, directly perceived by the senses.[12] The distinction between North and South is pertinent to Lemaire's case, as his work is affected both by the northern tradition, to which Molinet belonged, and by the idealizing tradition coming from Italy.

This combination is evident in Lemaire's use of imagery taken from Molinet and of the idealist forms that cast that imagery in a new light. If Molinet's flamboyant imagery in the *Chappellet des dames* reduced vibrant analogical symbols to a more decorative status, poems such as Lemaire's *La Couronne margaritique* revalorize symbolic forms and use them once again to reveal a hidden or higher meaning. In Lemaire's poetic world, which tends toward the Ideal, the internalized metaphysics of Molinet's *Le Chappellet des dames* once again come back into the open. If this idealizing influence is accepted as being operative in Lemaire's poetry, then it is no wonder that the "surreal" imagery of Molinet, which can be understood as a "mental sign," becomes the "magical" imagery of Lemaire as the conventional connections between things and between creature and God become "real" once again.

The question of Lemaire's Italian influence has divided modern critics. Georges Doutrepont sees the poet as influenced by Italian culture and places him in the Renaissance.[13] On the contrary, Pierre Jodogne understands Lemaire as having been barely touched by an Italian influence, though he emphasizes the importance of Lyons, the port of entry for much of Italian Neoplatonism into France, on Lemaire's poetry.[14] It is possible to understand Lemaire as being affected by both French and Italian influences and to read his work as both medieval and Renaissant. Lemaire can be understood as having opened up the private and subjective discourse of Molinet.[15]

Lemaire did not start out with such a viewpoint. A minor work called the *Petit Livret Sommaire* (1498) shows how Lemaire, very early in his career, was affected by the same Christian spirituality found in Molinet's poetry.[16] This small compilation of poems—by Ovid, Virgil, Seneca, Molinet, Chastelain, and Lemaire himself—is the only known document of Lemaire's literary activity before the *Temple d'honneur et de vertus*, written in 1503.[17] All the poems in this compilation are organized around the *Song of Songs*, and this structure gives even the poems of Ovid and Seneca a highly mystical and Christian flavor.[18]

The piety of Lemaire's works in the *Petit Livret* places the poetic imagination in a decidedly skeptical framework in relation to the divine. In one Marian poem by Lemaire, *Une Oroison composée par Jehan Le Maire de ladicte ville de Vallenciennes,* the epistemological constraint of Molinet's Marian poems is found. Here, Lemaire talks not only of contemplative knowledge of the divine but also of the limitations of human creation.[19] Lemaire's humility before the unsurpassable and unattainable quality of the Virgin ends in an impasse, since he is unable to describe the object of the poem. This poem, like the other Marian poems in this collection, is marked by the verbal virtuosity for which the *rhétoriqueurs* are famous. Running vertically and diagonally throughout the poem in red letters are acrostics, such as "Salve regina misericordie (Hail, queen of mercy)."[20]

It is not, perhaps, coincidental that this sort of wordplay occurs most often, both in Molinet and in Lemaire, in their religious poetry. It is as if the cognitive impasse that is at the thematic center of the poem forces the poet into a more material view of language. Since language cannot adequately bring imperfect subject and perfect object together, language twists and refashions itself into a more decorative form. The same epistemological difficulty that made the analogical symbol inoperative and more decorative in Molinet's *Le Chappellet des dames* makes the symbolic use of language undergo the same transformation. Unable to join the two terms of the analogy and unable to link the subject and object of a grammatical phrase, analogy and language lose their symbolic function and become decorative and formal. In fact, this sort of acrostic is rarely found in the nonreligious works of Lemaire and Molinet, where the authors can adequately express and describe the object of their poems.

Though it is possible that Lemaire had been exposed to Italian influences earlier than 1498, it is not evident in his *Petit Livret*. As Pierre Jodogne remarks, this collection hints very strongly that Lemaire was influenced by the mysticism that pervaded much of intellectual life in late fifteenth-century France.[21] The poetic imagery in the *Petit Livret* reflects the poet's inability to depict a transcendent referent. Likeness is reduced to a purely linguistic level; the acrostics and *rimes riches* that run throughout Lemaire's poems in this collection are the only way to bridge the gap between discrete phenomena. Ontological unity of being would seem resolutely absent from the *Livret*.

This situation soon changed, as Lemaire underwent the influence of

Lyonese Neoplatonism in the years following 1498. Lemaire spent the years from 1498 to 1503 at Villefranche-sur-Saône working as a *clerc de finances* for Pierre II of Bourbon; Henry Guy states that it was during this period that Lemaire met Neoplatonist intellectuals such as Symphorien Champier.[22] Pierre Jodogne places Lemaire's first real contact with Champier and other Lyonese intellectuals later, after 1506, when Lemaire stopped in Lyons on his way to Rome on a mission for Margaret of Austria. Though the exact date of Lemaire's contact with Lyonese Neoplatonism is unknown, Lemaire's imagery, poetics, and epistemology underwent major changes in the seven years between the *Petit Livret* and the *Couronne margaritique*. Where the Christian divinity was inaccessible to reason in the earlier work, in the latter, the pagan ideal is accessible.[23] The poetic imagery used to describe a higher meaning changes dramatically as a result, and the abstract character of such imagery in Molinet becomes much more concrete and luminous in Lemaire.

The *Couronne margaritique*, written in 1505 after the death of Philibert, Margaret of Austria's husband, offers an example of how Lemaire takes the conventionalized symbolic forms found in Molinet and inserts them in a poetic world in which the connection between transcendent and secular is reestablished. In this poem, the allegorical figure of Dame Vertus, seeing the grief of the Duchess of Savoy after the death of Philibert, takes pity on her ("luy en print au coeur une pitié incroyable") and wants to honor her with a triumphant and permanent halo ("sa bien aymée dune aureole triomphale et permanente.").[24] To this end she sends for a goldsmith named Merite as well as for ten philosophers and ten of her prettiest and most virtuous nymphs. She dresses the nymphs and attaches a stone to the forehead of each one "selon la mode italique" (according to the Italic way).[25] Martia, the daughter of Marcus Varro, makes a portrait of the ten nymphs, which Vertus places in a circle. Merite crafts a crown using Martia's portrait as his model, and the ten philosophers interpret the meaning of the ten stones placed on the nymphs' foreheads.[26]

Lemaire's *Couronne* sets Molinet's conventional etymology in a metaphysical environment, one that allows the image produced by the etymology to generate a higher meaning. As discussed in the preceding chapters, the nominalist practice of Molinet's *Chappellet* is motivated by a desire for a *plus hault sens* that would be revealed through the resemblance of word and thing. Molinet's etymology proves itself poetic or rhetorical rather than revelatory because the poet uses a conventional language that breaks down the relationship of word and referent. The etymology's meaning is produced through the relationship of the etymol-ogon and its mental representation. The image is a product of a mental operation, an *operatio intellectus*. The same etymological practice is at the heart of the *Couronne*, but the image is not a mental construct divorced from the real world. It corresponds to the vibrant, ideal world that surrounds the etymology. This ideal world, witnessed in geometrical, numerological, and astrological figures, places Molinet's nominalistically inspired etymology in a setting in which meaning is established in relation to the general and the universal. Resemblance between the contingent and the absolute, between the earthly and the divine, is reestablished.

The universal and ideal nature of Lemaire's poetic maturity is evident right from the beginning of the *Couronne*.[27] The narrator explains in the first prose section of the poem that the nymphs' circular configuration and their number—ten—have a universal and occult meaning.[28] This passage occurs at the end of a section that describes how various people discussed Dame Vertus's organization of the ten nymphs in a circle:

> Mais les poincts principaux de leur disputation sarrestoient touchant le nombre des dix Nymphes, et aussi touchant leur disposition en rondesse: *Car en ce leur sembloit il bien avoir quelque intelligence occulte.*
>
> Et leur motif procedoit, pour ce que le nombre denaire, c'estadire de dix unitez, veult denoter une chose totale et universelle: car cest le droit limité de tous autres denombremens ensuivans, lesquelz sont composéz de la dizaine reprinse par plusieurs fois: Si comme deux fois x. qui font vingt, et une fois x. et I. font onze, etc. *Il semble donques que le nombre de dix, tende à quelque perfection.* Et entant quil touche ce que lesdites Vertus estoient ainsi con-nexées ensemble par *une forme ronde, ilz affermoient concordablement que cestoit la figure la plus parfaite de toutes les autres,* comme il appert par la rondeur spherique du Monde et du Soleil, et des autres corps celestes: Si designoit la concatenation desdites Vertus, que toutes habitudes vertueuses sont conjointes ensemble lune à lautre en sorte perfective. Et pource conclu-oient ilz unanimement, que *Vertu la tresprudente dame y entendoit quelque mystere latent.*[29]

[But the principal points of their disputation all ended touching on the number of the ten Nymphs, and also touching on their circular configuration *since it seemed to them that there was some hidden meaning.*

And their motif continued, since the denary number, meaning ten unities, denotes a total and universal thing, since it is the *droit limité* of all the other following numberings, which are composed of the unit ten many times. As in two times ten, which makes twenty, and one times ten and one make eleven, etc. *It seems then that the number ten tends toward some perfection.* And as much as it happens that the aforesaid Virtues were thus joined together *by a round form, they affirmed harmoniously that it was the most perfect figure of all the others,* as it appears by the spherical roundness of the World, and of the Sun, and of the other celestial bodies. It was decided that the configuration of the said Virtues demonstrated that all virtuous habits are joined together one to the other in a perfect way. And for that, they concluded unanimously that *Virtue the very prudent Lady had placed there some hidden mystery.*]

The geometrical and numerological references in this passage place the *Couronne* in a Neoplatonic or Pythagorian context, in which forms and numbers offer proof of the infinite ideal. This is similar to Ficino's *Theologica platonica,* which explains how the immutability of the ideal form is necessary to understand the true essence of the circle. Ficino says that the mutability of the contingent circle can be understood only through an awareness of the ideal.[30] This obviously is very different from the nominalist discourse, which denied that human reason could penetrate the divine and held that any universalization of singular reality could occur only in the human mind. Here, things do come together *in re,* and human reason is capable of piercing the realm of the divine; the *via intellectiva* is a viable source of knowledge. The philosophers are to confirm that the contingent reality of the crown reflects the universal perfection of the form. They are able to rise above the contingent and consider the Ideal through the power of their reason. They can then judge the ability of the contingent form to reveal that Ideal reality.[31]

In this context, the objects that represent the virtues elaborated in the etymology are treated very differently than they were in Molinet's *Chappellet.* In the *Chappellet,* the flowers had almost no real physical existence and were basically emptied of any occult meaning, but in the *Couronne* the relationship of the gems and a hidden meaning is reestablished. The flowers' meaning in the *Chappellet* was remotivated by their insertion in the portrait of Mary of Burgundy, but in the *Couronne* the gems and stones that represent the virtues associated with Margaret of Austria remain closely related to the meanings found in lapidaries. Although the etymology remains highly conventional in its organization, as in Molinet's *Chappellet,* the magical or alchemical connection between stone and meaning denies the cognitive skepticism that underlay Molinet's etymology. Lemaire might appropriate the etymological structure of the *Chappellet,* but he does not appropriate its nominalistic epistemology.[32] Where Molinet's nominalistic practice destabilized the Idealist premise of the etymology, Lemaire's Idealist practice destabilizes Molinet's nominalist model.

Just as in Molinet's *Chappellet*, the initial theoretical premise of the *Couronne*'s etymology is based on the resemblance of contingent reality with the absolute. Dame Vertus invites ten philosophers to see if they can "former le nom de la plus vertueuse et plus fortunée Princesse qui soit aujourdhuy vivant sur terre" (form the name of the most virtuous and fortunate Princess who is today living on Earth), according to the general truth witnessed in the original configuration of the ten nymphs in a circle:

> Mais pour venir à la specification du particulier, sans plus vous en tenir icy suspens, nous mettrons en avant une chose que vous ferez, presupposant premierement et avant toute œuvre, que sans nulle doute toutes ces belles Vertus noz filles vous sont congnues nommeement et distinctement.[33]

> [But to come to the specification of the particular, without holding you in further suspense, we shall propose one thing that you should do, supposing first and before all else, that without any doubt, all these beautiful virtues, our girls, are known to you namely and distinctly.]

The presupposition that the philosophers and orators will first know the virtues establishes the fact that, in the *Couronne*, knowledge about the particular is based on a previous knowledge about the general or ideal.[34]

In the poem, all of the philosophers called upon to explain the meaning of the stones begin with the general. The first philosopher, the French humanist Robert Gaguin, for example, says: "Or en diray je donques deux mots en laissant la generalité, laquelle par la tienne ample discussion, ha esté si bien elucidée."[35] (And I shall therefore say two words, leaving the generality, which by your ample discussion has been so well elucidated). Gaguin's analysis shows how the virtue of the individual stone exists before the philosophers and orators express it. The stones must be in agreement with the virtues and not the other way around. As Dame Vertus says:

> Mais quant aux qualitéz et aux alliances des Vertus et des gemmes, nous voulons que vous nous sachiez à dire, si linvention comprinse en nostre imaginative, est bien conduite et mise à effect selon la raison, et sil y ha point de discrepance quant à lobiect pretendu. Cestadire si les excellences de ces dix Vertus, et les proprietéz des dix gemmes, ont concordance si mutuelle, que delles puist resulter, comme en un miroir trescertain, le vif exemplaire de la dame dessus mentionnée.[36]

> [But as for the qualities and alliances of the Virtues and gems, we want you to tell us if the invention understood by your imagination has been well attended to and brought to bear according to reason, and if there is no discrepancy regarding the claimed object. This is to say that if the excellencies of these ten Virtues, and the properties of these ten gems, have some mutual

harmony that can result, as in a very accurate mirror, in the exact exemplar of the above-mentioned lady.]

The role of the philosophers and orators is to confirm the "concordance mutuelle" between the stone (the "obiect pretendu") and the virtue that has been imagined in the mind of Dame Vertus. The philosophers and orators are to testify that Margaret of Austria's likeness is found in the virtues represented by the stones.

Unlike Molinet's *Chappellet*, this initial metaphysical premise is never dropped in the *Couronne*. Where Molinet's poem relied on the tension between a theoretical desire for higher meaning and a practice based in difference, Lemaire's poem exults in the principle of resemblance. And because the principle of resemblance determines the nature of human understanding in the *Couronne*, the ontological ordering of prior and posterior is in full force in Lemaire's poem. It is Margaret who must resemble the virtues, and not the virtues that must resemble Margaret. The stones and gems reflect the general values or virtues of which they are a part. The value or virtue is then identified in Margaret of Austria, who as a result resembles the greater or more universal whole of which she is a part. The reversal of analogical relationships noted in Molinet's poetics does not exist in Lemaire's *Couronne*.

The first philosophical explanation in the poem exemplifies this ordering of things. When Robert Gaguin gives the first explanation of the meaning of the pearl, or *margarite*, his account grounds the pearl's meaning in occult properties. The stone or gem's meaning or property is linked to a morphological or geographical resemblance with other phenomena. Gaguin's explanation illustrates how this system of resemblance works by identifying the pearl's medicinal properties with those of the moon:

> Oultreplus, touchant les vertus, proprietez et efficaces des perles, à fin que nous noublions rien du principal, selon les medecins elles sont froides et seiches au second degré, qui est qualité moderée. Et les Astrologues disent, que la Lune est leur maistresse: car elles sont procrées d'humiditéz. Si est la commune opinion des sages, quelles confortent le cœur, vallent contre le mal caduque, et sont aydables à toute debilité destomach, et syncopisation: cestadire, faute de cœur. Restraingnent le flux du ventre et du sang, et proufitent aux febricitans, quand elles sont mises en pouldre, et administrees avecques du sucre rosat.[37]

> [Even more, regarding the virtues, properties and powers of pearls, in order that we not forget anything of the principal, according to the doctors they are cold and dry to the second degree, which is a moderate quality. And the Astrologers say that the Moon is their mistress since they are procreated by

humidity. Such is the common opinion of wise men, that they comfort the heart, are helpful in preventing epilepsy, and are effective in curing all stomach problems, and syncope, meaning lack of heart. They restrict the flow of intestinal and sanguinary fluids, and are good for feverish patients when they are ground up into a powder and administered with rose sugar.]

This description of the pearl is nearly identical to those found in medieval lapidaries. The thirteenth-century *De virtutibus herbarum* by Rufinus explains that the pearl is "frigida" (cold) and "sicca" (dry) and that powdered pearl is given with rose sugar for heart troubles to feverish patients and for weakness and fainting caused by medicines and for intestinal and sanguinary flow.[38] The late fifteenth-century Peterborough lapidary describes the *margarita* as "helping to ease the feebleness of flux caused by medicine, and also easing the running of blood and easing the flux of the the womb."[39] These medicinal qualities are anchored in the pearl's relationship with the powers of the planets and stars. The connection between the contingent pearl and the cosmic forces of the moon opens up the semantic field in which Lemaire's poem grounds its meaning. The metaphysical connection between contingent and absolute allows the poem to escape from the purely mental and contingent resemblance of Molinet's *Chappellet*. Things really do resemble each other in the *Couronne*.

The virtues exhibited in the pearls in the *Couronne* fit into this metaphysical scheme of occult philosophers such as Henry Cornelius Agrippa, with whom Lemaire was familiar at Dôle. Agrippa explains that God, who is the end and beginning of all Virtues, gives the seal of the "Ideas" to his servants, the "Intelligences."[40] These Intelligences sign all things with an Ideal Virtue, which is then transmitted to contingent things on Earth. The virtues of stones, herbs, and metals all come from this initial Ideal. The gem's meaning is determined by its resemblance to an elemental "Intelligence." The pearl bears the signature of the qualities of the moon because it is cultivated in the sea, which is directly related to the powers of the moon. Just as the moon can control the tides in the sea, so too the pearl can provide a moderating influence on the movement of blood in the body. The pearl's *vis* is therefore established through its likeness with the moon and not through a contingent relationship with an earthly monarch.

Although the *Chappellet des dame*'s etymological principles provide the *Couronne* with its structural organization, the metaphysical association of stone and virtue overwhelms this underlying organization. In Molinet's *Chappellet*, the meaning of each flower is generated through an arbitrary connection with the poet's portrait of Mary of Burgundy. For example, the daisy's (*marguerite*) virtue, "Mundicité de corps," is an abstract value unassociated with the flower itself. It is produced *secundum placitum*, according to the needs of the portrait of Mary of Burgundy. In the *Couronne*, the pearl's virtue is medicinal and is grounded in its metaphysical relationship with the moon. All of the gems in the *Couronne* bear the mark of metaphysical resemblance.

Lemaire gives a geographical and historical overview for each gem, usually taken from Pliny, as well as a fairly detailed explanation of its medicinal properties. These properties are representative of the elemental powers that natural philosophy believed controlled the world. For example, the second gem, *adamas* (diamond), is identified as helpful in curing lunacy and those individuals having "quelque esprit malin dedens le corps."[41] The same treatment is accorded the third gem, the ruby, which is under the influence of Jupiter and Saturn and has the ability to prevent water from boiling over.[42]

Instead of having the metaphysical higher term resemble the lower, the *Couronne* makes the lower term resemble the higher. The portrait once again resembles its subject. The moderating effects of the pearl appropriated from the lapidaries are attributed to women from the past whose names all begin with the letter *M*. Alphabetical resemblance is not the only thing that unites these women; they all share the quality of moderation, which is, of course, best exemplified in the person of Margaret of Austria. The contingent resembles the absolute and can therefore reveal a higher or hidden meaning.

Whereas the use of *amplificatio* in Molinet accentuates the unreal quality of the objects described, the detailed description of the crown in Lemaire plays up its material reality.[43] Molinet's images of the Virgin Mary and Mary of Burgundy could exist only as mental images in the *Chappellet*, but Lemaire's crown flourishes as a tangible object whose esthetic quality elevates it above the commonplace and opens the eye to the possibility of a greater or absolute beauty. The description of the crown itself is far more plastic than the curiously disembodied images found in Molinet's poetry. Lemaire creates an image full of painterly detail that clearly establishes the crown as an object that exists in the real world:

> Martia donc la pucelle tressage
> Donne au pourtrait termes d'orfaverie,
> Et aux fleurons fait un double souage,
> Qui regne en cercle, et sert de bon
>   liage
> A dix pilliers portans l'imagerie.

Le souage est frisé d'œuvre jolie
A demy bosse, à Nymphes, et Pegases:
Les pilliers points d'esmaillure delie,
Et sont les noms des dix Vertus aux
    bases.

Entre pilliers, et souages gentilz,
Un fons semé de lettres se dispose.
Mais entremy les beaux fleurons faictis
De son sens propre, et de ses doigts
    traictis
Certainement elle feit noble chose.
Car entre deux Vertus, mit une rose
Avec couleur d'esmail, qu'elle luy
    baille.
Et entremy chacune estoit enclose
D'or fin massif une noble medaille.[44]

[Therefore Martia the circumspect virgin / Gives a goldsmith's turn to the portrait, / And places a double moulding round the flowers, / Which rules in a circle and makes a fine link / To the ten pillars bearing images. / The moulding is bordered with handsome works / in bas-relief of Nymphs and Pegasuses: / The pillars are marked with subtle enamel, / As are the names of the Virtues at the bases. // Between pillars, and noble moulding, / A background flecked with letters is set out. / But between the handsome flowers, / Made according to her sense and her / fingers, certainly she made a noble thing. / For between two Virtues she placed / An enamel-colored rose. / And on each one was enclosed / A noble medal of fine solid gold.]

The beauty of the crown, especially in the metaphysical context of the stone's alchemical meanings, places the notion of image in a very different light than it had been in Molinet's *Chappellet*. Within the context of sixteenth-century Neoplatonism, beautiful images had the power to overcome the limitations of singular contingency. Ficino's *Theologia platonica* explains how the beautiful object can raise the soul of the person who perceives it to the level of the divine. The human being is able to rise from an awareness of the beauty of a singular thing to a more general awareness of beauty. That beauty, finally, leads to an awareness of the infinite beauty of God.[45] In the same way, Lemaire's crown not only is a well-described image, it provides a means for the human mind to rise beyond the level of the contingent and singular. The particular beauty of the crown participates in the greater beauty of which it is a part. The wholeness of the universe, in turn, is revealed through the harmony of the parts.

In the *Couronne*, the universal oneness of the world is particularized into individual phenomena that allow for the connection of contingent to absolute, whereas the singularity of the world in Molinet's poetics forbids this connection. In the *Couronne*, the plastic reality of the crown shows a different relationship between imagery and reality. It is magical but realistic, because reality is itself considered magical.[46] The connection between the contingent and the absolute, between the pearl and the moon, creates a universe in which all objects can have a higher meaning. The crown is one of these objects, connecting the perfect and the imperfect, the divine and the secular.

The *Couronne* can be understood as lying atop and correcting the underlying *Chappellet*. Just as Molinet's meaningless analogical forms depend on a previous metaphysical age, so Lemaire's crown depends on Molinet's flamboyant imagery but invests it with new symbolic meaning. Here, the plastic arts can again offer a parallel that helps explain the poetic image. The *Couronne* is similar to Philibert's tomb in the Church of Brou at Bourg-en-Bresse.[47] Margaret of Austria had entrusted the construction of this church to Lemaire (1510–11). The tomb exhibits an aesthetic that borrows from both French Gothic and Italian styles.[48] The base of the tomb is made up of allegorical gothic figures of the Virtues. On top of this base lies a marble slab. The alabaster of the underlying figures contrasts with the Italianate marble slab and especially with the marble *putti* on top of the slab. Constructed by French and Italian sculptors in 1511, the tomb offers evidence of a similar juxtaposition of ideas that appears in the *Couronne*.[49] The initial form is in the French Gothic tradition. The Italianate form on top radically alters the underlying form, focusing attention on its discordance with the Gothic form. In a similar way, Lemaire's use of Pythagorean and Neoplatonic figures that open up the *Couronne* to an ideal world is radically at odds with the Christian and nominalistic imagery of its model, Molinet's *Chappellet*. The tension between the two traditions, one northern and the other southern, is a vital part of the *Couronne*, just as it is a vital part of the tomb at Brou.

This juxtaposition of two traditions leads to several questions: does the *Couronne* belong to the same tradition as the *Chappellet*, or is it new? Is Lemaire a poet in the tradition of Chastelain and Molinet, or is he a *poète lyonnais*?[50] Is he a medieval poet or a Renaissance poet? If we can talk of Lemaire at all, which Lemaire are we talking about, the author of the 1498 Marian poems or the author of the Neoplatonizing *Couronne*? The answer to these questions is ambiguous, like Lemaire's work itself. The *Couronne* is both northern and southern in temperament. It is both part of the medieval tradition and part of the Lyonese tradition of Maurice

Scève.[51] Lemaire is, as Paul Zumthor points out, astride two epistemic systems, and his poetry reflects that difference. He and his poems are, like Burgundy, both northern and southern, with characteristics of both Malines and Lyons. This confusion (or better, diversity) illustrates how the categorization of time into periods such as the Middle Ages and the Renaissance often obscures meaning as much as it elucidates it. Lemaire, equally divided between North and South, Middle Ages and Renaissance, Burgundy and France, is the perfect model for the problems brought about by this sort of periodization. He belongs to all of the categories and to none of them.[52]

The divided nature of Lemaire's poetics is also apparent in his *Concorde du genre humain*, in which he again appropriates Molinet's work, this time taking the analogy between the Virgin Mary and Mary of Burgundy from the *Chappellet des dames*. Lemaire wrote the *Concorde du genre humain* in 1508 to celebrate the signing of the Treaty of Cambrai, which established peace between France and Burgundy. The treaty was signed on December 10, 1508, and Lemaire took advantage of the proximity of the Feast of the Conception of the Virgin on December 8 to legitimate an analogy between Margaret of Austria's role in the signing of the Treaty of Cambrai and the conception of the Virgin Mary, using terms that are very close to those used by Molinet in the *Chappellet*. The underlying analogical form might be anchored in Molinet's poetics of difference, but the poem constructed atop the analogy exemplifies the world of resemblance and participation in which Lemaire could construct a poem like the *Couronne*. The contrast, as in the earlier poem, indicates clearly how Lemaire was a poet astride an epistemological divide.

The poem is a *prosimetrium*, with alternating sections in verse and prose. Made up of 919 lines divided into nineteen sections, it can be understood as consisting of four main parts: the first comprises the analogy of the Virgin Mary and Margaret of Austria; the second is a glorification of the town of Cambrai and the signatory parties of the treaty; the third consists of a dream in which an angelic figure or nymph intervenes to transform Margaret's epithet "Infortune" to "Auguste"; and the fourth comprises the poet's waking from the dream and a pastoral in which five shepherdesses praise the peace established by Margaret.

The poem was written in a very specific political context. Margaret of Austria, who had been named "gouvernante" of the Low Countries by Maximilian until his son Charles, the future Charles V, reached his majority, was unable to dominate her enemies, who favored the king of France.

As a result of this military impasse, she arranged for the opposing parties to meet in Cambrai. The coalition of Christian powers resulted in an anti-Venetian league desired by both the French king Louis XII and the Austrian emperor Maximilian. The *concorde* of the poem's title refers to this eventual Christian coalition allied against the infidels.[53]

The poem begins by drawing a parallel between the conception of Jesus Christ in the womb of the Virgin Mary and the conception of peace in the mind of Margaret of Austria. Just as a prince (Gabriel) came to announce the coming of Jesus Christ to the Virgin Mary, so too did a messenger (George d'Amboise, ambassador of King Louis XII of France) come with a message of peace for Margaret:

> Dieu a transmis des arcanges ung prince
> en Nazareth, qu'on dit fleur, germe ou monde,
> (c'est à Cambray, en belgicque province),
> vers une dame ayant vertu non mince,
> se vierge non, vesve au moins pure et monde.[54]

> [God sent a prince from the archangels / To Nazareth, which is said flower, seed or world, / (In Cambrai, in Belgian province), / Toward a lady having no small virtue, / If not a virgin, at least a widow, clean and pure.]

Lemaire makes a comparison between the story of the Virgin Mary and the story of Margaret of Austria's role in the Treaty of Cambrai. It is not difficult to see the influence of Molinet's *Le Chappellet des dames* in this comparison, since the terms Lemaire uses are often similar to those used by Molinet. For example, the human race (*le gendre humain*) is described as having been in Hell and as now waking to desirous joy:

> Le gendre humain, dés longtemps miserable,
> estoit ou lymbe ainsi comme dampné;
> mais à ce jour, au monde secourable,
> il se resveille en joyë desirable,
> car le doulx fruict, son redempteur, est né.

> [The human race, for so long miserable, / Was cast in limbo as if damned: / But on this day, in the pardonable world, / Wakes a desirable joy, / Since the gentle fruit, his saviour, is born.]

Molinet's comparison between Adam and Eve's Fall and the Burgundian people's demise from the *Chappellet* is the obvious model for this passage and many others in the first section of the poem (see chap. 2).

Besides individual lines, Lemaire also imitates the structure of Molinet's analogy from the *Chappellet*. Margaret is described as bearing a good but imperfect resemblance to the Virgin Mary: "hors sainctise et hors virginité, / c'est ton ymaige et qui mieulx te ressemble." (other than sainthood and virginity, / She is your image and who best resembles you) (55).

As in the *Chappellet*, the imperfect's similitude with the perfect becomes the theoretical basis for the comparison. Margaret's resemblance to the Virgin becomes a means for the imperfect human being to understand the divine:

> Ne t'en desplaist, Vierge saincte et sacrée,
> Se nous en elle admirons ta semblance:
> . . . .
> C'est la marine estoille clere et blanche,
> l'espoir du jour, qui n'est haÿe de ame;
> c'est, aprés toy, nostre plus seure planche;
> brief, ce nous est une autre Nostre Dame. (55–56)

> [We mean no offense, holy and sacred Virgin / If we admire in her your likeness. / . . . / She is the star of the sea, clear and white, / Hope of day, hated by no soul; / After you she is our surest hope / In short, she is for us another Notre Dame.]

Margaret is nearly the same thing, but not exactly, as the Virgin. This theoretical framework is very similar to both the theory and the practice of resemblance found in poems by Lemaire such as the *Couronne,* in which the pearl's connection with the moon made it a potent agent of change in the world. In this case, Molinet's analogy fits Lemaire's poetics of resemblance like a glove. The only problem is that Lemaire also appropriates Molinet's reversed analogical structure.

Lemaire's analogy, like Molinet's, ends up using the perfect to describe the imperfect. Margaret of Austria does not describe the Virgin, rather, the Virgin is used to describe Margaret. The structure might be that of an analogy that reveals the perfection of the divine through the participation of the imperfect in a common analogon, but the aim is identical to that in the *Chappellet*. The analogy praises the individuality of Margaret of Austria. The Virgin Mary and the coming of Christ are used as paradigms for understanding Margaret and her role in the Treaty of Cambrai. The relationship is less concerned with participation than it is with temporality. What happened to the Virgin Mary fifteen hundred years earlier now happens to Margaret of Austria: "Lors en Marie et or en Marguerite" (Then in Mary and now in Margaret) (52). The temporal relationship underlines the conventional connection between the two terms of the analogy. The link between the Virgin and Margaret is more logical than ontological, since there is no real connection between the two terms of the comparison.

As happened in Molinet's *Chappellet*, Lemaire's analogy reverses the ordering of *prius* and *posterius*, making the subject resemble the portrait and not the other way around. The glory of the Virgin Mary is now cast on Margaret, and it is Margaret who is the subject of the portrait:

> O Marguerite, o fille de Marie,
> perle et consaulde undoyant gemme et fleur,
> seul union, seul chief de pierrerie,
> en medecine et en tresorerie
> aidant et riche, effassant perte et pleur,
> cueurs unissant en grace et en valeur,
> consolidant les couraiges desjoingtz,
> tu rendz ou monde oudeur, vie et chaleur,
> qui presque estoit amorty de tous pointz. (57)

> [O Margaret, O daughter of Mary, / pearl and undulating bloom, gem and flower, / Sole union, sole queen of stones, / In medicine and in treasury / Helpful and rich, effacing loss and tears, / Uniting hearts, in grace and worth, / Strengthening disjointed courage, / You give to the world scent, life and warmth, / Which everywhere nearly was destroyed.]

This reversal is remarkable since in general Lemaire respects the ontological ordering of *prius* and *posterius*, as has been shown in his description of the powers of the pearl and the other gems and stones in the *Couronne*. It is only when Lemaire copies Molinet's analogy directly that the ordering is reversed. Throughout the rest of the *Concorde du genre humain*, the poem's imagery depends on the participation of the particular in the whole. Margaret's glory remains very much the subject of the poem, but the imagery elsewhere in the poem reflects a considerably different understanding of the principle of resemblance than that found in the analogy taken from the *Chappellet des dames*.

Throughout the rest of the poem, the principle of ontological resemblance provides the dominant paradigm. This is particularly evident in the central image of the poem after the initial analogy. After explaining that the city of Cambrai fits into a genealogical and numerological hierarchy of being in a prose section immediately following the analogy, the Acteur describes a vision he had concerning the *matiere*. He explains that he had a dream in which he saw two beautiful women. One is an angelic figure with feathers and wings. This is *Concorde du genre humain*, hereafter referred to as the Nymph, to avoid confusion with the title of the poem. Although the substance of her clothes is described as unknowable, she is easily recognized:

Ses membres rondz, plus blancs que fin velin,
monstroit l'abit, ne sçay de soye ou lin,
mais plus meslé, changant, versicolore
que l'arc en ciel vermeil et saphirin. (64)

[Her members round, whiter than vellum, / Wore a habit, I know not of silk or linen, / but more mixed, changing and multiform / than a vermillion and sapphirine rainbow.]

The other woman, as beautiful as the angel, wears armor ("harnois"), which makes her look like Pallas Athena:

L'autre non maindre, ains aussi belle encore,
portoit harnois qui si bien la decore
qu'on l'eust jugée une droicte Pallas
de port royal et magnificque gorre. (64)

[The other no less, and just as pretty, / wore a harness which complemented her so well / That she might have been thought a real Athena / Of royal bearing and magnificent elegance.]

This second figure is Margaret of Austria. The Nymph gives her solace by helping her take off her armor and fanning her face. She finally brings joy and laughter to the saddened princess.

In its form and in its depiction of the relationship of the particular and the general, this scene differs from the analogy between the Virgin Mary and Margaret of Austria. Formally, Lemaire uses a decasyllabic nine-line stanza for his analogy, very close to the decasyllabic ten-line stanzaic form used by Molinet in much of the *Chappellet*. The later scene, in which the Nymph appears, is much more "modern" in its form, composed of twelve quatrains followed by one five-line stanza. Its rhyme scheme is very close to the terza rima used by Lemaire later in the *Concorde des deux langages*: *a a b a / b b c b / c c d c*, with the third line supplying the lead rhyme in each following stanza. Lemaire's four-line stanza with connected rhymes indicates the development of his predecessor's French paradigm into a much more Italian style. Although Lemaire might not be as overt as his more famous successors in the Pléiade in imitating and developing Italian forms, the proximity of his more Italianate forms to Molinet's verse forms offers a revealing picture of the rapidly evolving French poetics in the early sixteenth century. These stylistic differences are also matched by an even greater and more fundamental difference in Lemaire's understanding of the relationship of the particular and the universal.

In the analogy between Margaret of Austria and the Virgin Mary, the Virgin plays a purely paradigmatic role. She does not intercede for Margaret. Just as in Molinet's *Chappellet des dames*, the Virgin Mary becomes an image that reflects the glory of an earthly monarch. The Nymph in the *Concorde du genre humain*, on the other hand, has the power to change Margaret's life. This represents a change not only from the analogy in the first part of the poem but also from the entire ethos of Molinet's poetic world. In Molinet's *Chappellet des dames*, Dame Vertus never actually intervenes in Mary of Burgundy's life. She simply weaves a garland of flowers, which Dame Experience then interprets for the Acteur. The split between Dame Vertus and Dame Experience in the *Chappellet* corresponds to the divide between the stars and human beings expressed in the *Roman de la Rose moralisé*. The absolute might have some message for human beings, but it is only experience that can provide meaning. The Nymph in the *Concorde du genre humain* enjoys a much greater ability to intercede in the lives of mortals than either the Virgin Mary in the analogy or any of the personifications from Molinet's poems. The Nymph is as efficacious as the pearl in the *Couronne margaritique*; she possesses real daemonic power.

The Nymph's daemonic powers reflect the Neoplatonic ambiance of Lemaire's poetics. The Nymph mediates between the perfection of the heavens and the imperfection of human existence in the same way that the pearl mediates between the perfect and the imperfect in Lemaire's *Couronne*. In his *Commentary on Plato's "Symposium,"* Ficino describes daemons as inhabiting the middle ground between Heaven and Earth.[55] Daemons, like Ficino's cosmology as a whole, depend on the hierarchical chain of being. Ficino says that "as the whole is more perfect than the part, in the same measure is the body of the world more perfect than the body of each thing" (ibid., 184). Daemons thus participate in both the perfect and the imperfect. Ficino describes the gods as immortal and incapable of feeling or suffering (*impassible*), and human beings as mortal and capable of feeling or suffering (*passible*). Daemons are immortal, like the gods, but capable of suffering like human beings (ibid., 185). They also "mix agreeably and eagerly in the governing of lower things, but especially of human affairs."

The daemonic structure described by Ficino is apparent in Lemaire's Nymph. She is described in angelic terms, having "plumes et esles / si tres luisans, gaillardes et nouvelles / que mieulx sembloit ung esprit angelin / que estre du reng ou nombre des mortelles"[56] (plumes and wings / so shining, light, and new / that she seemed more an angelic spirit / than of mortal rank or number). Although her description indicates that she is more angelic than human, she also feels compassion for human beings, as can be seen in her explanation of how she will help Margaret avoid misfortune in the future. The Nymph states that she has reestablished contact with human beings and is now allied with them by "lyens invisibles et plus que adamantines" (66). By these celestial connections, the Nymph promises that Margaret will no longer need to wear the "laboureux harnois de cure et sollicitude en bellicqueux effroy et seditieux tumulte, destrempé d'anxieté pensifve." Margaret will be able to live forevermore in the shade of the tree of peace. The Nymph functions like the herbs and stones described by Agrippa and Paracelsus, bringing the perfection of the hidden divine to the contingent and human realm. The "lyens invisibles" might be hidden from human sight but they are diamond hard ("plus que adamantines").

Even her clothing can be understood as expressing the hierarchical universe of Lemaire's poetics. Lemaire mentions her clothing as being of uncertain substance: "ne scay de soye ou lin, / mais plus meslé, changant, versicolore / que l'arc en ciel vermeil et saphirin" (I know not of silk or of linen, / but more mixed, changing and multiform / than a vermillion and sappharine colored rainbow) (64). In his discussion of daemons, Ficino also describes how pure bodies emanating from God must be clothed in a "certain heavenly and clear wrap" before they can be enclosed in earthly bodies. The cloth becomes the necessary third element that would allow the perfect being of the soul to become one with the impure body. The Nymph's clothing can be understood as representing such a prelapsarian kind of purer state; it indicates the purity of a being that is neither completely mortal nor completely immortal.[57] Although not a God, she participates in the perfection of God more fully than do the mortals with whom she interacts in the poem. The cloth represents one small link in the hierarchy of being that connects the smallest particle to the greatest metaphysical entity in Lemaire's poetics. The poem's political context also shows that harmony and concord dominate the individual and the singular in the poem.

This political reality is transparent in the final section of the poem, which begins with the poet waking from his dream and writing down what he has seen. The poet mentions that on December 16, 1508, Maximilian ratified the peace treaty concluded by his daughter, Margaret, and names the various notables who were at the ratification. The poem ends with a pastoral performed by five shepherdesses; each is dressed in a costume representing either Germany, France, Castille, England, or Savoy, and each proclaims the glory of Margaret and of the peace. The pastoral represents the political concord effected by the Treaty of Cambrai, a political concord directly related to the ideal harmony and concord represented by the Nymph, *Concorde du genre humain*. The individual differences between these countries are subsumed in the ideal concord of the poem's title. Each country's singularity remains but as part of a larger whole. Political concord becomes an integral part of the larger metaphysical harmony expressed in the poem.

Both Molinet and Lemaire were called upon to praise an earthly monarch, yet their different means of effecting that praise reflects the changing landscape of French literary history.[58] Where Molinet created artificial decorations to ornament his portrait of Mary of Burgundy, Lemaire creates poetic images that insert Margaret of Austria in a hierarchy of being. Both monarchs are equally praised; it is only the means of producing the *éloge* that change. The contrast is particularly strong in the *Concorde du genre humain*, since Lemaire works within the poetic influence of his predecessor in the first section of the poem. In the analogy between the Virgin Mary and Margaret of Austria, Lemaire's poetic images function as attributes that can be applied to the subject of the poem. Margaret does not participate in the Virgin's perfection, since the ordering of the comparison has been changed. The Virgin helps explain the glory of Margaret even though she is the prior term, ontologically. The subject ends up resembling its portrait.

It is only in the second part of the poem, when Lemaire moves away from his predecessor's poetic model, that the connection between divine and human is reestablished. In this second section, the Nymph participates in both the perfection of the divine and the imperfection of the human. The Nymph actively intervenes in the life of Margaret through real but invisible connections. The second half of the poem reestablishes the hierarchy of being connecting the smallest particle of matter to the largest possible universal and reimposes the ordering of *prius* and *posterius* that was reversed in the initial analogy. The end of the first part of the poem marks the furthest limits of Molinet's poetics of singularity, and the second part bears witness to Lemaire's own poetics of resemblance and participation.

Lemaire's *Concorde du genre humain*, like the *Couronne*, is built around a poetic model from Jean Molinet. Like the *Couronne*, this poem creates an overlay of metaphysical participation and resemblance that overwhelms the underlying model. The reversed analogy from the *Chap-*

pellet lies underneath the *Concorde du genre humain,* as the etymology from the *Chappellet* provides the foundation for the *Couronne.* The analogy is again grounded in the singularity of Margaret of Austria. The comparison with the Virgin Mary does not reveal anything about the divine as much as it glorifies a mortal but noble ruler. It is only when Lemaire gets away from his predecessor's influence that the principle of resemblance overwhelms the principle of singularity and difference. Margaret's greatness is not the product of poetic attribution, whereby the glory of a divine figure is associated with her through the comparison of artificially created "imaiges." Rather, her greatness comes from her participation in the divine and from the intervention of the daemonic Nymph. The poem moves from the singular praise of Margaret to the harmony of the poem's title in the final pastoral, and Margaret's glory is part and parcel of this greater harmony. The principle of resemblance, in a latent state in Molinet's poetics, exerts itself here, just as in the *Couronne,* effacing the underlying poetic image with a series of images connecting the imperfect to the perfect and the human to the divine.

The poem in which Lemaire most fully mixes northern and southern, and Italian and French, influences is undoubtedly the *Concorde des deux langages,* written in 1511. It is, as critics have noted, a curious mélange of French and Italian styles.[59] Although the title suggests that the work is about the union of French and Italian cultures, the poem rarely touches on this issue.[60] In the prologue, the narrator says that he intends to prove the equal worth of French and Italian "langages," which in the context of early sixteenth-century French must be understood as meaning "cultures." Yet the poem revolves around the story of a young man who offers his attentions first to Venus, the Goddess of Love, and then to Minerva, the Goddess of Reason.[61] It is possible that the *Concorde des deux langages* is an amalgam of two poems. Lemaire mentions one in a letter to Margaret of Austria, written in 1503, and proposes to title it the "Palais d'honneur féminin," and the other is the present version of 1511, which is ostensibly about political union.[62] Whether the poem is about amorous or political union, there is little doubt that the key word in its title is again *concorde.* As in the *Concorde du genre humain,* the idea of harmony provides both the thematic structure of the poem and the means to higher meaning.[63]

The prologue's allusion to the political or cultural union of France and Italy is grounded in Lemaire's situation at the court of Burgundy in 1511.

Increasingly out of favor with Margaret's advisors in Malines, Lemaire paved the way for his eventual move to the court of France in Blois in 1512 with the *Concorde des deux langages*'s gallican point of view.[64] Although the prologue says that the poem will expose the equality of French and Italian cultures, Lemaire's approach is decidedly pro-French. To proclaim, in 1511, that the French and Italian cultures were of equal worth was obviously a political act, because the French language and culture were very much *à la remorque* of Italian language and culture in the early sixteenth century.[65]

This political context helps explain the curious disjunction between the prologue, where cultural union is dominant, and the main body of the poem, where amorous union prevails. The "Palais d'honneur féminin," mentioned by Lemaire in 1503, becomes the basis for the *Concorde des deux langages*. The story of the Lover going first to the temple of carnal love and then to the temple of intellective love dominates the principal sections of the poem. The political intrigue of the union of French and Italian cultures, which dominates the prologue and the epilogue, contextualizes that amorous story in the reality of France in 1511. The amorous and the political, although never fully in agreement, coexist in a harmonious union of disparate parts, like the thematic structure of the poem itself.

The recurrence of the term *concorde* in the poem's title indicates just how important the idea of harmony was to Lemaire. Harmony was crucial to Neoplatonism because it allowed the totality of the whole to overcome the diversity of the contingent. Ficino defines beauty as "a certain charm which is found chiefly and predominantly in the harmony of several elements."[66] Both the political and the amorous narratives in the *Concorde des deux langages* fall under the aegis of harmony, since they both involve the overcoming of difference in a totalizing union. The higher meaning of the *Concorde des deux langages* is revealed finally through the harmonizing of the affective and the intellective parts of the protagonist's soul and the uniting of the French and Italian cultures. The poem works from an initial impulse toward harmony as a way of overcoming individual difference toward a transcendental revelation of higher meaning. This overcoming of individual difference provides the most telling divergence between the poetics of Lemaire and the poetics of his predecessor.

In the version of 1511, the poem is divided into five sections. The prologue, in prose, introduces the question of the relative superiority of the Italian and French languages. Here, Dante, Petrarch, and Boccaccio are equated with Jean De Meung, Froissart, and more recent French poets such as Chastelain, Saint Gelais, and Molinet. The second section, in terza rima, begins with the Acteur in the "verdeur du mien flourissant aaige" composing Petrarchan verses. A *concorde* of sorts is drawn between the Acteur and Petrarch, because they both left their native lands (the Haynault and Florence, respectively) to search out love. The Acteur falls asleep and has an allegorical dream in which he is transported to the Temple of Venus in Mère d'Amours's chariot. This Temple of Venus is inhabited by allegorical personifications, many of whom, such as Belaccueil and Dangier, are drawn from the *Romance of the Rose*. Genius, the high priest of this "Paradis corporel," makes a speech whose theme is the brevity of the spring of this life.

In the third section, written in prose and titled "Comment l'Acteur fut rebouté du Temple de Venus" (How the Actor Was Thrown Out of the Temple of Venus), the Acteur offers a gift, "ung petit tableau de mon industrie" (a small painting of my own making), which is rejected by Dangier. He leaves the Temple of Venus and wanders in the desert until he comes upon a "rochier treshault et tresmerveilleux" (a very high and very marvelous rock). At the end of this prose section he finds an inscription carved into the base of the "rochier." The fourth section, in Alexandrines, is composed of this inscription, which describes a Hesiodic Mount of Virtue: "tresdur, agu, poinctu, offendant piedz et palmes" (very hard, steep, pointed, offensive to feet and hands). At the top of this "mont" is the Palais d'Honneur, inside of which is the Temple of Minerva. In the fifth and final section, in prose, the Acteur falls asleep and in a dream, the "Esperit familier . . . nommé Labeur Hystorien" (familiar Spirit . . . named Historical Labor) appears and describes the temple to him. The final *concorde des deux langages* takes place in this temple.[67]

In the first sections of the poem, devoted to the Temple of Venus, the Acteur begins his journey toward harmony through carnal attraction. The power of love dominates this first section of the poem. Genius, the chief priest in the Temple of Venus, defines love as the unifying motor of the universe.

> Les elementz les ungz aux aultres
> riient,
> Celestes corps l'un à l'autre se jouent,
> Toutes choses d'amours ores se prient.
>
> Tous sexes or en concorde se vouent;
> Masle, femelle ont accord reciproque,

Jusque aux poissons qui soubz les undes
   nouent.

Mutuel meuf, unïon univocque
Font connexer la machine du monde.
Soubz ung moteur qui à paix les
   provocque.[68]

[The elements one with another laugh, / Celestial bodies / one with another
play, / All loving things now one to another pray. // All sexes now in concord
make vows; / Male, female have common accord, / Even the fish knot
beneath the waves. // Mutual motion, univocal union. / Make the earth's
machine adhere. / Beneath a motor which ushers them / To peace.

If love provides a basis for concord in the Temple of Venus, it is only a
physical love. "Masle" and "femelle" have a reciprocal "accord" that
binds them together; their union, however, is not transcendent in any way.
This love leads an individual to another human being through sexual
attraction, but the union does not produce higher meaning. This initial
move toward another is, as Ficino describes in his *Commentary on Plato's
"Symposium,"* a turning away from chaos and toward God.[69] The Acteur
turns toward harmony by being attracted to another human being in the
Temple of Venus. He cannot find true harmony in this temple because the
love described by Genius is purely carnal. Love, in the Temple of Venus,
binds male and female together but does not lead to God.

As long as he stays in the Temple of Venus, the Acteur is trapped in the
realm of the particular and the imperfect. In his *Commentary*, Ficino
explains that, initially, man was created whole and was equipped with two
lights, one natural and the other supernatural. The natural light allowed
him to see inferior and coequal things, and the supernatural light allowed
him to see supernatural things. When man "aspired to equal God," he
resorted to the natural light alone and fell immediately into bodies.[70] The
univocal union that Genius describes in the Temple of Venus applies only
to imperfect human beings. Real *concorde* can happen only through divine
love. And this divine love is not experienced through the body but through
the soul, specifically the upper part of the soul.

In Lemaire's *Concorde des deux langages*, the limits of carnal love are
reached in the great rush of aspirant lovers to fill the basins that Belaccueil has placed in front of Venus's altar with worldly goods:

Belacueil soubzdiacre faisoit resonner ses grandz bassins d'argent, dedens
lesquelz qui ne povoit advenir, il y ruoit or, argent, drogues aromaticques et
odoriferantes, riches bagues, aournemens sumptueux, et toutes especes de
richesse mondaine. . . .[71]

[Belacueil subdeacon made / his great silver basins sound, to / which no one could approach, he / threw in gold, silver, aromatic and odiferous drugs, / rich rings, sumptuous ornaments / and all sorts of worldly riches . . .]

The Acteur then offers a small "tableau" to Venus. The painting is rejected by Genius because it is not grand enough, and the Acteur is "rebouté dehors." The Acteur finds himself fleeing his fellow creatures "lesquelz par grande foule occupoient les chemins de toutes pars pour aller au sacrifice de Venus" (which in great crowds everywhere occupied the roads in order to go to the sacrifice to Venus) (36). He has reached the end of carnal love's influence and has come away with little or no notion of a higher meaning or harmony.

After being thrown out of the Temple of Venus, he makes for the desert, where he says "je parvins en une merveilleuse solitude, c'est à dire desert sterile, pierreux, areneux et tout heremiticque" (I arrived in a marvelous solitude, which means to say a sterile, rocky, sandy, and completely hermetical desert) (36). Here, in the desert, between the Temple of Venus and the Temple of Minerva that he has yet to discover, the Acteur becomes aware of the futility of his past endeavors and begins to have an inkling of what is to come. The only higher meaning he possesses at this point in the poem has been achieved by negative example; he knows that he cannot find the concord or harmony he is looking for in the Temple of Venus. Now conscious of the limitations of sensual desire, but still incapable of understanding where concord may lay, he begins to perceive the possibility that the meaning he is looking for is up above, beyond the contingent reality of human sensuality.

The first physical evidence of this higher plane is "ung rochier treshault et tresmerveilleux à regarder pour sa diversité," which he sees on his journey through the desert (36). This rock is the first example of a Hesiodic Rock of Virtue in French literature, representing the theme *per angustam ad augustam*.[72] The Acteur gives the following description:

> Or estoit la roche eschauffée de soleil meridional, si droite, si scopuleuse et si difficile à monter que je ne m'en osay oncques entremectre, ainçois aloie environnant son circuite, souhaittant par grant soing que je peusse recouvrer quelque source de fontaine, laquelle chose après grant traveil j'obtins heureusement, et parvins en ung lieu solitaire et umbrageux. . . .[73]

> [And the rock so scorched by the southern sun, / so steep, so abrupt / and so difficult to ascend that I dared not try, thus / I went round about its base, hoping / that much care might lead me to a / fountain, which thing I found / after much labor, and I arrived / in a solitary and shady place.]

The idea of elevation and distance is essential here. The rock is identified as possessing hidden meaning, but that meaning is still beyond the Acteur's ken. He is still incapable of understanding or expressing the place where harmony is found.

It is only in the "Inscription" found at the bottom of the rock that one finds a complete description of the "Rochier." The Acteur cannot yet understand the true nature of harmony and can read only a description of the place where this harmony might exist. This description offers a much more detailed picture of the rock than the Acteur's eyewitness account from its base. The inscription mediates the Acteur's understanding of the *plus hault sens* that is hidden at the summit of the rock. The *absconce* quality of the rock's meaning is accentuated by its elevation; it is above and beyond normal human understanding: "Vecy le noble roch qui les nuës surpasse, / Des plus haulx montz qu'on saiche au monde l'outrepasse" (Here is the noble rock higher than any cloud / Or the highest mountains known on earth) (ibid., 39).

Montaigne's later counterexample in *De l'institution des enfants* highlights the notion of alterity that dominates Lemaire's rock. Montaigne describes virtue as being located not at the top of an insalubrious peak but rather on a fertile plain. It is not "plantée à la teste d'un mont coupé, rabotteux et inaccessible" (planted at the top of a steep, rough, and inaccessible mountain) but is, rather, "logée dans une belle plaine fertile et fleurissante" (found on a fertile and flowering plain).[74] Lemaire's higher meaning is the exact opposite of Montaigne's virtue. Because it is ideal and absolute, it must be far off and difficult of access. Real higher meaning cannot be contingent and immediate in Lemaire's world; otherwise the Acteur would have found it in the Temple of Venus.

The different degrees of higher meaning found in carnal and intellectual knowledge are reflected in the poem's geography. The Temple of Venus is placed on a rock above the "confluentz d'Arar et Rhodanus" (the confluence of the Saône and Rhone rivers).[75] Although higher than the plain of lowly folk, Venus's temple owes much more to the high-brow discourse of the Lyonese intellectuals who meet on the hillside of the Fourvière than it does to the heavenly discourse, of the divine.[76] Minerva's temple, on the other hand, where the real *concorde* takes place, is atop a rock "qui les nuës surpasse."[77] Venus's meaning is still part of an earthly discourse, while Minerva's is divine. The Acteur hears Genius's speech with his own ears. He has the higher meaning of Minerva's temple revealed to him through the inscription and through the figure of Labeur Hystorien, who appears in a contemplative dream. Real spiritual meaning, which explains the nature of *concorde*, is high up, beyond the literal or historical level.

The final concord of the poem is revealed to the Acteur in a dream by Labeur Hystorien. While contemplating the inscription, the Acteur falls asleep and Labeur Hystorien appears to him: "En ceste contemplation je m'endormiz, et non guieres, car je fuz tantost esveillé par ung esperit familier, qui me sollicite aucunesfoiz, nommé Labeur historiien. . . ."[78] (In this contemplation I fell asleep, but only just when I was woken by a familiar spirit who tempts me sometimes, called Historical Labor). Labeur Hystorien explains to the Acteur that it was Jean de Meung who ordered the inscription made. Labeur Hystorien explains that Jean had been to French culture what Dante was to Italian culture. Noting that France and Florence, Dante's town, both begin with the letter *F* and that all these things being taken into account, Labeur Hystorien explains that it was "bien sëant" (fitting) for the "fleur de liz de Florence" to be joined with that of France.[79] Finally, the harmony that the Acteur has been looking for is at hand.

The rational nature of understanding in the Temple of Minerva is underlined both by Labeur Hystorien's name and by the description of Minerva, in whose palace the *concorde* is found. Labeur Hystorien's name epitomizes an intellectual approach to knowledge. There is nothing arational about the labor of the historian, who organizes the world according to intellectual categories. The intellectual endeavor in which the historian participates is applicable, in a Gersonian context, to purely human affairs. In Gerson, the historian would only lead man astray when he tried to understand the divine. In Lemaire, Labeur Hystorian does not mislead the Acteur but rather explains the meaning of a divine message. Minerva's palace is the locus of the union of French and Italian cultures, and she is described in terms that place her squarely on the intellective side of the soul rather than on the affective side:

> . . . Mynerve, laquelle aultrement se nomme Pallas, ou Bellona, deesse de science, d'estude, de vertu, de paix, qui est aussi quise par armes, maistresse de tout artiffice et ouvraige . . . .[80]

> [. . . Mynerva, who otherwise is called / Pallas, or Bellona, goddess of science, / of study, of virtue, of peace, which / is also had by arms, mistress of / all artifice and work . . . .]

The distant and hidden nature of higher meaning in the *Concorde des deux langages* is manifest in the Acteur's futile attempt to reach it himself. Even using the intellective means of the Temple of Minerva, the Acteur must still experience the *concorde* that the inscription and Labeur Hystorien have told him about. For the moment, although he has turned away from the carnal knowledge of the Temple of Venus, he is still incapable of describing either the Temple of Minerva or the *concorde*. Labeur Hystorien promises that the Acteur might some day "apres le decours de ma vie" (after the waning of his life) see "à plain la tresvertueuse et tresnecessaire concorde des deux langages" (plainly the very virtuous and very necessary concord of the two languages).[81] For the time being, Labeur Hystorien shows the Acteur a reflection of the two "langages" embracing one another in a mirror.

Although the true and complete revelation of a higher meaning is never achieved in the *Concorde des deux langages*, the possibility of such an understanding is never denied or contradicted. The harmony of the poem's title remains just beyond the grasp of the Acteur, because such a totalization is impossible, even within the context of sixteenth-century Neoplatonism. The Acteur is exposed to the existence of harmony first by his carnal attraction to another human and second by his intellective allegiance to Labeur Hystorien. Yet, the ultimate *concorde* remains a specular image at the end of the poem. The Acteur's imperfection prevents him from fully perceiving the totality of the whole that Labeur Hystorien points out to him. Like the circle in Ficino's *Theologia platonica*, the harmony that the Acteur perceives is imperfect in its materiality, but the perfect ideal of which it is a part remains.

The *Couronne margaritique*, the *Concorde du genre humain,* and the *Concorde des deux langages* show that Lemaire, although close to his predecessor at the court of Burgundy, is a very different poet. Where the imagery of the *Chappellet des dames* depended on the inability of the protagonist to understand a higher truth, Lemaire's imagery exploits the revelation of that *altior sensus*. In Molinet's *Chappellet* the divine was knowable only through a conventionalization of analogy. The Acteur in the *Chappellet* made images of the Virgin Mary and Mary of Burgundy so that they could become univocal terms in a comparative analogy. That which is "high" remains beyond comprehension or description.

In contrast, the philosophers in Lemaire's *Couronne* have an a priori knowledge of the universal virtues that allows them to ascertain whether the artificial image that Dame Vertus creates is in concordance with universal truth. The etymologization of the word *Marguerite* depends on their ability to rise from the particular to the universal. In the same poem, the circle and the number 10 indicate the existence of an ideal world hidden behind the mask of appearance. The poem unmasks that ideal by charting the linguistic correspondences with the real world. The cosmic and the particular are connected by the power of the philosophers's reason.[82]

In the *Concorde du genre humain*, when Lemaire imitates the reversed analogy found in Molinet's *Chappellet*, the whole process of resemblance becomes a means of praising a mortal monarch. The relationship of the two terms of the analogy is one of conceptual univocity. The Virgin Mary is used as a model for Margaret of Austria, whose singularity is ironically underlined by the comparison with the Virgin. If Margaret really had participated in the greater perfection of the Virgin, the final image would have been of the Virgin and not of Margaret, who appears as a magnificent court portrait surrounded by the accompanying glory of her divine counterpart. It is only when Lemaire comes out from under Molinet's influence in the later parts of the poem that the principle of participation and resemblance comes to the fore. The individuality of the town of Cambrai becomes part of a much larger mythical structure, and the individuality of the treaty is subsumed in the universalizing power of the number 3. The nymph who helps Margaret is both divine and mortal, a daemon who intercedes actively in her life. Throughout the latter two-thirds of the poem, the individual constantly becomes part of the larger whole. The hierarchical organization of the universe is reinstated, with the particular fitting into the larger whole, from which it receives both its beauty and power. Figures such as the Nymph intercede in the lives of human beings, overcoming the difference between perfect and imperfect that characterized Molinet's poetics.

In Lemaire's *Concorde des deux langages*, reason does not try to replace love as a way to God, as it did in Molinet's *Roman de la Rose moralisé*. It offers a logical continuation of the process begun by carnal love. Reason is simply a higher form of love. The Acteur's use of contemplation is not antithetical to the use of reason, as it would have been in the *Roman de la Rose moralisé*. Lemaire's poem is much more optimistic about human ability to understand the divine. Human reason is not defective, as it was in Molinet, and the world of ideas is a part of the oneness of the universe. The cognitive impasse that marked Molinet's work, which problematized his use of rational forms of expression such as analogy and allegory, does not exist for Lemaire.

In Lemaire's literary world, human beings can rise up through the soul and see the higher meaning of things through the eye of reason. Carnal love gives only part of the answer and reveals only a limited form of the beauty that reason reveals more fully. The ontology of Lemaire's *Couronne* and the two *Concordes* is rationally understandable from top to bottom and marks a return to the kind of ontology found in Aquinas.[83] Individual phenomena are connected one to the other like tendons to bones, and the human mind can ascend to the highest levels of existence by piecing these phenomena together. The philosophers and orators in the *Couronne* begin at the literal level of the letter and follow the traces of metaphysical correspondences that link the letter to its spiritual meaning. The Acteur in the *Concorde des deux langages* begins with physical concord and follows its correspondences until he arrives at the place where real "concorde" takes place. The poem's narrative development follows the contours of this metaphysical world. In the *Couronne,* the crown really exists, just as its ideal dimensions do. In this way, the duality of the allegorical form parallels the duality of spiritual and carnal.

In the works studied in this chapter, God and creature are distinct but connected all the same. The ontological rupture that characterized Molinet's *Chappellet des dames* is not evident in Lemaire's poetry. Lemaire's imagery is not conventionalized in the same way Molinet's was, because there is no need to bring equivocal terms into a univocal comparison that is essentially impossible. The images of the crown in the *Couronne* and the rock in the *Concorde des deux langages* relate to things that exist in a metaphysical world. They are not painted images that allow the secular and the divine to be compared, but rather they are symbols with cosmic meaning that bring the secular and the divine together. Lemaire's crown might be taken from Molinet's *Chappellet,* but it is transformed in Lemaire's more southern, or ideal, poetics.

To return again to Panofsky's geographical theory of a nominalist North and an idealist South, the decorative qualities of the necklace in the *Chappelet* become vital symbols in the *Couronne*'s crown. Both the crown and the *concorde* of Jean Lemaire share in a unifying wholeness of being, of which they are symbolic parts, offering a synthesis of symbol and form that escaped Molinet's more formal and abstract images.

CHAPTER FIVE

From *ius gentium* to *Gaster:*
A Rational Rabelais?

⚜   ⚜   ⚜

The depiction of analogical imagery in the novels of Rabelais follows a curious development that parallels that of the size of the two main heroes—Gargantua and Pantagruel. In the first two novels, *Gargantua* (1534) and *Pantagruel* (1532), the two heroes are depicted as giants, and analogical images prove capable, in theory if not always in practice, of bridging the gap between contingent and absolute. In the later novels, especially in the *Quart Livre* (1552), when Pantagruel is reduced in size, analogical images become horrendous and turn the whole premise of revelation of the absolute through the contingent on its head.

The giganticism of the first novels and the depiction of analogical imagery is not perhaps purely coincidental. In these novels, where Rabelais's gigantic heroes are thoroughly invested in the hopes and promise of the new learning and the new religion, plenitude of language and the direct, unmediated meaning of Scripture promise to bring human beings closer to the invisible but more essential truth of the transcendent. In the *Quart Livre*, when Pantagruel and his comrades confront the totalizing knowledge of the inhabitants of the islands they come across on their journey to the "Dive Bouteille," they fall back increasingly on their own contingent and empirical understanding. Language and meaning become conventional and the gap between contingent and absolute becomes ever greater as the range of the Pantagruelians' own rational capacities becomes ever smaller.

Buoyed by the spirit of humanistic learning, *Pantagruel* and *Gargantua* mock the perceived inanity of the scholastic age. One of the recurrent leitmotifs in Rabelais's early novels is the contrast between scholastic barbarism and humanistic eloquence. The polarities created in this polemic between humanist and scholastic often tended to exacerbate the differences between the two sides, though the differences sometimes were not as great as the humanists believed or, perhaps more correctly, wanted to believe.[1] It is very clear, however, that the humanists understood themselves as representing a break with the empty and vain logic of the scholastics. Humanistic eloquence, as opposed to the logic of Ockham and his epigones, was based in the plenitude of meaning that the new learning was thought to provide. Philology enabled the humanist to pierce the letter of the law and attain a true understanding of the spirit that lay behind it. Language, especially Hebrew—which maintained a vital connection with a pre-Adamic plenitude in which word and thing were one—was full of presence. Original meaning was available to the humanist scholar, albeit after years of study and hard work. Within the context of the humanistic optimism of *Pantagruel* and *Gargantua*, the high and the low, both culturally and linguistically, can be understood—in theory, if not in practice—as being in harmonic union.[2]

The dream of harmonic union of contingent and absolute, which is manifest in theoretical passages throughout the first books, becomes a nightmare in the last two books, the *Tiers Livre* (1546) and especially the *Quart Livre* (1552). Disillusioned by the wasted promise of the humanistic project, and especially by the increasingly venomous quarrels between the Protestants and the Roman Catholic orthodoxy, Rabelais's view of human understanding becomes much more modest. As a result of this disillusionment, human understanding of the relationship of the secular and divine is markedly reduced in the *Quart Livre*. Against this background of limited human understanding, analogical images become huge and misshapen, like those found in Molinet's poetry and prose. The skepticism of the *Quart Livre* cuts the contingent from the absolute; anyone or anything that presumes to reveal a secret connection between them is depicted as monstrous and misleading.

This chapter describes the trajectory of human understanding in Rabelais's novels, as well as in his *Almanachs* and *Prognostications*. From the optimism of *Gargantua*, in which an *ius gentium*, or natural law, would allow all peoples in all countries to understand the inherent meaning of the color white, to the despairing skepticism of the *Quart Livre*, in which misshapen children are created through analogy, Rabelais's novels run the gamut of cognitive possibilities. After establishing this trajectory from *Gargantua* to the *Quart Livre* in relation to questions of free will, language, and astrology, the production of analogical images will be treated in the following chapter.

As noted, the first two of Rabelais's four books exhibit a sense of hope and optimism in the promise of both humanism and the new religion.[3] These works are marked by a humanistic belief in the ability to pierce the veil of meaning through an analysis of ancient works in their original languages and by an evangelical belief in the direct experience of scripture. The optimism of the new humanistic and evangelical age that characterizes *Pantagruel* and *Garagantua* is often expressed as a satire or parody of scholastic life.[4] In these books, scholastics appear as buffoons, whose empty knowledge and poor Latin are compared unfavorably with the philological skills of the humanists. In chapter 9 *bis* of *Pantagruel*, for example, scholastic jurists are taken to task for their ignorance of Greek and of the emerging "human sciences" in general: "Et au regard des letres de humanité, et de congnoissance des antiquitez et histoires, ilz en estoient chargez comme ung crapault de plumes, et en usent comme ung crucifix d'ung pifre."[5] (In regard to humane letters and knowledge of antiquities and history, they were loaded with them like a toad with feathers, and used them like a crucifix handled by a smith).

In the intellectual vacuum of the scholastic age, as perceived by the humanists, knowledge was reduced to words that have little or no relation to the things to which they refer. Gérard Defaux underlines how the humanists of the early Renaissance criticized the empty word games of the late scholastics.[6] For the humanists, the schoolmen were guilty of concentrating on words rather than on things, thereby enabling the verbal universe to acquire its own autonomy.[7] Although the nominalists' intent was to make logic more precise by establishing the autonomy of the "verbal universe," as Defaux explains, the epigones of Ockham just as often turned theology into an exercise of empty words, a form of verbal jousting that had little or no connection with the meaning of the Gospels. Much of the humor of *Pantagruel* and *Gargantua* is grounded in Rabelais's humanistic mockery of the emptiness of scholastic debate.

In *Pantagruel*, the debate between the two jurists, Baisecul and Humevesne, whose very names satirize the pretensions of scholastic knowledge, is a cornucopia of meaningless words. In this debate, which occurs in chapter 9 *bis*, things are independent of words, which float meaninglessly in the air. Meaning becomes a game of *équivoques*, and language is not adequate to deal with the world in which it exists. It becomes a means of obscuring truth rather than revealing it.[8] Pantagruel's summation of Baisecul's and Humevesne's case exemplifies the sort of language in which words have no meaning but are given the syntax of logical argument. After

Baisecul and Humevesne present the two sides of the case, Pantagruel uses a syntax that offers the armature of a meaningful discourse but that proves as meaningless as the discourse of the Ecolier Limousin, the student who destroys the French language with pretentious academic jargon.[9] Pantagruel begins with a causal proposition, which offers little meaning even though its syntactic structure is logical: "Que, consyderé que le soleil décline bravement de son solstice estival pour mugueter les billes vesées qui ont eu mat du pyon par les males vexations des lucifuges nycticoraces"[10] (That, considering the horripiliation of the bat gallantly declining from the festival solstice to make passes at rifles that have been checkmated by the pawn by the evil vexations of the lucifugues). The result clause is little better. Once again, the syntactical and semantic structures slide apart, as words proliferate but signify nothing: "le demandeur eut juste cause de calfreter le gallion que la bonne femme boursouffloit, ung pied chaussé et l'aultre nud" (the plaintiff had just cause to caulk the galleon that the gammer was inflating, one foot shod and the other bare).

Both parties in this case are satisfied with Pantagruel's nonsensical and incomprehensible sentence. Even the "Conseilliers et aultres Docteurs," who are present at the disputation, are ecstatic about Pantagruel's judgment. There is little doubt that, in a system of knowledge that is built on meaningless words, where meaning is merely a game of empty signs, little or nothing of value is produced. The humor in *Pantagruel* and *Gargantua* often relies on similar parodies of sophistic disputation. Language is not at the service of wisdom but is simply an opportunity for sophists to exhibit their idle knowledge. This empty knowledge is contrasted with the useful and unequivocal science of the humanists.

Rabelais's parody of meaningless scholastic debate, which tended to obscure the relationship of words and things rather than to talk about things with words, reaches its high point in the disputation between Panurge and Thaumaste, "ung grand clerc de Angleterre" (a great cleric from England), in *Pantagruel*, chapter 13. In this episode, Thaumaste comes to Paris to debate with Pantagruel, having heard of his great wisdom. Instead of using words that are not capable of explaining the real world, Thaumaste proposes that he and Pantagruel debate using signs in a sort of metalinguistic discourse that would escape the slipperiness of human language.[11] Rabelais arranges a very important substitution in this episode when Panurge steps in for Pantagruel in the debate with Thaumaste.[12] Pantagruel, like Rabelais himself, does not participate in the idleness and vacuity of sophistic discourse. He is effectively removed from a potentially dirtying experience and thus maintains his validity as a spokesman for humanistic ideas. Pantagruel remains a faithful proponent of meaningful language, while Panurge shows himself a great adept of sophistic discourse.

The physical gesticulations of Panurge and Thaumaste are an astonishing parody of pointless debate. When Thaumaste, for example, places all the fingernails from his left hand against those of his right and opens his hands to form a circle and raises them as high as he can, Panurge responds in kind:

> A quoy Panurge soubdain mist le poulce de la main dextre soubz les mandibules, et le doigt auriculaire d'icelle en la boucle de la gauche, et en ce point faisoit sonner ses dentz bien melodieusement les basses contre les haultes.[13]

> [At which Panurge promptly put the thumb of his right hand under his jawbone, and the little finger of it into the ring of the left, and in that position clicked his lower teeth very melodiously against the uppers.]

The enunciations of Thaumaste and Panurge mean nothing. Thaumaste responds to Panurge's chattering teeth and twisted fingers with a great fart. All of these nonsignifying gestures—raised hands, clacking teeth, and farts—can be understood as parodies of a sophistic discourse that revels in the logical distinctions of language. In Rabelais's satire, the first, second, and third intentions of nominalist discourse have become the locus of philosophical and theological discussion.[14] Signs, rather than their meaning, are discussed, and a void develops between the spirit and the real world.[15]

While the sophists play with signs and meaningless words, the humanist, through philological research and close attention to the Gospel, tries to reveal the universal meaning or law that underlies or surpasses the differences of conventional languages. In chapters 8 and 9 of *Gargantua*, this universal law, or *ius gentium,* is posited as being revealed in emblems that bring word and thing together.[16] The narrator takes contemporary emblematists to task, in chapter 8, for using arbitrary signs for real emblems. He attacks those whose devices depend on "inept homonyms" such as "'pennes d'oiseaux' pour 'penes'" (bird plumes for pens) and "'ancholie' pour 'melancholie'" (columbine for melancholy).[17] He cites the ancient Egyptians as a counterexample. For the Egyptians, hieroglyphs offered a real language alternative, in which the image used to signify the thing and the thing itself were mysteriously related. There was, in these hieroglyphs, a combining of word and thing.

Bien aultrement faisoient en temps jadys les saiges de Egypte, quant ilz escripvoient par letres qu'ilz appelloyent hieroglyphicques lesquelles nul n'entendoyt qui n'entendist et un chascun entendoyt qui entendist la vertus, proprieté et nature des choses par ycelles figurées.[18]

[Very differently did the Egyptian sages act once upon a time, when they wrote with letters they called hieroglyphics, which no one understood, who did not understand and everyone understood who understood, the virtue, property, and nature of things represented by these figured.]

The opposition between contemporary emblematists and the Egyptians is an important one because it shows how in *Gargantua*, at least theoretically, language is held to have the potential for revealing the "vertus, proprieté et nature" of the things it represents. Much like the etymological theory of Isidore or the occult magic of Henry Cornelius Agrippa, Egyptian hieroglyphs were thought to be "signatures" of the reality they represent.[19] The linguistic sign participated in the virtue or property of the thing of which it was a sign, and there was a real, ontological connection between word and thing. The name did "correspond to the properties of things," at least in theory.

The same desire for natural language is expressed in the following chapter. Here, the narrator proposes that there are certain meanings understood by all people as true and not imposed by human will. This is the *ius gentium* or universal law:

Et n'est poinct ceste signifiance par imposition humaine institué, mais repceue par consentement de tout le monde, que les philosophes nomment "jus gentium," droict universel, valable par toutes contrées.[20]

[And this significance is not instituted by human imposition but received by universal consent, which the philosophers call *ius gentium*, universal law valid in all countries.]

The argument is based on the assumption that all peoples of all nations and languages demonstrate their unhappiness by wearing black (see 71–72). This universal consent is impossible, the argument goes, unless "nature n'en donne quelque argument et raison, laquelle un chascun peut soubdain par soy comprendre sans aultrement estre instruict de persone" (nature gives some argument or reason that any one can immediately understand by himself without in any way being instructed by any one else) (72). This intuitively understood sign is the complete opposite of Thamauste's and Panurge's arbitrary gestures, which have no meaning. The sophists depend on the arbitrary nature of conventional language, while

Rabelais's narrator argues for a natural language that would join words and things together in bounteous harmony.

In *Gargantua*, the harmony of the world, reflected in the adequacy and analysis of language, allows humankind to understand the real nature of the world. Things are synonymous for the narrator of *Gargantua,* and "inept homonyms" merely hide and obscure that true resemblance that is intuitively recognized. This plenitude of meaning offers a telling contrast to the dispute between Baisecul and Humevesne in *Pantagruel,* in which words are so removed from things that there is not even any homophonic resemblance. Signs are removed not only from their referents but also from their oral rendering. The plenitude of the *ius gentium* can be understood as bearing eloquent witness against the arbitrariness of the sophistic sign.

This opposition between the humanistic, evangelical tradition, on the one hand, and the scholastic tradition, on the other, is cast into even greater relief when Pantagruel's comments about those who had tried to understand Baisecul's and Humevesne's trial are considered. The people who attended the trial had not been able to understand it:

> Car je suis sceur que et vous et tous ceulx par les mains desquelz a passé le procès, y avez machiné ce que avez peu, "pro et contra," et, au cas que leur controverse estoit patente et facile à juger, vous l'avez obscurcie par sottes et desraisonnables raisons et ineptes opinions de Accurse, Balde, Bartole. (58)

> [For I am sure that you and all those through whose hands the lawsuit has passed have contrived whatever you could, pro and contra, and, in case their controversy was patent and easy to judge, have obscured it by stupid and irrational reasons and inept opinions of Accursius, Baldus, Bartolus.]

The jurists were incapable of understanding the meaning of the law because they had no "congoissance de langue ny grecque, ny latine" (knowledge of either Greek or Latin) and were dependent upon inept translations and ignorant commentary. Since the laws were first taken from the Greek and then "rédigées en latin," there was no way for the Bartolians to understand anything.[21] The humanists—Valla, Erasmus, Lefèvre d'Etaples, Rabelais, et alia— differed from their scholastic predecessors in that they were philologically trained and could experience both Scripture and the Greek texts directly. They were more likely to perceive the *ius gentium* because they were not blinded by the obscuring language of the sophist. Language was adequate to convey the meaning that lay hidden beneath the surface. The closer one got to the original language, the closer one got to the original, or universal, meaning. The humanists and the evangelicals of 1534 offered the hope that a new age was at hand, one that promised to avoid the mistakes of the "age des ténèbres" by turning to direct experience of Scripture and the study of the ancient languages. The *ius gentium* that underlay the Egyptian hieroglyphs would be made clearer by tearing away the equivocal word games of sophists like Baisecul, Humevesne, Thaumaste, and Panurge.

There are cracks in this promising monument to humanist and evangelical reform. These fissures are found in Rabelais's own use of the conventional language, which he parodies in Baisecul, Humevesne, Panurge, the Ecolier limousin, and others.[22] Puns, *calembours*, and other equivocal word games play a very important role in Rabelais's humor. Often these word games are part of the sophists's discourse, as in Baisecul's humorous misappropriation of "in verbo sacerdotis" (on the word of a priest) as "in sacer verbo dotis," or in Panurge's "femme folle à la messe" (mad woman at mass) and "femme molle à la fesse (woman soft in the ass)."[23] Because Rabelais himself includes passages attacking the "inept homonyms" of the court emblematists, it is difficult to know how to understand his own use of puns and word games.

If language, at least theoretically, is supposed to reveal its connection with things, what is to be made of these instances of conventional language in Rabelais's novels? What is to be made of the final stanza of the "Inscription above the Gate at the Abbey of Thélème," a particularly remarkable example of conventional language:

Or donné par don
Ordonne pardon
A cil qui le donne,
Et tresbien guerdonne
Tout mortel preud'hom
Or donné par don.[24]

[Gold given by gift / Gives a golden shrift / For the giver stored / And makes rich reward / As a wise man's shift / Given by gift.]

In passages such as these, Rabelais would seem to be caught in flagrant disregard of his explicit remonstrations about language. The "inept homonym," which Rabelais attacks in *Gargantua*, would seem to be crucial to the poetics of "Or donné pardon / Ordonne pardon."

Rabelais's explicitly theoretical pronouncements about language and his seemingly contradictory use of conventional language point to an underlying tension that will be worked out only in the *Quart Livre*, where language theory and practice exist in a fruitful if not somber symbiosis. In *Gargantua* and *Pantagruel*, François Rigolot's very succinct explanation of Rabelais's use of language is clearly demonstrated. Rigolot explains that there are two contrasting themes in Rabelais's thinking on language: on the one hand, there is a theoretical longing for the plenitude of a natural or Cratylic language, and on the other, there is a practical dependence and joy in the pleasures of conventional language.[25] The split between what Rabelais says explicitly about language and what he practices in many passages provides a clue to the problematic nature of *Gargantua* and *Pantagruel*. In these works, Rabelais, hewing to the humanist and evangelical line, expounds a belief in the plenitude of language. Underneath the optimism of these explicit passages, a skeptical understanding of the nature of contingent and absolute lies waiting to emerge in Rabelais's implicit practice.

Pantagruel and *Gargantua* are not only filled with hope for humanistic studies, they are also filled with hope for the new religion that promises to bring the Christian people back to a direct, unmediated experience of the Gospels, unfettered by the commentary and glosses of the "caphars" (humbugs), the term Rabelais uses to refer to hypocritical bigots. In these early books, as Michael Screech shows, Rabelais adopts a predominantly Lutheran position, even though he is not a Protestant.[26] Rabelais's evangelicalism is similar to that of Erasmus, Lefèvre d'Etaples, and Clichthove in its willingness to bring the Catholic Church back to the traditions of the Church Fathers without becoming openly schismatic like Luther and Calvin.

One of the most telling critiques of Roman Catholic doctrine concerned the question of free will. Luther attacked all of the scholastics for their voluntarism, proclaiming that they were all guilty of Pelagian heresy.[27] It is not surprising, then, that Rabelais condemns the *caphars* and "cagotz" (cretins) as he espouses a Pauline attitude toward free will that is very close to that of Luther.[28] In chapter 18 of *Pantagruel*, after Pantagruel has beaten the "Dipsodes" and the "Geans" (Giants), he is asked by a prisoner for mercy. Pantagruel replies:

Après que tu auras annoncé à ton roy, *je ne te dys pas, comme les caphars,* "Ayde-toy, Dieu te aydera": car c'est, au rebours, "Ayde-toy, le diable te rompra le col." Mais je te dys: metz tout ton espoir en Dieu, et il ne te délaissera point. Car de moy, encores que soye puissant, comme tu peuz veoir, et aye gens infiniz en armes, toutesfois *je n'espère point en ma force, ny en mon industrie: mais toute ma fiance est en Dieu, mon protecteur*, lequel jamais ne délaisse ceulx qui en luy ont mys leur espoir et pensee.[29] (emphasis mine)

[After you've announced everything to your king, *I will not tell you like the humbugs: "Help yourself and God will help you," since it is much to the contrary: "Help yourself and the devil will break your neck." But I will tell you: put all your hope in God*, and he will not forsake you; for as for me, although I am strong, as you can see, and have an infinity of men in arms, nevertheless *I hope not in my strength or my diligence, but all my trust is in God, my protector*, who never forsakes those who have put their hope and their thought in him.]

Rabelais's position is not unlike that of Martin Luther, who denies absolutely the power of free choice in his essay *On the Bondage of the Will*. No good, says Luther, can be done in the absence of grace: "It is settled, then, even on your own testimony, that we do everything by necessity and nothing by free choice, since the power of free choice is nothing and neither does nor can do good in the absence of grace."[30] Evangelicals, while remaining within the Catholic Church, took a similar position on matters of faith. For example, Lefèvre d'Etaples emphasizes the necessity of faith in matters of salvation and cites Saint Paul: "Par grace (dit sainct Paul) estes sauvez par foy, et non de vous" (By grace [says Saint Paul] you are saved by faith and not by you).[31]

This Lutheran and evangelical belief in the efficacy of faith instead of *bonnes oeuvres* is directly related to Rabelais's satire of Baisecul and Humevesne. The empty words of the "caphars" and their belief in the need for man to merit God's saving grace were, for theologians and intellectuals rallying to the Lutheran cause, part and parcel of late medieval scholasticism. When Ockham took his razor to the logical distinctions of realist theology, he not only made language purely conventional, he also cut human beings off from God. Protestants and Evangelicals criticized what they saw as Ockham's Pelagianism. In Ockham's nominalism, human beings first had to make a meritorious action in a state of nature before attaining a degree of cooperative and, finally, saving grace.[32] For anyone taking a Lutheran or semi-Lutheran position on the question of free will, the "Ayde-toy, Dieu te aydera" of the "caphars" reeks of scholastic sophistry. It is only natural, then, that if Rabelais rejects the sophistry of Baisecul, Humevesne, and Thaumaste, he also rejects the Pelagian belief in good works that was so integral a part of the late scholastic worldview, at least as it was construed by its sixteenth-century critics.[33]

In chapter 18, Rabelais reemphasizes the novel's evangelical leanings when he has Pantagruel submit himself entirely to the will of God in the prayer he says before doing battle with the fearsome Loupgarou. When Pantagruel prays, he does not presume to claim that he can save himself or even help God in effecting his salvation. He places himself whole-heartedly in the hands of God:

> Seigneur Dieu, qui tousjours as esté mon protecteur et mon servateur, tu voys la destresse en laquelle je suis maintenant. Riens icy ne me amène, sinon zèle naturel, comme tu as concédé ès humains de garder et défendre soy, leurs femmes, enfans, pays, et famille, en cas que ne seroit ton négoce propre, qui est la foy; car en tel affaire tu ne veulx nul coadjuteur, sinon de confession catholicque, et ministère de ta parolle.[34]

> [Lord God, who hast always been my Protector and Savior, thou seest the distress I am now in. Nothing brings me here but natural zeal; as thou hast vouchsafed to humans to guard and defend themselves, their wives, children, country and family in a case where it would not be thy affair, which is faith; for in such matters thou wilt have no collaborator but that of Catholic confession and service of thy word.]

Pantagruel's prayer reflects a position that is entirely consonant with the theology of Luther and Erasmus. For the Protestants and the evangelicals, God does not need any help or "coadjuteurs" in effecting human salvation. The only thing human beings can to do to effect their own salvation is have faith and spread the word of God. Pantagruel finishes his prayer by criticizing the obfuscations of the Catholic tradition and promises to spread the word of the Gospel:

> je feray prescher ton sainct Evangile, purement, simplement et entièrement, si que les abuz d'ung tas de papelars et faulx prophètes, qui ont par constitutions humaines et inventions dépravées envenimé tout le monde, seront d'entour moy exterminez. (154)

> [I will have thy Gospel preached pure, simple, and entire, so that the abuses of a bunch of hypocrites and false prophets, who, by human institutions and depraved inventions, have envenomed the whole world, will be driven forth from around me.]

Pantagruel's serious promise to "prescher" the "sainct Evangile, purement, simplement, et entièrement" is not inconsistent with the humor of the novel as a whole. The satire of Rabelais's early novels cannot be understood apart from their serious evangelical message. The satire directed against the Scholastics makes sense only if the perceived emptiness of scholastic discourse is contrasted with the fullness of the evangelical message. The book's humor and seriousness could not function one without the other. Erasmus's *Praise of Folly* (1511) is remarkably similar to *Pantagruel* both in its condemnation of the subtleties of the scholastics and in its praise of the simple truths of the Gospel:

> And then these most subtle subtleties are rendered even more subtle by the various "ways" or types of scholastic theology, so that you could work your way out of a labyrinth sooner than out of the intricacies of the Realists, Nominalists, Thomists, Albertists, Occamists, Scotists—and I still haven't mentioned all the sects, but only the main ones.
>
> In all of these there is so much erudition, so much difficulty, that I think the apostles themselves would need to be inspired by a different spirit if they were forced to match wits on such points with this new breed of theologians. Paul could provide a living example of faith, but when he said "Faith is the substance of things to be hoped for and the evidence of things not seen," his definition was not sufficiently magisterial. So too, he lived a life of perfect charity, but he neither distinguishes it nor defines it with sufficient dialectical precision in the first epistle to the Corinthians.[35]

Both the *Praise of Folly* and *Pantagruel* are characterized by their optimism concerning the new religion and their satire of the scholastics. In both books, the subtleties of the scholastics and their poor Latin are juxtaposed with the simple faith of the Gospels and the Apostles. The aim of both Rabelais and Erasmus, it seems, is to tear down the scholastic edifice constructed of words and replace it with a simple faith in the all-powerful God of Saint Paul.[36] It is impossible to separate the critique of scholastic language from the evangelical insistence on faith in matters of salvation. Pantagruel's belief in the efficacy of the Gospels is an essential counterpart to the satire of the dispute between Panurge and Thaumaste. Pantagruel's confidence in the power of faith and his advice to his prisoner that, if he tries to help himself the Devil would break his neck, are as telling a commentary on scholasticism as Thaumaste's arbitrary and meaningless gestures.

Things change, however, and both Erasmus's and Rabelais's early satires of the scholastic age would be tempered by their experience with some of the chief proponents of the Reformation. Erasmus's rejection of the scholastics in the *Praise of Folly* becomes much more nuanced in his *On the Freedom of the Will* (1524), in which his position on free will ends up much closer to Ockham than to Luther.[37] This change in position came at the end of a long and painful debate with Luther, during which Erasmus found himself more and more alienated from the Reformation by Luther's increasingly virulent attacks. Erasmus says, for example, that

Pelagius has no doubt attributed too much to free choice, and Scotus quite enough, but Luther first mutilated it by cutting off its right arm; then not content with this he thoroughly cut the throat of free choice and despatched it. I prefer the view of those who do attribute much to free choice, but most to grace. . . . The result of this moderation will be the achievement of some good work, albeit imperfect, from which no man can arrogate anything to himself: there will be some merit, but such that the sum *is* owed to God.[38]

Erasmus's call for a middle road, after having been confronted by the extremism of both Luther and the Sorbonne, is repeated by Rabelais in the *Quart Livre*. By 1548, Rabelais himself had been attacked not only by the Sorbonne but also by the "Demoniacles Calvins, imposteurs de Geneve."[39] Calvin, in the *Traité des scandales,* attacks Rabelais and others, saying that they,

apres avoir gousté l'Evangile, ont esté frappez d'un mesme aveuglement. Comment cela est-il advenu, sinon que desja ils avoyent par leur outrecuidance diabolique profané ce gage sainct et sacré de la vie eternelle? . . . Vray est qu'ils s'insinuent par petis broquards et faceties, sans faire semblant de tascher sinon à donner du passetemps à ceulx qui les escoutent. Neantmoins leur fin est d'abolir toute reverence de Dieu.[40]

[after having tasted the Gospel, were struck by the same blindness. How did this happen, if they had not already, by their diabolical presumptuousness, profaned this holy and sacred pledge of eternal life. . . . It is true that they insinuate themselves by little gibes and facetious jests, effortlessly, seeming only to divert those who listen to them. Nonetheless, their end is to abolish all reverence of God.]

If Calvin's criticism of Rabelais was virulent, the Catholic orthodoxy was no less energetic in their attack on the author of *Pantagruel* and *Gargantua.* They went so far as to make one of the most serious charges possible in the sixteenth century: they accused Rabelais of atheism. For example, Gabriel de Puy-Herbault (Putherbus), doctor of theology at the University of Paris, accused Rabelais in his *Theotimus*

de se damner, chaque jour ne faire que se souler, goinfrer, vivre à la grecque, flairer les odeurs des cuisines, imiter le singe à longue queue . . . lancer la calomnie et l'injure . . . attaquer les honnêtes gens, les pieuses etudes . . . faisant si peu état de Dieu et des choses divines . . . qu'il ne semble reconnaître aucun culte.[41]

[of damning himself, of doing nothing other than every day getting drunk, living "à la grecque," smelling the odors of the kitchen, of imitating the long-tailed monkey . . . of proffering calumny and curses . . . of attacking honest folk . . . and making so little case of God and divine things . . . that he seems to recognize no cult.]

In 1552, Rabelais found himself embroiled in the theological vortex that led to the outbreak of religious war in 1562. Disillusionment and despair replaced hope and promise as both sides of the theological dispute hardened their positions and become increasingly extreme.[42] Rabelais found himself between "Andouilles et Quaresmeprenant . . . entre l'enclume et les marteaulx" (Andouilles and Quaresmeprenant . . . between the anvil and the hammer).[43] The promise of the evangelical Reformation was crushed by the extremism of Calvin, and the position of the Catholic orthodoxy was strengthened at the Council of Trent. Rabelais, like Erasmus after his quarrel with Luther, found himself taking a more centrist and moderate position as he was repulsed by both the Protestant and the Catholic extremists.

The prologue to the *Quart Livre* is in many ways a plea for *mediocritas*, for moderation. In the prologue, Rabelais recounts the story of a woodcutter named Couillatris who loses his axe. Although full of double entendres concerning the sexual connotation of the word *coignée*, or axe, the prologue places the question of moderation at the center of its narrative. Couillatris loses his axe and pleads with the gods to have it returned. The gods decide to grant Couillatris his wish and offer him the choice of three axes: one gold, one silver, and his old one. When he chooses his own, Mercury tells him: "Et, pour ce que as opté et soubhaité mediocrité en matiere de coingnée, par le vueil de Juppiter je te donne ces deux aultres. Tu as de quoy dorenavant te faire riche; soys homme de bien."[44] (And because you wished for and chose moderation in the matter of the hatchets, by the will of Jupiter I give you these two others. You have enough to make you rich from now; be a good man). When his neighbors see how rich he becomes when he sells the gold and silver axes that Mercury gave him, they also lose their axes and demand restitution from the gods. However, instead of receiving gold and silver, they lose their heads because they do not practice *mediocrité*.

The *Quart Livre* as a whole can be read as a critique of those people who do not show the moderation of Couillatris. Throughout the *Quart Livre* the pretensions of those who claim to understand the hidden design of the universe are contrasted with the moderation and empirical skepticism of the Pantagruelians. In the *Quart Livre*, only the knowledge arrived at by personal experience is acceptable, whereas the totalizing knowledge of those who claim to have understood God's design produces monsters and ends up making human beings slaves.

Truth in the *Quart Livre* is less a matter of universals than of personal experience.[45] Although the desire for a totalizing system of knowledge might motivate the voyage that the Pantagruelians undertake, the actual narrative development of the *Quart Livre* is founded on the confrontation of the Pantagruelians' empirical knowledge with the totalizing knowledge of the inhabitants of the islands they discover on their voyage. The Pantagruelians might undertake their voyage in order to "veoir, apprendre, congnoistre, visiter l'oracle de Bacbuc et avoir le mot de la Bouteille, sus quelques difficultez proposées par quelqu'un de la compaignie" (see, learn, know, visit the oracle of Bacbuc and to have the word from the Bottle about certain difficulties raised by someone in the company); however, the voyage itself constantly places the Pantagruelians in opposition to all those peoples who, like the Engastrimythes, claim to have some oracular knowledge.[46] In fact, the Pantagruelians continuously find themselves up against various forms of deterministic knowledge, which they all reject.[47]

The *Quart Livre*'s distance from the joyful satire of the scholastics in *Pantagruel* and *Gargantua*, and from the early belief in faith to the detriment of works, can easily be illustrated by considering the "Tempête en mer" (chapters 18-24). The Pauline belief in the efficacy of faith that characterized *Pantagruel* disappears in the *Quart Livre*. Now, in the "Tempête en mer," voluntarism enters into Rabelais's understanding of salvation.[48] Whereas in *Pantagruel* God needed no "coadjuteur" to help save human beings, in the "Tempête en mer," humankind must cooperate with God.[49] This increased belief in free will marks a subtle yet profound change from Rabelais' denial of merit and total confidence in faith some twenty years earlier.

The "Tempête" is not written solely against Calvinist fideism. The Catholic orthodoxy, with its belief in relics and its cult of the saints, also comes in for attack.[50] Rabelais steers a course between the extremes of both sides and pleads for the advantages of a "middle way."[51] Panurge becomes the focus of Rabelais's attack on both extremes. On the one hand, because he does nothing to help the Pantagruelians save themselves in the storm except to make empty promises to build churches should he ever escape alive, Panurge represents the sort of empty sacramental posturing that Rabelais and other humanists objected to in the Catholic orthodoxy. On the other hand, Panurge's inaction in the storm becomes the counterpart of the activism of the Pantagruelians and sets the scene for their decidedly voluntaristic philosophy.

Although his own actions represent a caricature of Catholic liturgical excesses, Panurge also allows the author to attack the fideistic point of view of the Calvinists. Throughout the storm, the Pantagruelians (with the exception of Panurge) place their trust in God and work to save themselves when they have the chance, depending on the technical expertise of the ship's captain. In contrast, Panurge is reduced to empty posturing. When the energetic monk Frere Jan enjoins Panurge to "icy nous ayder" (help us here), Panurge refuses. The Pantagruelians work to save themselves, thereby offering a positive counterexample to the Calvinist philosophy of predestination and to the Roman Catholic belief in the power of relics. The Pantagruelians, who combine grace and merit, seem to embody the position Erasmus sketches out in his *On the Freedom of the Will*: they are like "those who do attribute much to free choice, but most to grace."

Panurge sets the tone of the episode in chapter 18, when he interprets the passing of a ship full of monks on their way to the "Concile de Chesil" as a good omen.[52] Panurge's superstition is counterbalanced by the captain's empiricism, for the captain notices a strange movement in the sails after the monks' ship passes and, based upon his knowledge of the sea, orders his own ship to make ready for a storm. The sea immediately becomes very rough and soon resembles "l'antique Cahos, on quel estoient feu, air, mer, terre, tous les elemens en refractaire confusion" (antique Chaos, in which fire, air, sea, and earth, all the elements, were in rebellious confusion).[53] Although the juxtaposition of the two events, the monks and then the storm, creates a certain metonymic connection that allows a doubt to hover over the incident, nothing is said about an occult influence at this point. Here, as elsewhere in the *Quart Livre*, the pragmatic philosophy of the Pantagruelians places human action within the human sphere and humility within the divine sphere in a positive light. The opposition of the Pantagruelians' secular activity and humility in divine matters with the secular inactivity and arrogance in divine matters of the peoples they meet is one of the principal motors in the plot of the *Quart Livre*.[54]

In the storm there is a telling conjunction of theology and language. Panurge, scared to death, prays to the saints and the Virgin Mary. These prayers appear as a satiric commentary on the cult of the saints and the cult of the Virgin Mary, both of which were targets of Evangelical and Protestant criticism. Many of the saints beatified by the Catholic Church in the Middle Ages were not accepted by the Protestants, and the cult that had developed around these saints was considered an example of how the Catholic orthodoxy had moved away from the simple and eloquent truth of the Gospel. For the Protestants and Evangelicals, the divine Logos is present in the word of Christ, and one has only to read the Scriptures to have evidence of divine truth. The Protestants and Evangelicals saw the Catholic Church's straying away from the primacy of the Gospel and its use of relics, images, and the cult of the saints as examples of how the traditional church had lost the true meaning of Christianity, which was the word of Christ as it is expressed in the Gospels.

After Panurge prays to the saints and the Virgin Mary, his language falls apart. This glossolalia appears to be a linguistic corollary of his theological sins, for his words mean nothing. They are cut off from their referents, just as his use of dubious saints cuts him off from the simple truth of God as revealed through Scripture. He says, for example: "Bou bou, bou bou! Otto to to to to ti! Otto to to to to ti! Bou bou bou, ou ou ou bou bou bous bous! Je naye, je naye, je meurs. Bonnes gens, je naye."[55] (Bou, bou, bou bou! Otto to to to to ti! Otto to to to to ti! Bou bou bou, ou ou ou bou bou bous bous! I'm drowning, I'm drowning, I'm dying. Good friends, I'm drowning).

The breakdown of language occurs when the referent is ignored or obscured by the vanity of words. The effect is comparable to Pantagruel's summation of Baisecul's and Humevesne's trial. In both Panurge's empty praying and the jurists' inane trial, the syntax offers the promise of a meaning, which is refused. In the "Tempête en mer," Panurge's inability to express himself adequately in language is directly related to his incomprehension of the real meaning of God. Just as his use of relics and dubious saints cannot save him in the storm, his use of language cannot express meaning. His "Bou bou, bou bou! Otto to to to to ti." bears a syntactical relationship to significant language in the same way that Pantagruel's syntax in his summation of the trial of Baisecul and Humevesne bears a resemblance to logical discourse. The syntax bears witness to a significant symbolic structure that no longer functions. As Rigolot states in regard to Baisecul and Humevesne, it is as if the speaker were well versed in the use of *elocutio* and *dispositio* but completely ignorant of *inventio*.[56] Panurge's language is as dysfunctional as his use of ineffective religious symbols.

The beginning of chapter 19 stands in marked contrast to the glossolalia of the final lines of chapter 18. Where Panurge's empty gestures result in nothing but meaningless sounds, Pantagruel's honest humility results in effective action and clear speech. Pantagruel, having "préalablement" prayed to God, turns to the captain of the ship for advice and council in earthly matters. The captain is the lord and master of his vessel, and it is from him that necessary knowledge is obtained. Pantagruel grabs hold of the tiller "par l'advis du pilot" (on advice of the pilot).[57] Frere Jan, Epistemon, and Ponocrates get ready to help the sailors. Panurge remains, crying and complaining, on the deck. Immediately, the contrast between the language of Panurge and that of the other Pantragruelians is clear. Efficacious action and clear speech go hand in hand.

The distance the Pantagruelians have traveled since 1532 in regard to free will is also noticeable. When Panurge sits blubbering on the deck of the ship, Frere Jan tells him that "tu feroys beaucoup mieulx nous aydant icy que là pleurant comme une vache, assis sus tes couillons comme un magot" (you would do much better to help us here than crying like a great cow, sitting on your balls like a great macaque).[58] Frere Jan's imprecation to "help us here" is, metaphorically, a double-edged sword. It attacks the empty gestures of Panurge, who is reduced to mouthing meaningless sounds. It also attacks, or begins to attack, the fatalism of Calvinist doctrine. Frere Jan repeats his call to action when he reacts to another of Panurge's nearly incomprehensible litanies, saying: "Vien, pendu au Diable . . . icy nous ayder, de par trente legions de Diables, vien!"[59] (Come here . . . and lend us a hand! In the name of thirty legions of devils, come on!).

Throughout the "tempête," Frere Jan accuses Panurge of doing nothing and exhorts him to help the Pantagruelians save themselves. He says: "parle tu de testament à ceste heure que sommes en dangier, et qu'il nous convient evertuer ou jamais plus" (108) (are you talking about a will, at this moment when we're in danger and when it's up to us to our damndest now or never). And later: "Ce diable de fol marin est cause de la tempeste, et il seul ne ayde à la chorme" (110) (That devil's sea-calf is the cause of the tempest, and he alone won't help the crew). In chapters 22 and 23, Frere Jan's imprecations take physical form in the hands of Epistemon, which are bloodied from his efforts on the ship's deck. Epistemon's hands become a synechdocal symbol of the need to cooperate with God in order to achieve salvation.

Frere Jan's "Vien . . . ici nous ayder" steers a middle path, seeming to paraphrase Erasmus's position in the *On the Freedom of the Will*. Erasmus's *via media*, which gives some efficacy to works but the lion's share to God's grace, avoids the pitfalls of both Pelagian arrogance and Calvinist fatalism. The position of Rabelais might appear somewhat more voluntaristic than that of Erasmus, but the idea is the same. Man cannot depend wholly on faith in God to effect his salvation, nor can he depend on useless relics; rather he must exercise his proper will in order to merit God's saving grace. He must cooperate with God. This new voluntarism is clearly expressed in Pantagruel's speech in chapter 23:

> Je consydere que si vrayement mourir est (comme est) de necessité fatale et inevitable, en telle ou telle heure, en telle ou telle facon mourir est en la saincte volunté de Dieu. Pourtant, icelluy fault incessamment implorer, invocquer, prier, requerir, supplier. *Mais là ne fault faire but et bourne: de nostre part, convient pareillement nous evertuer, et, comme dict le sainct Envoyé, estre cooperateurs avecques luy.*[60]

> [I consider that if really it is of necessity fatal and inevitable to die (as it is), at such or such a time, to die in such or such a way, is in the holy will of God. However, we must ceaselessly implore, invoke, pray, ask, supplicate him. *But we must not set our goal and limit there; for our part, we should likewise put forth our utmost effort, and, as the Holy Envoy says, be cooperators with him.*]

Here, Rabelais has moved a considerable distance from the "Ayde-toy, le diable te rompra le col" of *Pantagruel*.[61] God is still responsible for our living or dying, but within the context of secular life, man must do all he can to save himself. The Pantagruel of the *Quart Livre* is closer to Molinet's Friar Jehan, who hit the old woman on the head for saying that the death of the young girl in the flood was predestined by God, than to the earlier Pantagruel of the first novel, who seemed to reject all forms of voluntarism in salvation.[62] Both Molinet's Friar Jehan and the Pantagruel of the *Quart Livre* take responsibility for their own salvation, unlike the Pantagruel of *Pantagruel*, who puts all his "faith and confidence in God," to the exclusion of his own agency.

Effectively, man is further from understanding God's will in 1552 than in 1532. Obviously, Rabelais does not adopt the position of the Catholic orthodoxy in the *Quart Livre,* as his treatment of Panurge in the "Tempête" shows. But it is clear that by 1552 he had moved away from the more strictly Lutheran stance he held in 1532, perhaps in reaction to the extremism of certain Calvinists. Faith is not sufficient, and man is once again in the position of *viator*, struggling to find his way with imperfect knowledge of the divine. Whereas in 1532, God needed "nul coadjuteur," twenty years later, man must be a "cooperateur[s] avecques luy." Although it would be impossible to qualify Rabelais as a nominalist, his position in 1552 is "semi-Pelagian" in its insistence on the need for man to exercise his will in achieving his own salvation.

Pantagruel and his crew are human beings who for salvation depend on their own experience and on that of earthly experts like the captain in the "Tempête." They are cut off from God and the divine. Whatever God's will, it is beyond their understanding, and anyone who attempts to understand that will is going against nature. Knowledge is limited to direct observation in the secular world and to faith and Scripture in the divine world. Predestination might exist, but it is beyond the powers of man to know who is to be saved. Man must "s'evertuer" and "cooperer" in his own salvation.

The epistemological humility that marks the "Tempête en mer" approaches the attitude that Rabelais takes toward astrology throughout his works. If in *Pantagruel* or *Gargantua* Rabelais could write about an *ius gentium* with a fair amount of optimism, in his *Almanachs* and *Prognostication* he maintains a skeptical viewpoint toward a humanly understood universal.[63] His *Pantagrueline Prognostication pour l'an 1533* is remarkable for its similarity to Molinet's *Prenostications*. In both Rabelais's and Molinet's astrological predictions, the ordinary is satirically inflated with transcendental signification. In Molinet, the usual course of events—the rising and setting of the sun, the passing of comets—is arranged in such a way that it seems to have a causal relationship with the events that transpire during the year.[64] Yet this relationship is entirely factitious, as the events described would happen no matter what the stars and the planets did. Molinet says as much in his *Prenostication de la comette* (1477):

> Nous arons ceste annee plus grande esclipse de pecune que de lune et, a ceste cause, s'engendr[er]a une maladie nommee podenaire, fort melancolieuse et dommageuse; le souverain remede sera faire grande provision de vif argent, le porter sur luy et autour de luy et en oindre tres bien les palmes de ceux qui en seront entechiés, il n'est riens meilleur.[65]

> [We will have this year a greater eclipse of coins than of the moon and, on account of this, a most melancholy and injurious sickness will breed itself, called lack of cash. The supreme remedy will be to make great provision of quicksilver and carry it on you and rub well the palms of those who will be so afflicted; there is nothing better.]

Here, Molinet satirizes the pretensions of the court astrologers, much as he did in the *Roman de la Rose moralisé*; the suffering of the world will continue with or without the astrologer's vain speculation about God's will.

Rabelais takes a similar tack in his *Pantagrueline Prognostication*. In his predictions about the future, Rabelais underlines the banality of day-to-day existence and mocks the pretensions of the astrologer by cloaking his predictions about this sort of existence in orotund tones.

For example:

> Ceste année les aveugles ne verront que bien peu, les sourdz oyrant assez mal, les muetz ne parleront guieres, les riches se porteront ung peu mieulx que les pouvres, et les sains mieulx que les malades. . . . Vieillesse sera incurable ceste année à cause des années passées.[66]

> [This year the blind will not see much, the deaf will be a little better off than the poor, and the healthy will stay better than the sick. . . . Old age will be incurable this year because of the past years.]

Here, as in the *Roman de la Rose moralisé* and in Molinet's *Prenostications*, the sun will rise, the sun will set, it will be hot in the summer and cold in the winter. This is the limit of man's knowledge, and beyond this constrained field of inquiry lies God's will, which is unknowable. Rabelais places his *Prognostication* under the aegis of an impenetrable and all-powerful God.[67] In the first chapter, he says:

> Doncques le gouverneur de ceste année et toutes aultres, selon nostre veridicque resolution, sera Dieu tout puissant. Et ne aura Saturne, ne Mars, ne Jupiter, ne aultre planete, certes non pas les anges, ni les sainctz, ny les hommes, ny les diables, vertuz, efficace, puissance, ne influence aulcune, si Dieu de son bon plaisir ne leur donne.[68]

> [So the governor for this year and all others, according to our truthful resolution, will be Almighty God, and not Saturn, nor Mars, nor Jupiter, nor any other planet, certainly not the angels, or saints, or men, or devils, will have any virtue, efficacy, or influence, unless God, in his good pleasure, gives it to them.]

As the rest of the "prognostications" show, the stars and planets reveal nothing to humans that could not be known by more empirical methods. It is not that there is no truth in the stars, it is just that, if it is there, then it is by definition unavailable to humans. Saint Paul is the "celeste Astrologue" because he was exposed to God's truth when he was "ravy jusques au Ciel," but unless an individual is exposed to a similar direct experience of God, transcendental knowledge of this sort is unavailable to him or her. The *Pantagrueline Prognostication* is a parodic exercise in which the "infiniz abus" of the "Prenosticqueurs" become the fuel for Rabelais's wit.[69]

The skepticism underlying the *Almanachs* and *Prognostication*, like the puns and other word games in *Pantagruel* and *Gargantua*, seems to belie the optimism that Rabelais manifests in human understanding of an *ius gentium*. While the hopes inherent in the evangelical and humanistic projects might have pushed Rabelais into taking optimistic positions regarding human understanding of the relationship of the contingent and absolute, his own language stays resolutely conventional in his mockery of the excesses of the scholastics. Even as early as 1533, when the concerns of the evangelicals and humanists were not directly addressed, Rabelais was leery of all systems that pretend they can reveal the hidden but real structure of the universe. This skepticism, like the practically exuberant use of conventional language in *Pantagruel* and *Gargantua*, emerges as a dominant trait in the *Quart Livre*.

As in his astrological predictions, Rabelais does not completely deny the power of the skies in the *Quart Livre*. The heavens can be instruments of God's will, as in chapter 26, where the skies are said to yield meaning in the same way a human body reveals meaning to a doctor. The storm that has nearly killed the Pantagruelians in the "Tempête en mer" is now interpreted by "le bon Macrobe" as an augur of heavenly intention, as an indication that a great human being is about to pass away. In chapter 27, Pantagruel explains:

> Semblablement les cieulx benevoles, comme joyeulx de la nouvelle reception de ces beates ames, avant leur decés semblent faire feuz de joye par telz cometes et apparitions meteores, les quelles voulent les cieulx estre aux humains pour prognostic certain et veridicque prediction que, dedans peu de jours, telles venerables ames laisseront leurs corps et la terre.[70]

> [Likewise, the benevolent heavens, as if joyful at receiving another of these blessed souls, before their decease seem to light bonfires of joy by such meteoric apparitions, which the heavens wish to be to humans as a certain prognostic and truthful prediction that in a few days such venerable souls will leave their bodies and the earth.]

Out of context, it would seem that Pantagruel is saying that the skies can generate meaning in and of themselves. However, when understood in relation to the medical metaphor, it becomes apparent that the signs in the sky ("cometes et apparitions meteores") have been appropriated by a human system of signification. These signs can be understood only in relation to a human message, which is bound by the limits of human discourse. The comets and meteors do not reveal God's will, although God's will might be evident in them to a beatified mind, such as that of Saint Paul. These heavenly signs do, however, remind men that they should pay attention to their great men, because once they are gone their knowledge will be unattainable. Pantagruel says:

Ainsi, par telz cometes, comme par notes aetherées, disent les cieulx tacitement: Homes mortelz, si de cestes heureuses ames voulez chose aulcune
sçavoir, apprandre, entendre, congnoistre, preveoir, touchant le bien et utilité
publicque ou privée, faictez diligence de vous representer à elles, et d'elles
response avoir; car la fin et catastrophe de la comœdie approche. Icelle
passée, en vain vous les regretterez.[71]

[Thus by such comets, as if by ethereal signals, the heavens tacitly say: "Mortal men, if from these happy souls you want to find out, learn, understand,
take in, foresee anything concerning the public good or private utility, make
haste to come before them and get their answer from them, for the end and
denouement of the comedy is at hand. Once this is past, you will regret them
in vain."]

Pantagruel makes an important distinction in this passage. He does not
say the stars will teach man something "touchant le bien et utilité publicque" (concerning the public good and utility) but rather that the "heureuses ames" (happy souls) provide this knowledge. The relationship between the hidden truth of the stars and mortal man is not the same as an
astrological prediction. The truth indicated by the skies is neither transcendental nor fully revealed. The comets and meteors are indices, which
indicate to human beings that they should pay attention to the great men
who live among them. Stars do not express meaning themselves.

The stars serve a deictic function in this chapter: they point to the central figure of an earthly portrait. The great man whose death was pre-
figured by the stars was Rabelais's late protector, Guillaume Du Bellay,
the "docte et preux chevalier de Langey" (the learned and brave Lord
Langey).[72] Epistemon remembers the "prodiges tant divers et horrificques" (varied and horrific wonders) that they saw five or six days before
Du Bellay's death.[73] In this way, Du Bellay is recognized as a great man
who had much to offer his country. The glory of the "preux chevalier de
Langey" is ensured by his association with the "precedens signes formez
contre tout ordre de nature" (134), but the precise message or meaning of
those signs is never given by Rabelais.

Rabelais's understanding of astrology in these chapters comes very close
to that of other evangelicals. Lefèvre d'Etaples says that observation of
the stars is most profitable when it is restricted to simple contemplation
of them.[74] It is even possible for humans to have some knowledge from
this observation.[75] But, he also cautions that we should limit ourselves to
the simple contemplation of stars and planets and to praises of and thanks
for divine wisdom and goodness.[76] He specifically excludes the use of
horoscopes and other means of speculation from the beneficial sort of
astronomy.[77] Lefèvre d'Etaples, like Rabelais, allows for meaning in the

stars since they are the creation of God; he simply denies that human beings can understand that meaning.

In the *Quart Livre*, astrology is a means of figurative discourse and resembles Molinet's analogy and etymology in the *Chappellet des dames*. In neither case can real knowledge be gained by astrology, analogy, or etymology. In both Rabelais and Molinet, the theoretical possibility of transcendental meaning is exploited yet denied in the same image. The stars are used to illustrate Guillaume Du Bellay's greatness, but they reveal no meaning. Like the divine analogate in the *Chappellet des dames*'s analogy, the stars point to an earthly fact or phenomenon. In Rabelais, the human element is the source of knowledge and power, while the transcendent image is used to extol the greatness of the human.

Rabelais does not deny that there may be meaning in the stars, but this meaning is beyond human understanding except in the most general fashion. That there is a divine truth in the stars is attested to in his calling Saint Paul the "celeste Astrologue," but this truth is always understood "tacitement" by humans. The sign used to express this truth is conventional, being dependent on the fallen human's imperfect reason. Humans cannot understand anything of a precise nature through the observation of the skies, but they can have a notion of the magnificence of God's works. Observation of the skies does not reveal the meaning of God's will, but it can at least allow one to observe the nature of God's works, even if their meaning is still beyond comprehension.

Things, be they stars, comets, or meteors, do not signify in the *Quart Livre*. They can allow one to have knowledge of God's workings, yet unless one has a supernatural experience of God, like Saint Paul had, these workings must remain enigmatic. Metaphysical meaning is promised in the stars but denied to human intelligence. For the author of the *Quart Livre*, as for Molinet and Gerson, God's will is impenetrable, and any "understanding" of it must be conventional; symbolic use of the stars or planets must also be conventional. The coexistence of a nonhuman, metaphysical system, such as astrology, with a skepticism about just such a system produces a symbolic confusion. The metaphysical symbol that is a part of a semiotic code independent of human interpretation is made problematic when that metaphysics is refuted and understood as the product of a human intelligence. The symbol—star, planet, comet—no longer signifies some hidden truth: it signifies itself, as form. This form then becomes an ornament in a different, humanly grounded code. Signification is not transcendental or "real" in the medieval sense. It is conventional and equivocal. Meaning is a product of human mediation, and resemblance—between sky and earth, macrocosm and microcosm—is due only to convention. The relationship of human and God implied in analogical understanding is the product of human intelligence. Things come together as mental signs, not in and of themselves.

Rabelais adopts a position in the *Quart Livre* in which human reason assumes a much less lofty role than in the earlier books. In this he resembles those *frères lubins* (an expression Rabelais uses to describe medieval clerics) he mocks so eloquently in the early novels. In the following chapter, it will be seen how the monstrous figures in the *Quart Livre*—the Papimanes, the Andouilles, the Engastrimythes, the Gastrolatres—are all guilty of the same sin as the metaphysicians described in Gerson's *De modis significandi*. They take the phantasms of their thoughts for reality and then become slaves to the unnatural creatures they create.

The humanist dream of bringing man closer to the original truth through the powers of philology, and the evangelical dream of understanding the divine through a direct experience of Scripture, evaporate as the techniques used to attain the oneness of being prove ineffective or error ridden due to feeble human reason. In the *Quart Livre*, the divine is more than ever an unattainable "other" that excites desire and yet remains unknowable. Real wisdom is gained not through human understanding of the divine but through experience. Like Couillatris, human beings do best in the *Quart Livre* when they recognize their limits. In Rabelais's *Quart Livre*, human beings would do well to follow the advice given in another sixteenth-century essay on the feebleness of human reason, "L'Apologie de Raimond Sebond": "Tenez chauts les pieds et la teste; Au demeurant, vivez en beste" (Keep your feet and your head warm; for the rest, live like a beast).[78]

CHAPTER SIX

Fractured Resemblance in the *Quart Livre*

❦   ❦   ❦

In Rabelais's novels the increasingly human size of the heroes bears witness to the increasingly limited scope of human understanding. In the first two novels, Gargantua and Pantagruel were as enormous as the hopes of the new religion and the new learning, while in the *Quart Livre*, Pantagruel's human size reflects the reduced extent of human understanding. In 1552, the heroes' measure is established by their moderation; it is their monstrous enemies who are gigantic. These enemies are all guilty of the same crime: they claim to understand the design of the universe. The empirical understanding of the Pantagruelians, who trust only in their own experience or in experts with long practical experience is contrasted with the a priori knowledge of those who believe they know the one and only truth of the universe. The Pantagruelians might not know much in the *Quart Livre*, but they do recognize what they do not know; thus they stand in sharp contrast with those they meet on their travels, who do not realize that what they know is untrue.

The Pantagruelians' skepticism, which contrasts with the monstrous and monolithic systems of the peoples they meet on their voyage, can be read as a commentary on the increasingly gloomy religious debates of the mid-sixteenth century. The Council of Trent, which had begun in 1545 in order to reconcile the reformers and the Catholic Church, had by 1552 become a means of polarizing the two factions even further. The polemic between the forces represented by Luther and Erasmus had long since degenerated into a virulent diatribe, and there was little chance of evangelical moderation ever having any effect either in the reformed or the Catholic churches.[1] Caught between the extremism of the Calvinists on one side and the Catholic orthodoxy on the other, evangelical moderates like Rabelais were increasingly excluded from both camps. The *Quart*

Livre can be read as the funeral eulogy of Erasmian moderation, a moderation that was killed by the extremism of both sides of the religious quarrels that would lead to the bloody and fratricidal wars that ripped France apart at the end of the sixteenth century.

By the end of the *Quart Livre*, it is clear that human understanding is much more limited in 1552 than it had been twenty years earlier, when Rabelais began his novels. In the *Quart Livre*, human experience rather than some erroneous comprehension of the hidden structure of the universe becomes the model of understanding. Already in the *Tiers Livre*, the Pantagruelians were exposed to a panorama of all-too-human sages who proclaimed that they could resolve Panurge's dilemma: whether he should get married. One after another, these sages—the Sibylle de Panzoust, Nazdecabre, Raminagrobis, Her Trippa, Hippothadée, Rondibilis, Trouillogan, Triboullet, and the Judge Bridoye—fail to solve Panurge's problem. When these human sources of knowledge prove themselves incompetent, the Pantagruelians decide to visit the "Oracle of the Dive Bouteille" for a more complete answer. Their desire for oracular knowledge provides the motivation for the *Quart Livre*. Yet even if the *Quart Livre* is motivated by a desire for a totalizing answer, the Pantagruelians' experiences in the *Tiers Livre* make them extremely wary of any system that proclaims to reveal the entire truth.

For the inhabitants of the islands visited by the Pantagruelians in the *Quart Livre* it is possible to understand the absolute through contingent forms. For people such as the Andouilles, the Papimanes, and the Engastrimythes, humanly generated words and images can reveal the perfect reality of the divine; for the Pantagruelians, human reality remains intransigently contingent. Time and again in the *Quart Livre*, analogical discourse turns a normal human event or phenomenon into a horribly misshapen divinity that enslaves the people who have elevated it to a divine status. The Pantagruelians must repeatedly fight those who have not observed the Erasmian moderation of Couillatris. Human understanding of the divine becomes twisted and misleading because human beings repeatedly make up what is not there. The limited optimism of *Gargantua* and *Pantagruel*, which made it at least theoretically possible to hope that an *ius gentium* existed, gives way in the *Quart Livre* to a pessimism about human understanding that precludes the contingent from ever revealing anything about the absolute and the imperfect from ever being joined with the perfect.

The somber skepticism of the *Quart Livre* illuminates modern critical arguments concerning the nature of likeness and difference in the six-teenth century. As already mentioned, Michel Foucault and Jean Paris represent two opposing tendencies in modern scholarship about the Mid-dle Ages and the Renaissance. Foucault and like-minded critics see the Middle Ages and the Renaissance as one continuous period dominated by an epistemology of likeness. Paris sees the Renaissance as representing a break with the Middle Ages, a break whose modernity was grounded in an empirical refusal of the principle of likeness. Rabelais's novels offer abundant evidence to support both positions at various points in the author's career. The *Quart Livre*, however, offers eloquent proof of the demise of analogical likeness in Rabelais's literary world.

In Foucault's analysis, the contingent and the absolute are connected through the power of resemblance. For Foucault, resemblance is at the heart of sixteenth-century epistemology: "Resemblance is the most uni-versal thing in 16th-century knowledge; it is at the same time what is most visible and what must be looked for in order to be discovered, since it is also the most hidden."[2] According to this reckoning, the dualistic rela-tionship of the world would reveal the invisible through the visible in Rabelais's texts. Paris criticizes Foucault, saying that his conclusions are valid only if Rabelais is excepted.[3] Paris, instead, sees Rabelais as break-ing with the medieval tradition, as representing a new conception of the world. Writing about the "Blason de couleurs" from chapters 8 and 9 in *Gargantua*, Paris says that Rabelais mocks "these fools [who] repeat in this way the error of the Middle Ages: they suppose the particular and the contingent as a universal; they raise to the absolute a fortuitous relation-ship."[4] Rabelais, says Paris, in order to denounce the inconsistency of the fortuitous relationship, compares it to the most fragile relationship that exists: the pun.

The genius of Rabelais is to provide evidence of both the resemblance Foucault talks about and the contingency that Paris identifies as marking Rabelais's modernity. As Paris explains, Rabelais does condemn the "hom-onymies tant ineptes" (so inept homonyms), which would seem to repre-sent a break from a "medieval" understanding. But Rabelais also extols the *ius gentium*, which "n'est poinct ceste signifiance par imposition hu-maine institué, mais repceue part consentement de tout le monde" (is not instituted by human imposition but received by universal consent).[5] As usual, what Rabelais gives with one hand, he takes away with the other. In the context of *Gargantua*, it would seem that Rabelais rejects the inept homonyms that join *ancholie* (columbine) and *melancholie* in the courtiers's emblems, just as he rejects the arbitrariness of Thaumaste's empty language. Yet Rabelais rejects the inept homonyms also because they depend on the equivocal nature of things, and he contrasts them to the true hieroglyphs of the Egyptians, which convey their "vertus, proprieté et nature des choses par ycelles figurées" (the virtue, property, and nature of the things represented).[6] Screech has remarked that the opposition of the inept homonyms and the true hieroglyphic emblems of the sage Egyptians goes hand in hand with the "restitution des bonnes lettres" (restoration of good learning) and points out that "the sense of emblems and hieroglyphs is, for Rabelais and the other emblematists, by no means arbitrary."[7]

With his praise of hieroglyphs and his desire for an *ius gentium*, it is difficult to understand how Rabelais represents a break with a Middle Ages, in which, as Paris puts it, "the universe, according to the evidence of the faith, was divided into concrete but constant qualities, which were articulated by invisible structures further and further spread out, right up to the source of their coherence: the divine."[8] On the contrary, it would seem that in *Gargantua* Rabelais is arguing for a true system of analogy, which would be part and parcel of the new learning. The significance of true emblems and hieroglyphs and the availability of an *ius gentium* seem to show that in *Gargantua* Rabelais is not representative of a new empirical age. In fact, at this point, it appears that his attitude is more akin to Lemaire than to Molinet. In *Gargantua* and in *Pantagruel*, the obvious parody of late scholastic logical discourse, in which words have no meaning, stands as a counterpart to the plenitude of Neoplatonic dualism and Pauline faith.

Both Foucault's and Paris's arguments might be overdetermined by their need to prove a point. Foucault wants to explain the analytical discourse of the classical age in contrast to the analogical discourse of the Renaissance, while Paris seeks to show how Rabelais's attack on the inept homonyms is an indication of the Renaissance's break with a totalitarian order of society intimately related to "a substantialist conception of language."[9] Paris explains that, since the Renaissance wanted to put an end to both this substantialist view of language and totalitarian society, Rabelais must necessarily come down against an analogical understanding of the universe. For Paris, totalitarian politics and a substantialist understanding of language go hand in hand, and therefore if Rabelais is a modern, he must reject totalitarian regimes and the medieval confusion of fortuitous and absolute.

Rabelais's novels show that neither Foucault nor Paris is entirely wrong or entirely right. Foucault's paradigm of resemblance can be understood as existing in a latent state of desire in Rabelais's early works, and Paris's paradigm of contingency manifests itself in Rabelais's linguistic practice in the first two novels. Although Paris's argument comes closer to the truth of the *Quart Livre*, it does not take into account the desire for resemblance that can be perceived in the earlier novels. Two other modern critics, François Rigolot and Guy Demerson, offer analyses more sensitive to the complex and ambiguous nature of Rabelais's novels. Rigolot sees Rabelais as proscribing arbitrary language, which is the source of lies and, as a good Pantagruelist, as affirming his "mépris des choses fortuites" (disregard for fortuitous things).[10] At the same time, according to Rigolot, Rabelais's constant recourse to word games invites the reader to participate in a poetic vision of the world in which the contingent alliance of words (consonance) authorizes the necessary alliance of things (concordance). The paradigm of resemblance can be understood as existing within the humanist vision of Rabelais's novels at the same time that contingency exerts its influence in Rabelais's language.

The same sort of complex analysis is proffered by Guy Demerson, who views Rabelais's work as being marked by a medieval episteme that functions according to the law of analogy and yet that also represents a new humanistic spirit that is pulling away from the abstract systems of the logicians.[11] For both Demerson and Rigolot, Rabelais was neither medieval nor Renaissant; he was both. His propensity for word games that depend on phonetic resemblance and that underline the equivocal nature of things exists alongside his theoretical belief in the ultimate correspondence of things. As the previous chapters show, the developments identified by Rigolot and Demerson in Rabelais's novels were part of a larger evolution. As early as the *Chappellet des dames* by Molinet, writers were being torn between a desire for resemblance and a practice based in difference. Rabelais's work represents a culmination of these tendencies, as the analogical paradigm began its final death throes.

Demerson's analysis of analogy attacks one of the most enthralling yet perhaps misleading of modern interpretations of Rabelais, Mikhail Bakhtin's *Rabelais and His World*. Bakhtin interprets Rabelais's novels as representing an upwelling of popular culture through the carnival. Bakhtin's carnivalesque critique of Rabelais, according to Demerson, places Rabelais squarely in a medieval mold:

When Bakhtin claims to explain the global thought of Rabelais, he looks for its foundation in the culture of the Middle Ages; and it is the central notion of analogy that unifies the system of the Russian theoretician: he brings to light a likeness of functions, of structures, which, within the popular consciousness, would link the body to the cosmos, biology to history, language to a revolutionary consciousness raising.[12]

As Demerson explains, Bakhtin insists on the reality of the carnival in the lives of the people. Bakhtin believes that the carnival was not simply a spectacle seen by the people, it was, rather, something they lived.[13] The reversal of high and low was not merely a theatrical effect—it had a real effect on the fabric of society. That which is high (spiritual, ideal, abstract) becomes the material (earth and body), in very real terms.[14]

Although extremely persuasive, Bakhtin's analysis is perhaps flawed, as Demerson's analysis shows. For if popular culture truly does well up and determine Rabelais's work, this would imply that the analogical relationship of low and high is operational. The microcosmic and the macrocosmic could be reversed as univocal terms of a symbolic formula. This conception could perhaps be said to be valid in *Gargantua* and *Pantagruel*, in which the dualism of secular and divine can be argued for fairly convincingly. But even in the first two books, this analysis tends to lose sight of the parodic element in Rabelais's novels. Elements of high and low culture do not simply well up in *Pantagruel* and *Gargantua*; Rabelais puts them there. Jacobus Bragomardus and Thaumaste serve an ironic function and fit into Rabelais's general scheme of medieval parody.[15] Rabelais exploits them as conventions, as parts of a code, which he manipulates. Panurge does not represent an unconscious surfacing of popular culture but, like all the other characters, is a tool that the author deploys in his parody. Far from naïve, the oppositions that Rabelais uses between high and low in *Pantagruel* and *Gargantua* are indicative of the highly contrived nature of the "realist" portrait being drawn. The dualism of high and low, old and new, profane and secular is an artistic device, which Rabelais exploits. The terms of high and low are not equal. The author plays with them the way he plays with words.

If Bakhtin's analysis is problematic in the first two books, in which analogy is manifest as a state of desire, it becomes peculiarly inappropriate when talking about the *Quart Livre*. In the *Quart Livre*, the underlying equivocity of *Gargantua* and *Pantagruel*, revealed in Rabelais's language, comes to the fore both thematically and stylistically. The relation of high and low, of perfect and imperfect, is shown in Rabelais's last novel to be resolutely contingent. If in *Gargantua* and *Pantagruel* the desire for an *ius gentium* counterbalanced an inherent lust for the inept homonym, in the *Quart Livre*, this equilibrium breaks down as all attempts to understand the concordance of things in the universe are rejected. In the *Quart Livre*, things (like words in *Gargantua* and *Pantagruel*) are recognized as being alike by convention and not by some rationally comprehensible universal law. Analogical likeness, even of the most tenuous sort, becomes fuel for Rabelais's satirical fire. The relation of visible and invisible is beyond human understanding. The sublime remains the sublime, and the corporal remains irrevocably locked in contingency.

In the *Quart Livre*, the Pantagruelians fight battle upon battle with individuals who have lost sight of the contingency of human existence. In the *Quart Livre*, to ignore this fact is to risk destroying the fabric of society and nature. Whether they be Papimanes or Papefigues, the Andouilles or Quaresmeprenant, the Engastrimythes or the Gastrolatres, these individuals claim to understand the total picture of the universe. The point raised by the Pantagruelians throughout this book is that it is impossible to know what the high and low in life are like. In the *Quart Livre*, such an understanding is bound to be misleading, since only empirical knowledge is a valid source of wisdom. The demise of analogical understanding and expression is nowhere better illustrated than in Quaresmeprenant, a monster described in analogical terms in chapters 29 through 32. The Quaresmeprenant episode demonstrates how the relationship between visible and invisible is entirely contingent in the *Quart Livre*. Both Foucault's theory of resemblance and Bakhtin's theory of reversal of high and low come to naught in the face of Quaresmeprenant's monstrosity.

The Pantagruelians are told about Quaresmeprenant by Xenomanes, who is their guide to the Dive Bouteille as they sail by "L'isle de Tapinois" (Island of Coverup). Quaresmeprenant's name, which roughly translated means Shrovetide, is obviously related to the developing religious quarrels between the Roman Catholics, who observed Lenten fasting, and the Protestants, who saw this fasting as merely one more meaningless rite that separated modern human beings from the true meaning of the Gospel. The reference to contemporary religious strife is made especially clear when Quaresmeprenant's enemies are described as the Andouilles, or sausages, who live on a neighboring island, "l'isle farouche" (Wild Island). Those who fast (Quaresmeprenant) are opposed to those don't (Andouilles).

In chapters 30, 31, and 32, Xenomanes makes an anatomical description of Quaresmeprenant, using long lists of his internal and external parts. Each organ is described by comparison with a completely unrelated object. The stomach is likened to a harness, or "baudrier," and the tendons are likened to a hawking glove, or "un guand d'oyseau."[16] At the end of this long anatomical description, Pantagruel remarks that Quaresmeprenant reminds him of Amodunt and Discordance. When Frere Jan asks Pantagruel what these two characters looked like, Pantagruel explains that they were the children of Antiphysie, "laquelle de tout temps est partie adverse de Nature"[17] (who has always been the adverse party to Nature). He describes them as having

> la teste sphærique et ronde entierement, comme un ballon; non doulcement comprimée des deux coustez, comme est la forme humaine. Les aureilles avoient hault enlevées, grandes comme aureilles d'asne; les oeilz hors la teste, fichez sus des os semblables aux talons, sans soucilles, durs comme sont ceulx des cancres; les pieds ronds comme pelottes; les braz et mains tournez en arriere vers les espaules. Et cheminoient sus leurs testes, continuellement faisant la roue, cul sus teste, les pieds contremont.[18]

> [heads spherical and completely round, like a balloon, not gently compressed on each side, as the human shape is. Their ears were raised up, big as donkeys' ears; their eyes, sticking out of their heads, on bones like heel bones, without eyebrows, hard, as are crabs' eyes; their feet round as balls; arms and hands turned around backward toward the shoulders; and they traveled on their heads, doing continuous cartwheels, head over heels, with their legs in the air.]

Despite their monstrous form, Antiphysie praises the unusual shape of her children:

> Antiphysie louoit et s'efforçoit prouver que la forme de ses enfans plus belle estoit et advenente que des enfans de Physis; disant que ainsi avoir les pieds et teste sphæriques, et ainsi cheminer circulairement en rouant, estoit la forme compétente et perfaicte alleure retirante à quelque portion de divinité: par laquelle les cieulx et toutes choses eternelles sont ainsi contournées. Avoir les pieds en l'air, la teste en bas, estoit imitation du créateur de l'Univers: veu que les cheveulx sont en l'home comme racines, les jambes comme rameaux. Car les arbres plus commodement sont en terre fichées sus leurs racines que ne seroient sus leurs rameaux. Par ceste demonstration alleguant que trop mieulx, plus aptement estoient ses enfans comme une arbre droicte, que ceulx de Physis, les quelz estoient comme une arbre renversée. (151)

> [Antiphysie praised her children's shape and tried to prove that it was more beautiful and attractive than that of the children of Physie, saying that thus to have spherical feet and heads, and thus to make one's way in a circular fashion by wheeling around, was the proper form and perfect aspect derived from

some part of the divinity, by which all the heavens and all eternal things are thus shaped. To have one's feet in the air and one's head below was an imitation of the creator of the universe, seeing that hair in man is like roots, legs like branches, for trees are more conveniently fixed in the ground on their roots than they would be on their branches; by this demonstration arguing that her children were much better and aptly like an upright tree than those of Physis, which were like a tree upside down.]

Antiphysie makes an analogical comparison between her children and a tree: since a tree's roots look like a human being's hair and its branches are like are a human being's legs, it is normal for Amodunt and Discordance to have their heads close to the ground like a tree's roots and their feet in the air like a tree's branches. The resemblance between the tree and the creator of the universe is implied even if it is not explicitly stated; therefore, Amodunt and Discordance must resemble the creator of the universe. Within this analogical framework, Antiphysie's children are creatures in God's image. The heavy dose of irony in this passage indicates that Antiphysie's backward understanding of the universe is, like her name implies, against nature.

Amodunt and Discordance, like Quaresmeprenant, are constituted by the comparative "comme": their heads are "like" balls, their ears are "like" those of an ass. According to Antiphysie, they hold their feet in the air and have spherical heads because they resemble the "forme compétente et parfaicte alleure" of the divine, whose perfect model provides the organization and form of the universe. They are, Antiphysie explains, more comely than Physie's children, who have their heads in the air and their feet on the ground. Instead of basing her understanding of the universe and of what is natural on what she sees, Antiphysie creates an understanding based on comparisions that are beyond her comprehension. Hopelessly lost in the comparative relationship of trees, human bodies, and the creator of the universe, Antiphysie creates her children in a world of impossible resemblance.

In this passage, Rabelais, even more than any nominalist, destroys the connection between contingent and absolute. The reality of Quaresmeprenant, Amodunt, and Discordance is composed of arbitrary or misleading connections of contingent parts that form monstrous shapes. Quaresmeprenant's monstrosity owes more to his perceived construction through analogical comparison than it does to any inherent evil. Quaresmeprenant cannot exist as material being; he can exist only as a compilation of gratuitous comparisons of discordant phenomena. His abnormality is rooted in the conjoining of purely normal body parts with inapplicable analogates. By equating his body parts with often impossible or nonexistent phenomena, Rabelais makes Quaresmeprenant a chimera. His power derives from the imperfect interpretation of perfectly ordinary phenomena. The Pantraguelians never see Quaresmeprenant; they merely hear about him. His monstrousness is due more to the compilation of comparative terms that describe him than it does to any essential quality.

For Antiphysie, the children of Physie are "renversés" because they do not represent analogical ordering of the universe, while Amodunt and Discordance, with their feet in the air and their round heads on the ground, represent correct thinking. Antiphysie is, however, guilty of what Gerson accused speculative theologians of doing: she believes that she can understand the truth of the "major" term of the analogy. She understands the reality of the "creator of the universe" through the image of the tree. A tree has its branches in the air and its roots in the earth. Therefore, since the microcosm of the creature resembles the macrocosm of the heavens, and since creatures must resemble their creator, the creature must also look like a tree. And, since legs look like branches and hair looks like roots, a correctly shaped creature must have its legs in the sky and its head on the ground.

Pantagruel ends the episode by naming some of the human producers of these monsters. He explains that Amodunt and Discordance were held in great admiration by "toutes gens éscervelez et desguarniz de bon jugement et sens commun," whom he describes as "Matagotz, Cagotz et Papelars; les Maniacles Pistoletz, les Demoniacles Calvins, imposteurs de Geneve, les enraigez Putherbes"[19] (Matagotz, Cagotz, Papelars, the maniacal Pistols, the demoniacal Calvins, the rabid Putherbeuses). Rabelais, having been attacked by the Catholic orthodoxy (Putherbes) and by Calvin, puts both in the same bag.[20] Although Calvin cannot be understood as being guilty of analogical representation, like the speculative theologians who offered evidence of God's existence through analogy, he was guilty of telling his followers what God's message was. Within the context of the *Quart Livre*, Calvin's *Institutes of the Christian Religion* was simply a new form of scholasticism. Throughout the *Quart Livre*, only the empirical knowledge of the Pantagruelians is finally accepted as adequate. All other forms of knowledge that depend on a human understanding of a deterministic a priori become monstrous, like Quaresmeprenant, Amodunt, and Discordance.

The Quaresmeprenant episode, especially Antiphysie's defense of Amo-

dunt and Discordance, shows the sorry plight of analogical understanding and expression in the *Quart Livre*. Although similar to Molinet's reversal of analogical ordering in the *Chappellet des dames* and the *Paradis
terrestre*, Antiphysie's description and defense of her children is presented
much more explicitly. Molinet's reversal of analogical prior and posterior
terms might have been the result of epistemological shifts the poet was
not aware of, but the ironic presentation of Antiphysie's defense of Amodunt and Discordance underlines how analogical reversal is consciously
inserted in the *Quart Livre*'s narration. The high and low are reversed not
out of some carnivalesque irruption of popular culture but as a commentary on the insanity gripping France in the mid-sixteenth century, when
people all around Rabelais, both the "Demoniacles Calvins" and the "enraigez Putherbes," were claiming to understand the intention of the creator of the universe.

Caught between "Andouilles and Quaresmeprenant," as Panurge expresses the Pantagruelians' dilemma, Erasmian moderates like Rabelais
trust only in their own understanding.[21] The analogical "like," or "comme,"
is a sign of madness, and resemblance between high and low or between
contingent and absolute exists only in the minds of the deranged. The
prose du monde, which would allow the human eye to read the "book of
the world," is shown in this episode to be severely misleading, and the
high and low cannot be reversed. The contingent and the absolute, the visible and the invisible, do not resemble each other in the *Quart Livre*, and
the connection between the secular and the divine is beyond human understanding. The contingency and difference found in the the language of
Gargantua and *Pantagruel* become the dominant paradigm in the *Quart
Livre*.

In *Gargantua*, language held out the possibility of bridging the gap
between contingent and absolute, of representing a very real form of ontological resemblance. Implicitly, in the very same book, Rabelais's puns
and contrived rhyme schemes showed that linguistic resemblance was
purely contingent and did not overcome the overwhelming singularity of
human existence. Meaning remained implicitly on the side of the contingent, even if in explicit passages it was posited as theoretically grounded
in the immutable and transcendent. In *Gargantua*, as in the other novels,
a desire for revelation motivated language, while at the same time language was just as often revealed to be contingent. Yet signification was
grounded decidedly in human experience and was in constant conflict
with the desire for a higher truth.

In the *Quart Livre*, the desire for linguistic plenitude is exploited to more explicitly rhetorical ends. Perhaps Rabelais's most graphic use of language's revelatory capacity to rhetorical ends is found in chapter 37 of the *Quart Livre*. In this chapter, titled "Comment Pantagruel manda querir les capitaines Riflandouille et Tailleboudin, avecques un notable discours sus les noms propres des lieux et des persones" (How Pantagruel sent for Captains Gobblechitterling and Chopsausage, with a noteworthy discourse on the proper names of places and persons), Pantagruel sends for soldiers who are waiting in two ships before the battle the Pantagruelians are to fight with the Andouilles. The colonel of the first group is called Riflandouille, and the colonel of the second group is named Tailleboudin. Epistémon says to Pantagruel that the names of these colonels augur well for the coming battle. Pantagruel replies that he too is well pleased by the arrival of these men:

> Vous le prenez bien, dist Pantagruel, et me plaist que par les noms de nos coronnelz vous prævoiez et prognosticquez la nostre victoire. Telle maniere de prognosticquer par noms n'est moderne. Elle feut jadis celebrée et religieusement observée par les Pythagoriens.[22]

> [You take it rightly, said Pantagruel, and I'm pleased that from the names of our colonels you foresee and predict our victory. Such a manner of prognosis is not modern. It was celebrated and religiously used, long ago, by the Pythagoreans.]

Pantagruel elaborates on this theory of natural language by citing Plato's *Cratylus* and explaining how the Pythagorians could understand by numbers and names that Patroclus would be killed by Hector, Hector by Achilles, Achilles by Paris, and Paris by Philoctetes. Theoretically, Pantagruel would seem to believe in the ability of etymologies to reveal a hidden truth through the natural resemblance of word and thing. The Pantagruelians's victory is assured by Riflandouille's and Tailleboudin's names: the Pantagruelians would rip through their enemies, the Andouilles, like so many sausages.

The rhetorical nature of Pantagruel's use of etymology is, however, clear from the start. The names of the two colonels are determined by the immediate context of the war with the Andouilles.[23] Pantagruel uses the proper names of Riflandouille and Tailleboudin to rally his troops. Although Pantagruel cites a long history of etymological revelations to authorize his predictions of victory in the coming battle with the Andouilles, the two colonels' existence depends on the accident of the war itself. The relation between proper name and its referent is contingent; it has no existence beyond the limits of the immediate and arbitrary. Without the war with the Andouilles, the names *Riflandouille* and *Tailleboudin* would have no meaning.

A theory of resemblance provides the basis for this passage, but this theoretical ground is vitiated by the purely conventional nature of Taille-boudin and Riflandouille's names. Their *vis* is grounded not in the thing they represent but rather in the name of the Pantagruelians' enemies. Like the remotivated meanings that Bernardino, Mombaer, and Molinet gave to the virtues that corresponded to the letters of the name *Maria,* the meaning of *Riflandouille* and *Tailleboudin* is not grounded in the objects they represent. Pantagruel uses the names as a means of amplification; he uses them as an augur of success for his men. The theoretical desire for linguistic plenitude sanctions a purely rhetorical use of etymology.

The truth revealed in Pantagruel's use of proper names is as determined as it was in Molinet's *Chappellet des dames.* In both cases, the name used to reveal a hidden meaning depends on the rhetorical needs of the moment and on the difference of the word from its referent. The *Chappellet des dames*'s garland of flowers must show a connection between the name *Mary* and its ascribed virtues, and the *Quart Livre*'s two colonels must show a connection between their names and a victory for the Pantagru-elians. The explanation is predetermined by the context, yet in both Molinet and Rabelais, there could be no rhetorical amplification without the theoretical desire for revelation through resemblance. Both Molinet and Rabelais exploit this desire for resemblance to rhetorical ends.

A small but telling incident in chapter 54 illustrates how language is used implicitly in the *Quart Livre* and helps clarify the explicit definition of language found in the episode about Riflandouille and Tailleboudin. In this passage, Homenaz, the high priest of the Papimanes, offers the Pantagruelians some fruit. When Pantagruel asks Homenaz what the name of the fruit is, Homenaz replies: "Non aultrement, respondit Homenaz. Nous sommes simples gens, puys qu'il plaist à Dieu. Et appellons les figues figues, les prunes prunes, et les poires poires."[24] (We call them no other way, replied Homenaz. We're simple folk, since God so pleases. And we call figs figs, plums plums, and pears pears). To which Pantagruel responds:

> Vrayment, dist Pantagruel, quand je seray en mon mesnaige (ce sera, si Dieu plaist, bien toust), j'en affieray et hanteray en mon jardin de Touraine sus la rive de Loyre, et seront dictes poires de bon Christian. Car oncques ne veiz Christians meilleurs que sont ces bons Papimanes.[25]

[Truly, said Pantagruel, when I'm back home (that, God willing, will be soon), I'll plant and graft some in my garden in Touraine on the bank of the Loire, and they shall be called good-Christian pears. For I've never seen better Christians than these good Papimanes are.]

For the Papimanes, the word and the thing are one and the same.[26] Here, the difference is clear between the Papimanes, who live in an artificially prelapsarian world constructed from an erroneous understanding of the papacy and the decretals, and the fallen yet truthful world of the Pantagruelians. For the Papimanes, the names for things exist in an Adamic state of univocity. For the Pantagruelians, living in a world in which the relationship of things and the words that represent them is conventional, names must be given by convention to the thing. The word and the thing are different, and the distance between them is mediated by human intelligence. The relationship between the thing and the name given to it is equivocal, as more than one name could be given. The resemblance between word and thing for the Papimanes is, although admirably simplistic and antisophistic, false.

For the Pantagruelians, the word corresponds less to the thing than to the qualities of the people who gave the thing to them. Pantagruel explains why he named the pears as he does: "Car oncques ne veiz Christians meilleurs que sont ces bons Papimanes" (for I've never seen better Christians than these good Papimanes are). In the fallen world of the Pantagruelians, language is a contingent reality, changeable and ephemeral. In the world of the Papimanes, the ontological difference between language and things is nonexistent, in the same way that the ontological difference between themselves and God is also nonexistent. In both cases, the Papimanes's understanding is as erroneous as their initial principle, that the archetype of the pope is truly informative.

The idea of the fallen nature of human language is further developed in chapters 55 and 56. In these chapters, devoted to the "Parolles gelées," Rabelais opposes an idealist or metaphysical conception of language to a more materialistic one. The situation is this: following their departure from the Isle of the Papimanes, the Pantagruelians are sailing across the sea when Pantagruel hears voices and asks his companions if they hear them too: "Compaignons, oyez vous rien? Me semble que je oy quelques gens parlans en l'air, je n'y voy toutesfoys personne. Escoutez?"[27] (Mates, do you hear anything? It seems to me I hear people talking up in the air, but all the same I don't see anyone. Do you hear?). He then offers an explanation for these voices that places words and things in an ideal world:

J'ay leu qu'un Philosophe, nommé Petron, estoyt en ceste opinion que feussent plusieurs mondes soy touchans les uns les aultres en figure triangulaire æquilaterale, en la pate et centre des quelz disoit estre le manoir de Verité, et le habiter les Parolles, les Idées, les Exemplaires et protraictz de toutes choses passées et futures: autour d'icelles estre le Siecle.[28]

[I've read that a philosopher named Petron was of the opinion that there were several worlds touching one another in the form of an equilateral triangle, in the magma and center of which he says were the abode of Truth and the habitat of Words, Ideas, the Exemplars and images of all things past and future, and all around these was the Worldly Life.]

Some critics see this passage as representing a Platonic belief that the "parolle" should express the idea represented by the object, that "Rabelais's metaphorical frozen words melt and thereby reveal their meaning."[29] Others, such as V. L. Saulnier, see "the impotence of words, the danger of words. To claim to pass in verbal, oral, or written formulas, the wholeness of a thought: what a strange undertaking."[30] If the episode were to end here, it would be reasonable to accept the Idealist argument, as there would seem to be a certain equality between "Parolle" and "Idée" in this "manoir de Vérité." However, the episode continues in such a way that Saulnier's interpretation would seem to be more exact.

The following chapter deflates the pretensions of this ideal conception of language and casts it back into the fallen world of human existence. Just as in the "Tempête en mer," it is the ship's captain who offers expert advice. He responds to Pantagruel's Neoplatonic theory by placing the phenomenon in a real-world setting:

Seigneur, de rien ne vous effrayez. Icy est le confin de la mer glaciale, sus laquelle feut, au commencement de l'hyver dernier passé, grosse et felonne bataille, entre les Arismapiens et les Nephelibates. Lors gelerent en l'air les parolles et crys des homes et femmes, les chaplis des masses, les hurtys de harnoys, des bardes, les hannissemens des chevaulx et tout aultre effroy de combat. A ceste heure la rigueur de l'hyver passée, advenent la serenité et temperie du bon temps, elles fondent et sont ouyes.[31]

[Lord, don't be afraid of anything! Here is the edge of the glacial sea, on which, at the beginning of last winter, there was a great fierce battle between the Arismapiens and the Nephelibates. Then in the air froze the words and cries of the men and women, the clashing of maces, the banging of harnesses, of men and horses, the neighing of horses, and every other tumult of combat. Right now, with the rigor of the winter past, and the serenity of the good weather coming on, they are melted and are heard.]

Here, "Parolle" exists in exactly the same way that the cries of men and women or the noises of harnesses and the whinnying of horses do. Words and ideas are not coterminous, and words certainly do not correspond to the things they represent. When the frozen words (which the Pantagruelians haul on board) begin to warm, the Pantagruelians can see the words materially, "mais ne les entendions, car c'estoit languaige barbare" (but we did not understand them, since it was a barbarous language).[32] To understand the words, the Pantagruelians need to possess the code that gives the words meaning. Without this code, the words are no different from the sounds of battle with which they are intermixed. Instead of revealing meaning when they melt, the words remain meaningless.

If the words existed in a metaphysical system in which their *vis* or force was grounded in their resemblance with their referents, they would reveal their meaning when they melted. As the contingent covering of the linguistic sign melted, the meaning would slowly emerge as the *res* was revealed. But meaning is not grounded in the thing, or *res*, to which the word refers. It is imposed *ad placitum*. In chapter 56, the words melt, and the Pantagruelians are left with meaningless sound, or at least with sounds that they invest with a meaning based on their own experience. When one word, "assez grosset" (a rather large word), melts, it makes a loud bang like a chestnut thrown on a fire. The bang frightens the Pantagruelians but does not reveal any meaning. It is Frere Jan who gives the noise meaning: "C'estoit, dist frere Jan, un coup de faulcon en son temps"[33] ("It was," said Frere Jan, "a falconet shot in its day"). Signification is a product of the intellect in this chapter; instead of revealing meaning, the word's explosion simply makes a noise. Meaning is less revealed than it is applied to the word after the fact.

In the chapters devoted to the "Parolles gelées," as in chapter 54, language appears highly conventional. As Jean Paris puts it: "One thing seems sure: it is that the signifier ceases here to participate with the signified, the link between them is from now on cut."[34] Though Paris identifies the problem with the quarrel about universals in the Middle Ages and Ockham's criticism of Thomistic essentialism, he persists in placing Rabelais "au futur." He concludes his discussion of the "Parolles gelées" by saying: "The rejection of symbols just like that of the 'age of shadows' comes with the rejection of their communal transcendance: it marks the beginning of the era of a rational knowledge in which signs and language change entirely."[35] Paris would seem to identify the modernity of Rabelais with the conventionalization of language as it was worked out by Ockham and other nominalists. Rabelais's futurity is difficult to understand when it is described as being just like the very Middle Ages against which his modernity is measured.

The problem perhaps is not whether Rabelais represents a break with the Middle Ages or whether the Renaissance and the Middle Ages are a consistent whole but, once again, whether the complexity of both Rabelais's work and of history in general makes terms such as *Middle Ages* and *Renaissance* more a hindrance than a help. If Paris can identify a break with analogical thought in the Middle Ages at least two hundred years before Rabelais, how can he then say that Rabelais is ahead of his time if he bases this contention on Rabelais's break with analogical thinking? Perhaps Rabelais did not break with a homogeneous medieval tradition based on analogy for a more modern point of view. Perhaps he abandoned a contemporary, or "modern," analogical understanding of the universe and slid back into a nonanalogical outlook that was born of the failure of the "modern" outlook. If, in the early books, Rabelais mocks the equivocations of late scholastic logic and praises the new hope in a linguistic plenitude, in the *Quart Livre* it is the absolutist tendencies of Quaresmeprenant, the Papimanes, et alia, based on a mythical univocity, that are the butt of his humor. In the *Quart Livre*, language is conventional, and meaning cannot be had by "melting" words of their contingency.

Language and meaning in the *Quart Livre* exist in the fallen world of humanity. Things, by and large, do not signify in and of themselves; they must be part of a humanly determined code in order to have meaning, as the reality of the "Parolles gelées" illustrates. Equivocity, rather than univocity, is both philosophically and linguistically dominant. The Pantagruelians are cut off from God and must act as free agents to ensure their salvation, and any understanding they have of God is achieved only by faith or convention. The analogical understanding that Antiphysie represents is based on the mistaken notion of univocity. Human and God are inescapably equivocal in nature, and any attempt to overcome this difference has to be either conventional or erroneous. Words share this equivocity. They too are cut off from some Adamic origin. It is only in the false utopia of the Papimanes that words and things coexist naturally and in an unmediated fashion. Univocity in the *Quart Livre* exists solely as a mental construct. The Pantagruelians know or learn this. This is what separates them from the peoples they visit, who believe it exists in reality.

Allegory, like analogical and etymological discourse, undergoes a distinctive change over the course of Rabelais's novels. As the optimism of the first books gives way to the skepticism of the last, the *doctrine absconce* takes on a new appearance. In the prologue to *Gargantua*, one of the most famous passages in sixteenth-century literature, the narrator invites the reader to look for a hidden meaning beneath the coarse outer covering of the literal meaning and to do with the book what the hungry dog does with a marrow bone: break it open and look for the "substantificique moelle."[36] Although this passage would seem to support an allegorical reading of his text, the narrator, in the following paragraph, mocks anyone foolish enough to think that an allegorical meaning might exist.[37] The ambiguous nature of allegory in the prologue to *Gargantua* is not that dissimilar to Rabelais's attitude toward linguistic plenitude in the same novel. The narrator vaunts the idea of a *plus hault sens*, but he also warns against abusive allegorizing of texts like Homer's *Odyssey* and *Iliad* that do not need interpretation. In theory, allegory might seem a good idea, but in practice it often produces more problems than it is worth due to excesses of the "frères Lubins."

If a *plus hault sens* is seen ambiguously in the prologue to *Gargantua*, it is viewed much more suspiciously in the *Quart Livre*, where allegorical meaning is opposed to literal meaning to the distinct advantage of the latter. That which is higher and distant does not bear a fuller meaning in the *Quart Livre* so much as it bears the mark of a sick mind. Where the literal meaning of *Gargantua* was held to conceal an *absconce* truth that could be revealed to the diligent reader, the literal meaning is betrayed by the hidden meaning in the *Quart Livre*. The ability to understand the relationship of literal and *absconce* is challenged and, eventually, rejected; finally, only the insane believe that they can comprehend that which is distant from immediate human perception.

Perhaps even more than the question of analogy, the question of allegory has generated considerable debate in modern Rabelais scholarship. Some critics understand allegorical meaning in Rabelais as being transparent; then there are those who think such a meaning is impossible to discern in the work of Rabelais or, perhaps, any other writer.[38] A chronological approach explains how allegorical meaning can be construed as both present and absent in Rabelais's novels. In the early books, allegorical meaning is explicitly identified as lying above and beyond the coarse outer layer of the literal meaning. Even if this allegorical meaning is troubled and seen as misleading, it exists as a virtual or latent possibility that the reader should make an effort to find—in the same way that linguistic plenitude exists as a hypothetical possibility in Egyptian hieroglyphics. In the later books, any ascertainable higher meaning is rejected, and only the literal level of meaning is accepted as valid.

The question of allegorical understanding and expression perhaps has less to do with whether or not allegory exists in Rabelais's novels than with what allegory meant for Rabelais and his contemporaries.[39] This is a difficult question to deal with because of allegory's highly contested status in the sixteenth century. When Rabelais speaks of allegory, what does the word mean? And even if it does have a stable meaning for Rabelais at any one time, does that meaning apply to all of his novels? As has been suggested earlier in this book, the sixteenth-century understanding of allegory was fluid, to say the least. There were almost as many definitions of allegory as there were writers interested in the question. Rabelais's position on allegory at different times of his life reflects this fluidity. A quick survey of some of these positions reveals the extent of the problem. Each group or individual had a peculiar take on the problem, and no one definition could adequately describe what allegory meant in the Renaissance.

There is perhaps no greater witness to allegory's force in the sixteenth century than the muzzle the Council of Trent placed on exegetical interpretation.[40] The tradition of biblical interpretation had eventually led to many heretical readings of Scripture, as Gerson noted in the fifteenth century.[41] The Council of Trent stipulated that the only accepted meaning was that of "mother church," which was responsible for the "true meaning and interpretation of Holy Scripture."[42] By threatening punishment of anyone who interpreted Scripture without the "imprimatur" of the Church, the council effectively bore witness to the power of scriptural interpretation. Within the Catholic Church the existence of spiritual meaning in the Bible was never questioned; it was considered so important that it had to be controlled and placed under tight surveillance. For the Catholic Church, it was less a question of establishing allegory's efficacy than it was of controlling its evident and often misleading force.

The reformers attacked the very efficacy of allegory that the Catholics tried to contain. Instead of controlling allegory, the Protestants denied its validity altogether. Calvin accused Origen and other allegorizers of "torturing Scripture, in every possible way, away from the true sense."

> They concluded that the literal sense is too mean and poor, and that, under the outer bark of the letter, there lurk deeper mysteries, which cannot be extracted but by beating out allegories. And this they had no difficulty in accomplishing; for speculations which appear to be ingenious have always been preferred, and always will be preferred, by the world to solid doctrine.[43]

Calvin's critique of allegory leads him inevitably into conflict with Saint Paul, a figure whose writings were so important to the Protestant doctrine on faith. Saint Paul's development of a figural meaning from the literal meaning of Scripture, particularly the Old Testament, is reduced by Calvin to catachresis rather than to allegory. Calvin writes that when Paul states, "The letter kills, but the spirit gives life" (II Corinthians 4 [3:6]), he did not mean that an allegorical *altior sensus* was hidden behind the literal meaning of Scripture.[44] Calvin explains that Paul merely borrowed the name of one thing to express another. Calvin's rejection of allegory, like the Council of Trent's shackling of biblical interpretation, demonstrates the perceived power of allegory.

Luther's reading of allegory is similar to Calvin's in its denial of the need to interpret Holy Scripture. He too attacks Origen and Jerome for looking for a "spiritual meaning" that would add to the literal meaning of Scripture.[45] He also defends Saint Paul, explaining that Paul's maxim, "The letter kills, but the spirit gives life," does not imply the existence of an allegorical meaning in the Bible (80–81). Luther proposes that Paul does not make a distinction between literal and spiritual meaning but rather between "grammatical, historical" meaning and spiritual meaning (81). Paul's maxim harmonizes the historical reality of the Old Testament with the spiritual meaning that Jesus Christ's coming provided. Higher meaning for Luther was more a matter of history than of allegory: before Christ, the letter of the law was supreme. His birth infused that letter with spirit; allegory had nothing to do with it.

For evangelical humanists such as Josse Clichtove and Jacques Lefèvre d'Etaples, allegory was a natural part of reading Scripture, although it was important not to abuse the text itself. Clichtove's sermons stay close to the text of the Bible, highlighting practical and moral applications in a particular scene or parable.[46] As Jean-Pierre Massaut notes, Clichtove's preaching style avoids the excess, the "mauvais goût" often found in the sermons of the fifteenthth and sixteenth centuries, without denying the power of allegorical exegesis.[47] Within the evangelical community, spiritual meaning needed to be found without doing violence to the text itself. One of the most fervent defenders of spiritual meaning in the sixteenth century was undoubtedly Lefèvre d'Etaples.[48] He reacted strongly against the literal interpretations of Nicholas of Lyra, who in the late thirteenth and early fourteenth centuries spoke of the Bible as having a "double literal sense" rather than a literal and spiritual meaning. Lefèvre d'Etaples accused Lyra of being a dangerous "Judaizer." Like Lyra, Lefèvre d'Etaples wanted to have only one sense of Scripture, but his sense was a "literal-spiritual" one as opposed to Lyra's "historical-literal."[49] Lefèvre d'Etaples believed that real spiritual meaning inspired by the Holy Spirit infuses the literal letter of Scripture with higher meaning. The historical "literal" meaning is merely the outer bark, while the real "literal" meaning is that which led to the intention of the Holy Spirit.[50] The four levels of traditional exegetical allegory represented four modes of spiritual interpretation.

Lefèvre d'Etaples, like other evangelicals, was inclined toward a moderate stance regarding interpretation and believed that it was not required to allegorize every passage in the Bible.[51] Only certain passages needed to have allegory applied to them and, then, only according to the appropriate level of meaning. Literal passages should be read literally and allegorical passages allegorically. The problem, of course, is knowing when to apply which kind of reading to which passage.

The interpretation of allegory that comes closest to Rabelais in his early novels is that of Erasmus. Although Erasmus, like the Protestants, professes a scriptural theology that strives to avoid the erroneous meandering of exegetical allegory, he cannot avoid the problem of unclear or contradictory scriptural passages. The "middle way" that Erasmus adopts concerning allegory, like his use of *mediocritas* in so many other areas, entails a certain amount of contradiction, thereby escaping the more extreme positions adopted by the Calvinists and the Catholic orthodoxy. Thus, in Erasmus's *Ratio seu methodus compendio perveniendi ad veram theologiam*, he rejects the allegorizing that he sees as typical of "gothic" ignorance, on the one hand, and on the other, he explains why allegory is necessary to understand the Old Testament. Like Clichtove and Lefèvre d'Etaples, he rejects "idle" allegorizing, which gives figurative meaning to even the most literal utterance but defends allegory when it is used with care:

> There are those who reject all allegories as arbitrary things similar to dreams. With these I would vehemently disagree, since I see that without allegories there are many meanings that are absurd, pernicious, and futile, feeble and pointless, and when it is seen that Christ used allegories and that Saint Paul interpreted some passages of the Old Testament through allegory. Still, I cannot help but disapprove the inept allegorizing of some who themselves make the thing up, which they explain allegorically: a weary traveler sits on the back of a huge dragon, thinking it to be a tree trunk. The dragon wakes and devours the wretch. The traveler is man, the dragon is the world, which destroys those leaning on him. And other even greater frivolities are produced in very righteous books by some people and are read with extraordinary care by not a few. It is better to apply allegory to things that are found in the

sacred writings only if the thing itself requires it, so that we do not add or make up something that is not there.[52]

In Erasmus's understanding of allegory, a reader should not add meaning to what is sufficiently clear, but the reader should also not simply stop at the literal. As Terence Cave explains, this passage defines the boundary between an authentic and an inauthentic representation of biblical meaning.[53] The Holy Scripture might have an allegorical meaning, but that meaning should not be sought in every passage. What is essential for Erasmus is the direct experience of the text itself. Erasmus contrasts this experience with the mediated message of the schoolmen. He says in the *Paraclesis*, the introduction to his translation of the New Testament, that

> so may all Christians hold the Gospels and Letters of the Apostles as so holy that in comparison with them these other writings do not seem holy. What others may wish to concede to Albert the Great, to Alexander, to Thomas, to Egidio, to Richard, to Occam, they will certainly be free, as far as I am concerned, to do, for I do not wish to diminish the fame of anyone or contend with the studies of men that are now of long standing. However learned these may be, however subtle, however seraphic, if they like, yet they must admit that the former are the most tried and true.[54]

The simple, direct experience of Scripture is sufficient for an understanding of Christ's word. Erasmus's translation of the New Testament spoke for Renaissance optimism and faith in reason; his aim was to discover the Apostles' actual words and their meaning. For Erasmus, the allegories and commentaries of the Middle Ages represented nothing so much as an unnecessary imposition of a third party to the relationship between Scripture and the devout reader. When that original text was obscure or difficult to understand, parables and allegories might be of some help, but they should not obscure the words of the Apostles or the Gospels.

Rabelais's early ambivalence about allegory belongs to this new liberating spirit. Human beings have no need of the old interpretive grid, which imposed meaning arbitrarily.[55] Yet, like Erasmus, Rabelais sees a need to search for a *plus hault sens* that would give life to an otherwise dead letter. Allegorical meaning exists to the same extent that a plenitude of meaning exists in his early novels. The spirit gives life to the dead letter in both sacred and profane texts. To get beyond the contingency of the literal level of meaning, the reader must plunge in and search out the "substantificque moelle," which lies hidden beneath the coarse outer coat of the text. Allegorical meaning does not, nonetheless, authorize the illegitimate interpretation of texts, like Politiano's reading of Homer or the "frères Lubins'" reading of Holy Scripture, to which Rabelais refers in the prologue to *Gargantua*.

Allegory exists as a liberating means of understanding, unlike the idle word games of the late scholastics. Real allegory allows not for idle conjecture but rather for the deeper meaning of life to express itself in the written word. Erasmus's defense of limited allegory saw true meaning, not enigmas, in Christ's parables. Rabelais's defense of allegory in the prologue to *Gargantua* opens up the text in the same way. If Christ's parables opened the literal level of language to the full meaning of the Gospel, then Rabelais's enigmas and prophecies also opened up his text to the full meaning of the evangelical and humanistic project. Signification was not simply a game of imposed meanings but was part of a process, revealing the rich promise of the early Renaissance's optimism.

The demise of allegory in the *Quart Livre* would seem a direct result of the weakest point in Erasmus's argument. For when Erasmus says that it is better to allegorize only when a passage requires it in order to avoid making up what is not there, he leaves a large part of the interpretive effort to human reason. It is human reason, a belief in a certain *mediocritas*, that allows one to know what is to be allegorized and what is not. If Rabelais's early work reflects an Erasmian optimism in the powers of language and reason, in the *Quart Livre* this optimism disappears.

Rabelais's imagery in the *Quart Livre* can be understood as a parody of what happens when the human mind makes up what is not there. The Papefigues, the Papimanes, Gaster, et alia offer themselves as allegorical images that promise a *plus hault sens* that is just as quickly deflated or disfigured or both. These figures are examples of what happens when the principle of *mediocritas* is abandoned. Thematically, they impose horrendous meanings on things that in and of themselves do not necessarily have a *plus hault sens*. The hidden meaning is literalized so that it becomes deterministic. Allegory, instead of being an aid to understanding, becomes an impediment when it is applied inappropriately. Instead of clarifying, it mystifies and obscures.

The allegorical ambiguity of *Gargantua* becomes a nightmare in the *Quart Livre*, as the moderation of Couillatris is abandoned by both sides of the theological debate. In many ways, the *Quart Livre* becomes an illustration of allegorical excess. Human beings give up their independence and "Christian liberty" to the false gods they have created. The portraits of Quaresmeprenant and the Andouilles can be seen as imaginative illustrations of the heretical dangers that Gerson wrote about in essays such as *De sensu litterali sacrae scripturae* and *Contra curiositatem studentium*. The human mind, when it deserts its innate moderation, gives birth to all sorts of blasphemous creatures. Just as Reason in the *Roman de la Rose moralisé* became Lucifer or Behemoth when she attempted to pierce the realm of the divine, now human reason gives birth to unnatural and horrible creatures when it turns away from its moderate place in nature. Couillatris knew not to ask for what was not his and was rewarded famously by the gods.

The creators of Quaresmeprenant are like Couillatris's companions, who ask for more than is their due and who die for their hubris. The natural *mediocritas* allows human beings to know when to limit the scope of their transcendant investigations. If Rabelais allowed for a *plus hault sens* that would be dependent on the ability to know when to apply an allegorical interpretation in *Gargantua*, in the *Quart Livre* he would seem to deny that possibility. Where the giganticism of *Gargantua* and *Pantagruel* focused a figurative light on the protagonists so that their actions could be taken as a spiritual truth denied characters like Thaumaste, in the *Quart Livre* the same sort of giganticism focuses on Quaresmeprenant and Gaster.

Rabelais does not suppress the effort to interpret divine reality, because this sort of censorship can also become the victim of human irrationality. Where Gerson supported the use of decretals in *De sensu litterali sacrae scripturae*, Rabelais creates the Papimanes, who venerate the "Sainctes Decretales" (Holy Decretals) instead of God.[56] Instead of literalizing the figurative the way the Andouilles literalize the "Idée de Mardigras" (Idea of Mardigras), the Papimanes give a transcendental truth to a literal meaning. The error is the same, however, as both abandon their powers of common sense and mistake the product of human imagination for reality.

The construction of the archetype by which the Papimanes know their "Dieu en Terre" (God on Earth) (and whose power gives authority to the decretals) is an exercise in the kind of logic that both Molinet and Rabelais mock in their astrological predictions. Homenaz, the high priest of the Papimanes, shows Pantagruel and his companions an "imaige paincte assez mal" (a rather badly painted picture), an image that has been hidden in a coffer locked inside an altar with "trente et deux claveures et quatorze cathenatz" (thirty-two locks and fourteen padlocks).[57] When Homenaz asks the Pantagruelians what the picture looks like, Pantagruel identifies it as the image of a pope. He recognizes it as such by the details adorning it, which are easily identifiable with a pope. Homenaz tells Pantagruel that he is correct and pronounces that it is "l'idee de celluy Dieu de bien en terre" (the idea of that good God on earth). Homenaz, like an astrologer, takes contingent reality for signs of an absolute and invests the purely human grouping of these imperfect details with the meaning of a divinity.

In the *Quart Livre*, Rabelais denies the re-creation of an *ius gentium*, or universal truth, from contingent reality. Quaresmeprenant, a giant accumulation of such details, is understood as a universal truth, albeit a horrible one. The Papimanes's archetype is equally fictitious and equally monstrous, since his power eventually goes beyond the limits that Rabelais elsewhere describes as "jusques au feu exclusivement" (up to but exclusive of fire). Homenaz, using the decretals as an authority, condemns to death those who do not recognize his truth as the absolute truth:

> Encores ces diables hæreticques ne les voulent aprendre et sçavoir. Bruslez, tenaillez, cizaillez, noyez, pendez, empallez, espaultrez, demembrez, exenterez, decouppez, fricassez, grislez, transonnez, crucifiez, bouillez, escarbouillez, escartelez, debezillez, dehinguandez, carbonnadez ces meschans Hæreticques, Decretalifuges, Decretalicides, pires que homicides, pires que parricides, Decretalictones du Diable.[58]

> [Besides, these heretic devils will not learn and know them. Burn them, tear them with pincers, cut with shears, drown, hang, impale, break their shoulders, disembowel, chop to bits, fricassee, grill, slice up, crucify, boil, crush, quarter, smash to bits, unhinge, charcoal broil these wicked Heretics, Decretalifuges, Decretalicides, worse than homicides, worse than parricides, Decretalictones of the Devil.]

This condemnation relies on the identification of the image, which Homenaz shows Pantagruel, as the "Dieu de bien en terre." The power invested in this image results from its supposed archetypal nature, but as Pantagruel notes, the image is the product of human imagination. The Papimanes become victims of their own imagination. They do not practice the restraint that Erasmus advises and allegorize what does not need such interpretation. They see a tree trunk rising and eating a traveler, where a simple literal interpretation is sufficient. The excessive nature of their interpretation of earthly phenomena, be it a picture of the pope or the decretals, is paradigmatic of an analysis that takes human concepts for metaphysical truths.

Allegory's disparate appearance in *Gargantua* and in the *Quart Livre* shows that there is a historical development in Rabelais's approach to the revelation of a *plus hault sens*. Throughout his novels, a theoretical desire for a higher meaning motivates the text. A hidden meaning lies beneath the jocular appearance of the novel. This *plus hault sens* is what pulls the reader into the text. Yet due to the fallen nature of human beings in these novels, a higher truth remains forever beyond the pale of human understanding. Allegorical meaning can only be imposed, in secular texts, the way Politiano imposed an allegorical meaning on Homer's text. In the early books, the notion of a higher meaning finds a receptive, if problematic, intellectual context. Because the *ius gentium* allows the human mind to rise to the general or universal, at least theoretically, the *plus hault sens* exists as a lure for the reader, enticing him or her beyond the ludic cover that hides the *substantificque moelle*. This process is never fully successful, however, because of the fallen nature of human understanding in *Gargantua*. In practice, meaning is resolutely on the side of human contingency. Although the Pantagruelians and Gargantua might aspire to a transcendent higher meaning, their desires always crumble under the weight of human imperfection.

The varying degrees of allegorical transparency in the early books and in the *Quart Livre* cast the critical debate regarding allegorical meaning in Rabelais in a new light. If allegorical meaning remains theoretically plausible in the early books, it is completely discounted in the *Quart Livre*. In 1552, allegorical meaning, like analogical meaning, is the product of deficient human reason. The inability to accept the literal level of meaning, or the immediate level of existence, leads human beings to create monsters, who end up enslaving those who produced them. Throughout the *Quart Livre*, the Pantagruelians contest the hidden meaning of the Papimanes, the Andouilles, the Papefigues, et alia. In every one of these cases, the inhabitants of an island invested a creation of their own imagination with transcendent power. This imaginative figure becomes a tyrannical power, enslaving the very people who gave it life. By making up what is not there, the Papimanes, the Andouilles, et alia commit the error that Erasmus warned about. What was clear and comprehensible became confused and troubling.

The culmination of the *Quart Livre*'s bitter parody of allegorical expression is found in the Gaster episode.[59] Here, in chapters 57 through 62, the figurative as a place that is distant, removed, and occult is opposed to a literal that is immediate, material, and obvious.[60] The question of how the hidden nature of the figural or allegorical is derived from the literal level of comprehension provides the narrative thread in these chapters. These chapters illustrate the procedure that places the figural above the literal at the expense of those who create the structure. They end with a circular twist, which brings the figural down to the level of the literal. This final deflation collapses the allegory of Gaster in on itself and shows how allegorical understanding amounts to very little in the world of the *Quart Livre*.

The Gaster episode also represents a crucial point in this study as it shows how the analogical symbol, reinflated with meaning in Lemaire's metaphysical universe, is deflated in Rabelais to an antianalogical form like that found in Molinet. Theoretical conjecture about either the continuity or the discontinuity in analogical understanding is proven most problematical in this episode. It begins with Pantagruel and friends arriving at a steeply sloped island, "scabreuse, pierreuse, montueuse, infertile, mal plaisante a l'œil, tresdifficile aux pieds et peu moins inaccessible que le mons du Daulphiné"[61] (rugged, stony, mountainous, infertile, unpleasing to the eye, very hard on the feet, and hardly less inaccessible than the mount in Dauphiné).

As Marichal and Cave note, this insalubrious place is most likely influenced by Jean Lemaire de Belges's *La Concorde des deux langages*, discussed here in chapter 4. Lemaire places his "Palais d'honneur" on top of a rock of similar composition:

> Vecy le noble roch qui les nuës surpasse,
> Des plus haulx montz qu'on saiche au monde l'outrepasse,
> Dont le sommet attaint l'air du ciel tressalubre.
> Or est tout ce rochier divers, glissant et lubre,
> Tresdur, agu, poinctu, offendant piedz et palmes . . .[62]

> [Here is the noble rock higher than any cloud, / Or any of the highest mountains known on earth, / Whose summit reaches the most healthy heaven. / Yet is this rock overhung, slippery and slick, / Hard, sharp, pointed, offending feet and hands . . .]

As Marichal points out, if Lemaire's rock is the first example in French literature of the revival of Hesiod's Rock of Virtue, then Rabelais's use of the Rock of Virtue is essentially parodic.[63] Instead of the Goddess Minerva, found at the top of Lemaire's Rock of Virtue, Messere Gaster appears on Rabelais's rock as a figurative image of human hunger. In place of an abstract quality such as learning or virtue, Rabelais's *altior sensus* is a material need.

Minerva and Gaster not only share their elevated positions on top of high, distant mountains, they also are both origins of technology and science. Lemaire describes Minerva as

> laquelle aultrement se nomme Pallas, ou Bellona, deesse de science, d'estude, de vertu, de paix qui est aussi quise par armes, maistresse de tout artiffice et ouvraige, inventeresse d'armures et de tous aultres acoustremens qu'on scet deviser ou souhaitter de main ouvriere en linge et en soye . . . [64]

> [otherwise called Pallas, or Bellona, goddess of science, of study, of virtue, of peace, which is also had by arms, mistress of all artifice and work, inventor of arms and of all other tools that have been devised by or wished for by a worker's hand in linen or silk . . .]

Likewise, Rabelais's Gaster is described as a master:

> Le gouverneur d'icelle estoit messere Gaster, premier maistre es ars de ce monde. Si croyez que le feu soit le grand maistre des ars, comme escript Ciceron, vous errez et vous faictez tord. Car Ciceron ne le creut oncques. Si croyez que Mercure soit premier inventeur des ars, comme jadis croyoient nos antiques Druides, vous fourvoyez grandement. La sentence du Satyricque est vraye, qui dict messere Gaster estre de tous ars le maistre. [65]

> [The governor of the island was Messere Gaster, first master of arts in the world. If you think that fire is the great master of arts, as Cicero writes, you are mistaken and are going wrong, for Cicero never did believe it. If you think that Mercury was the first inventor of the arts, as our ancient Druids believed long ago, you are far off the track. The statement of the Satirist is true, who says that Messere Gaster is master of all the arts.]

The materialistic Gaster, placed atop the distant mountain, disrupts the expected relationship of ideal and material. What is structurally elevated is, in fact, low and immediate. The parody is heightened by Rabelais's coupling of Gaster with "dame Penie, aultrement dict Souffrete, mere des neuf Muses" (lady Penie, otherwise called Want, mother of the nine Muses). Penie, according to the narrator, gave birth with Porus, "seigneur de Abondance" (lord of Abundance), to "Amour le noble enfant mediateur du Ciel et de la Terre, comme atteste Platon in *Symposio*" (Love, the noble child mediator between Heaven and Earth, as Plato attests in the *Symposium*).[66] Gaster is therefore placed in the same position as a divinity. With Gaster ensconced on top of the Rock of Virtue, the entire concept of a *plus hault sens* is destabilized. The notion of a hidden sense that would bring the reader to a plenitude of meaning is the crucial distancing element in his parody. Gaster represents a twisted desire for hidden meaning that would give life to the dead letter of literal meaning and material reality. The distance between the literal reality of hunger and the figurative reality of Gaster provides the focal point of the chapters's dark humor.

In Hesiod's *Works and Days* and in Lemaire's *La Concorde des deux langages*, virtue is difficult of access and acquired at great cost. In Rabelais's "manoir de Areté," Gaster represents hunger, a need so immediate it needs no verbal mediation. Hunger's meaning is revealed through the most elemental of stimulus-response semiotics: "Il ne parle que par signes" (He only speaks by signs).[67] Gaster has no mouth or ears: "c'est à dire sans bouche, ainsi Gaster sans aureilles feut crée" (that means to say without a mouth, thus Gaster was created without ears). Hunger does not need a mediated language, it transmits its desires directly through impulses. The mistake is to understand hunger's meaning as being revealed through Gaster's distant position on top of the manoir de Areté.

By favoring the figurative meaning, which gives Gaster a deterministic power over the organization of the universe, human responsibility is relinquished to a *plus hault sens,* which exists only because the human mind allows it to. The idolaters of Gaster, the Engastrimythes and the Gastrolatres, invest the figurative meaning of hunger with divine powers. The Gastrolatres

> tous tenoient Gaster pour leur grand Dieu, le adoroient comme Dieu luy sacrifoyent comme a leur Dieu omnipotens, ne recongnoissoient aultre Dieu que luy; le servoient, aymoient sus toutes choses, honoroient comme leur Dieu. (237)

> [all held Gaster as their great God, worshipped him as God, sacrificed to him as to their omnipotent God, recognized no other God than him, served him, loved him above all things, honored him as their God.]

The Engastrimythes and the Gastrolatres show how Gaster's power is much less a product of some innate quality than the result of his idolators investing the natural power of hunger with some hidden meaning. The Engastrimythes are called diviners and enchanters, who abuse the "simple people" by making believe that they speak from the stomach rather than the mouth. They are likened to a certain Jacobe Rodogine, an Italian woman who was said to be able to call a spirit from her stomach. This spirit, called Crespelu, when called upon to talk about the present or the past responded well, but

> si des choses futures, tousjours mentoit; jamais n'en disoit la vérité. Et souvent sembloit confesser son ignorance, en lieu de y respondre, faisant un gros

pet, ou marmonnant quelques motz non intelligibles et de barbare termina-
tion. (236)

[if about future things, he always lied; never told the truth about them. And
often he seemed to confess his ignorance, instead of answering, letting a great
fart, or muttering a few unintelligible words with barbarous endings.]

Jacobe Rodogine and her spirit are no more effective in foretelling future
events than the Engastrimythes. The spirit can depend on his memory for
past or present events but when called upon to "prognostiquer" the
future, his answers reflect an exceptionally human perception. Jacobe
Rodogine is invested with meaning she does not possess. She and her
spirit become a metaphor for an artificial *plus hault sens*. They symbolize
the false and misleading knowledge of the Engastrimythes, who mythol-
ogize the normal grumblings of a hungry stomach and invest them with a
special meaning.

If the Engastrimythes abuse the simple folk through their ventriloquism
and phoney prophecies, the Gastrolatres have Manduce, the monstrous
effigy who offers a perverse mirror image of Gaster:

C'estoit une effigie monstrueuse, ridicule, hydeuse, et terrible aux petitz
enfans, ayant les œilz plus grands que le ventre, et la teste plus grosse que
tout le reste du corps, avecques amples, larges et horrificques maschoueres
bien endentelées, tant au dessus comme au dessoubs; les quelles, avecques
l'engin d'une petite chorde cachée dedans le baston doré, l'on faisoit l'une
contre l'aultre terrificquement clicquetter, comme à Metz l'on faict du dragon
de sainct Clemens. (238)

[It was a monstrous effigy, ridiculous, hideous, and terrifying to little children, having eyes bigger than its belly and a head bigger than all the rest of
its body, with ample, wide horrific jaws with plenty of teeth, both upper and
lower, which, by the device of a little cord hidden in the gilded pole, were
made to clatter frighteningly together, as they do at Metz with Saint Clement's
dragon.]

This effigy parodies Gaster's own power and person. Its features are the
exact opposite of Gaster's (its eyes are bigger than its belly), yet its misshapen form places it in the same imaginative realm as Gaster. Both Gaster and Manduce represent abstractions or elaborations of reality that
play on fear and human weakness. Humans submit themselves to Gaster,
and children are terrified by Manduce. And both Manduce's and Gaster's
ghastliness stem from human manipulation. Manduce's jaws clack together in monstrous fashion because there is someone to pull the string
hidden in the stick holding up the statue. Gaster is placed on the top of

the manoir de Areté by the Gastrolatres and the Engastrimythes. The truth of Manduce lies in his poorly painted characters and rigged jaws, and the truth of Gaster lies in the pit of the human belly, which must be filled. Both the occult power that Gaster has over adult humans and the fear that Manduce produces in children result from the displacement of literal truth by figurative truth.

The need to elevate the immediately accessible to the metaphysical, which motivates the Engastrimythes and the Gastrolatres, also has a direct impact on how history is perceived. The immediately apparent history of civilization as a response to clear-cut needs is obfuscated in the land of Gaster; the figurative rendition ends up destroying the material and creating impossible myths. In the land of Gaster, the material reality at the base of this figural rendition is finally eaten up and destroyed. Gaster has the same effect on history that he does on ordinary understanding of hunger: he twists it until it is no longer recognizable.

Immediately after the sections on the Engastrimythes and the Gastrolatres, in chapter 61, the narrator explains how Gaster was responsible for inventing methods of producing and conserving grain:

> Vous sçavez que par institution de Nature, pain avecques ses apennaiges luy a esté pour provision adjugé et aliment, adjoincte ceste benediction du ciel que pour pain trouver et guarder rien ne luy defauldroit. (245)
>
> [You know that, by arrangement of Nature, bread and its appurtenances have been adjudicated to him for food and maintenance, besides this added blessing from Heaven that he should lack nothing to find and keep bread.]

This passage clearly expresses the notion that there is a material cause in nature that motivates the development of producing and conserving grain. Nature is identified as the creator of bread; however, Gaster is described as the creator of agriculture, which produces the grain, of military arts, which protect the grain from other peoples, and of medicine and astrology, which protect the grain from the weather. Hunger, as a natural phenomenon, is superseded by Gaster, the human interpretation of that natural event. Once Gaster has been inserted into the picture, the very course of history no longer holds, and what began in nature ends up being unnatural.

Here, the material reality of history is inflated with a higher meaning, which eventually erases the material level altogether. After explaining how Gaster invented agriculture, astrology, and the military arts, the narrator describes the workings of a bullet shot from a rifle according to the principles of sixteenth-century physics.[68] The materiality of the bullet disappears once Gaster's figural interpretation is allowed to intervene. Gaster not only invents gunpowder and rifles, he also invents ways to make bullets turn back on the people who shot them:

> Mais il inventoit l'art et maniere de faire les boulletz arriere retourner contre les ennemis, en pareille furie et dangier qu'ilz seroient tirez et en propre parallele. Le cas ne trouvoit difficile; attendu que l'herbe nommée *Æthiopis* ouvre toutes les serrures qu'on luy præsente, et que Echineis, poisson tant imbecille, arreste contre tous les vens, et retient en plein fortunal les plus fortes navires qui soient sus mer. (250)
>
> [But also he invented an art and method of making bullets turn back upon the enemy, with the same fury and danger as they had been fired with, and the same trajectory. He did not find the matter difficult, considering that the herb named dittany *Ætheopis* opens all the locks presented to it, and that remora *Echineis*, such a feeble fish, in the teeth of the tempest, stops the mightiest ships there are at sea.]

By transposing the physical reality of the bullet to the figurative plane of Gaster, the narrator allows it to be influenced by the forces of sympathetic magic. The narrator compares the bullets to the fantastical attractions and supernatural repulsions found in Pliny's *Natural History*.[69] The bullet is like herbs that open locks and furious bulls that are tamed when they approach wild figs.[70] The bullet, like the lock or the bull, submits itself to a secret force that exerts an influence on its material existence. The bullet loses its physical presence and becomes subject to the power of a higher meaning.

It would be easy to dismiss the story of the bullet, and of Gaster in general, as extravagant games of free association if it were not for the final section of the Gaster episode. In this passage, the relationship between contingent bullet, herb, or plant and a higher meaning or power is shown to be completely imaginary. This passage connects the arrested flight of the bullet and Gaster's power over the Gastrolatres and the Engastrimythes by showing that only singular reality has any meaning; any other kind of meaning is simply the result of an overactive imagination.

In the final section of the Gaster episode, the narrator describes the qualities of the domestic and wild elder trees, explaining that the wild elder tree is superior to the domestic elder in the making of flutes because it is unaffected by the crowing of a cock: "attendu pareillement que le suzeau croist, plus canore et plus apte au jeu des flustes, en pays on quel le chant des coqs ne sera ouy" (251) (considering likewise that the elder grows more melodious and suitable for flute playing in lands where cock crowing would not be heard). The narrator recounts different ways of understanding this strange phenomenon. The first way esteems that the wild elder is better because it has not been softened and stunned by the cock's song:

> ainsi qu'ont escript les anciens sages, scelon le rapport de Theophraste, comme si le chant des coqs hebetast, amolist et estonnast la matiere et le boys du suzeau; au quel chant pareillement ouy, le lion, animant de si grande force et constance, devient tout estonné et consterné. (251)

> [as the ancient sages have written, according to Theophrastus's report, as if cock crowing numbed, softened, and stunned the matter and wood of the elder; at which crowing similarly heard, the lion, an animal of such great strength and stamina, becomes completely astounded and dismayed.]

Because the wild elder grows where cocks are not found, there must be a secret connection between the cock's crowing and the quality of the wood.

The second way of looking at the tree's superiority as a wood for making flutes simply states that the wild elder is grown in areas far from the barns and farms where cocks are found:

> Je sçay que aultres ont ceste sentence entendu du suzeau saulvaige, provenent en lieux tant esloignez de villes et villages que le chant des coqs n'y pourroit estre ouy. Icelluy sans doubte doibt pour flustes et aultres instrumens de musicque estre esleu et preferé au domesticque, lequel provient autour des chesaulx et masures. (251)

> [I know that others have understood this saying about the wild elder, coming from places so remote from towns and villages that cock crowing could not be heard there. This no doubt is to be chosen and preferred for flutes and other musical instruments over the domesticated kind, which grows around dilapidated houses and ruined walls.]

Thus, the presence or absence of the cock's crowing is purely incidental as the wild elder just happens to grow far away from villages and farm where cocks are found and happen to crow. The singular reality of the wood and the cock singing is undisturbed, and no figurative meaning is allowed or needed.

These two explanations are opposed and explicated in a paragraph that provides a key to understanding the Gaster episode in particular and to the nature of allegory in the *Quart Livre* in general. In this paragraph, the last of the Gaster episode, the narrator explains that the wild elder can be understood allegorically:

Aultres l'ont entendu plus haultement, non scelon la letre, mais allegoricque-
ment scelon l'usaige des Pithagoriens. Comme quand il a esté dict que la
statue de Mercure ne doibt estre faicte de tous boys indiferentement, ilz l'ex-
posent que Dieu ne doibt estre adoré en façon vulgaire, mais en façon esleue
et religieuse. Pareillement en ceste sentence nous enseignent que les gens
saiges et studieux ne se doibvent adonner à la musique triviale et vulgaire,
mais à la celeste, divine, angelique, plus absconse et de plus loing apportée:
sçavoir est d'une region en laquelle n'est ouy des coqs le chant. Car, voulans
denoter quelque lieu à l'escart et peu frequenté, ainsi disons nous en icelluy
n'avoir oncques esté ouy coq chantant. (252)

[Others have chosen a loftier interpretation of this, not according to the letter, but allegorically, after the habit of the Pythagoreans. As, when it was said
that the statue of Mercury is not to be made indiscriminately of just any kind
of wood, they expound it to mean that God is not to be worshipped in a
common way but in an elevated, religious way. Likewise in this saying they
teach us that wise and studious people should not devote themselves to trivial
and vulgar music but to the celestial, divine, angelic kind, more abstruse and
coming to us from a greater distance: to wit, from a region where cock crowing is not heard. For when we want to define some out-of-the-way place
where few people go, we say that in it, cock crowing has never been heard.]

The rapport established between the first explanation of the elder's superiority and allegory reveals both how Gaster ends up in his Godlike
position and why allegory in the *Quart Livre* is such a problematic concept. The narrator clearly shows the relationship between the "musique
. . . celeste, divine, angelique, plus absconse" and the "region en laquelle
n'est ouy des coqs le chant." Both are far from domestic, immediate experience of human needs, and neither possesses any intrinsic truth. Just as
the wild elder's superiority for flute making is construed as being due to
the absence of cock's crowing, so too the "celeste musique" owes its superiority to its distance from common barnyard reality. In both cases, the
absence of the commonplace is what supplies the occult meaning, for
what cannot be seen must have a hidden meaning. Yet as the wild elder
story illustrates, real meaning is in the literal, and the figurative meaning
merely obscures the literal. The allegorical *altior sensus*, like the elder's
figurative explanation, has nothing to do with real meaning or literal
truth. It is, rather, concerned with imagination.

Gaster, like the wild elder, has qualities that owe little or nothing to
reality and everything to the argumentations of the Gastrolatres and the
Engastrimythes. Like the wild elder, he finds himself enjoying a supernatural or occult reputation that owes nothing to his real character and
everything to the human need to invest an *absconce* meaning into what is

obvious.[71] The Engastrimythes and the Gastrolatres, who place Gaster on top of the rock and proclaim him the "maistre es ars," make up something that does not exist in reality; they do not allow the immediate and clear meaning of hunger to go uninterpreted. They give a *plus hault sens* to something that does not need to be allegorized.

Rabelais's treatment of the *musique absconse* shows just how different the Gaster episode is from the "Palais de Mynerve" episode in Lemaire's *Concorde des deux langages*. In Lemaire's *Concorde*, the far-off summit of the rock is described as a place where "L'air . . . retentist de tresdoulce armonie" and a place of "estude et labeur et soucy."[72] The significance of the Palace of Minerva is underlined by its otherness, by its distance from everyday life. Its meaning is *altior,* both geographically and semantically. Rabelais's manoir de Areté is very much the opposite. Its real value is inherent in its own properties, and its *absconce* meaning is due to faulty human reason, which imposes meaning where there is perhaps none. Gaster's *altior sensus* is a product of the human imagination. The distant place, far from the madding crowd, has the same value as the absence of the cock's singing: none. Just as the fact that the innately superior quality of the wild elder has nothing to do with its distance from towns where cocks sing, the superiority of one meaning over another has nothing to do with its distance from common experience. The *absconce,* or hidden, meaning is like the connection between the cock's singing and the quality of the wild elder as a source of wood for flutes: it is entirely artificial.

In the *Quart Livre,* real meaning is not distant and difficult. It is as accessible as the explanation of the wild elder's superiority: it is the product of common sense. Gaster, placed high atop the manoir de Areté, owes his special status to his inaccessibility, for there is nothing essentially terrifying about him. His power comes from the need humans have to give an *altior sensus* to that which is immediately understandable. They turn an adequate earthly existence into a hellish experience by looking for the "vray Jardin et Paradis terrestre."[73] Gaster becomes the monster that he is because humans invest him with a meaning and a power that he does not possess. He is the *absconce* meaning of simple human hunger.

Throughout the *Quart Livre,* real meaning is found in material phenomena. Hunger, like music, can have no *plus hault sens.* Hunger and music are both material facts; they are given obscure meanings through the agency of the human imagination. Hunger becomes Gaster through the doings of the theologians, who argue about the exact location of the manoir de Areté and by the sycophantic Engastrimythes and Gastrolatres, who, once they create their figurative god, become its slaves. Yet, they do not explain his power any more than the allegorical understanding of the wild elder's superiority in the making of flutes explains its superiority. Occult meaning is the product of the inappropriate application of figurative meaning to that which does not need it.

The word for *hidden* is used in the explanation of the wild elder's powers in a very different way than it had been used in *Gargantua*. It is also spelled differently. In the prologue to *Gargantua*, the word was spelled as it appears in modern French: *absconce*, and it was used to denote a meaning that would exist above and beyond the coarse literal meaning of the book. In the *Quart Livre*, the word is spelled *absconse* and now describes the meaningless crowing of a cock. These two versions of the word represent two poles of understanding in Rabelais's opus. The *absconce* of the prologue to *Gargantua* represents the nearest Rabelais ever comes to accepting the paradigm of resemblance, while the *absconse* of the *Quart Livre* represents the principle of difference. The distance from *absconce* to *absconse* is great, and although the spelling change does not involve any semantic change, this slight morphological shift points to the very different meanings Rabelais applies to the word in these two books.

In *Gargantua*, an *absconce* meaning was not only possible, it was also necessary within the context of an *ius gentium* that would resolve the infinite differences of contingent existence. Somewhere beyond the horizon of human existence, a hidden meaning joined all the pieces of the universe together, in theory if not in practice. The plenitude of meaning in Egyptian hieroglyphs and the universality of meaning implied in the *ius gentium* both necessitate a hidden quintessence that would provide the link between contingent and absolute. The *absconce* doctrine of *Gargantua's* prologue relies on the existence of such a metaphysics. The hermetic and the hidden held out the promise of a higher meaning, which would make the discordant and individual part of the whole. If not in practice, this concept of *absconce* dominates *Gargantua* in theory.

In the *Quart Livre*, the *musique absconse* is identified as something that does not really exist. Like the absence of cock's crowing in the story about the wild elder, it has no bearing on material existence. That which is *absconse* in the *Quart Livre* is a figment of the imagination. Figures such as Amodunt and Discordance, Gaster and Quaresmeprenant owe their existence to the overexcited imagination of those who invent them: *absconce* loses its ontological ground when it becomes *absconse*.

This textual development points to, and is determined by, the sixteenth-century debates about the ability of human beings to understand the divine. The claims that both the Calvinists and the Roman Catholic orthodoxy make concerning their ability to understand the will of God place Erasmian evangelicals like Rabelais in a precarious situation. For moderates in the late sixteenth century, damned on their left and on their right, Pyrrhonian skepticism is the only mode of discourse available.[74] The *Quart Livre*'s *musique absconse* is the literary equivalent of the pretensions of all those theologians claiming to speak the word of God. These theologians, like the Engastrimythes, the Gastrolatres, the Papimanes, and the Papefigues, create their own Gasters, either in the *Institutes of the Christian Religion* or at the Council of Trent.

Rabelais's itinerary from the optimism of *Gargantua* to the skepticism of the *Quart Livre* is a journey back to the future in the sense that he returns to the skepticism found in Molinet. Amodunt and Discordance are clearly identified as the misshapen offspring of analogical thought. When Antiphysie applies the imperfection of human existence to the perfection of the divine in her description of her children, the results are necessarily erroneous. All of the inhabitants of the islands they visit make the same kind of mistake. They all understand the transcendent through a comparison with an earthly phenomenon. The intelligence of the Pantagruelians resides in their not mistaking the contingent for the absolute. They do not take the image of the pope for a true likeness of a higher truth. The Pantagruelians, like the miller in Molinet's story about the astrologer and the miller in the *Roman de la rose moralisé*, understand that the relationship between contingent reality and the stars and the planets is strictly nominal.

In Lemaire's *Couronne margaritique* and in Rabelais's early novels, human beings could—in theory if not in practice—rise from the contingent and singular to the universal truths of the Ideal. The individual and the imperfect participated in the perfect whole of which they were a part. This wholeness of being is absent in the *Quart Livre*. The Pantagruelians cannot reconstitute the archetype of the pope from his resemblance, any more than Antiphysie can adequately construct her children through her incomplete understanding of the creator of the universe. Homenaz and the Papimanes sincerely believe that the contingent image of the pope resembles his true higher nature, which becomes the paradigm for all other popes. The Gastrolatres and the Engastrimythes believe that Gaster truly was the "maistre es ars" of the world, but it is only their imagination that allows him to exist; he has no more power in the real world than the cock's crowing had in the making of flutes. Only the misled and the insane can reconstruct the connection of the contingent and the absolute in the *Quart Livre*.

In the *Quart Livre*, difference rather than resemblance dominates understanding. Reality is resolutely singular, and analogical thinking produces only monsters. In the *Quart Livre*, contingency (which had been seen only in word games in *Gargantua*) dominates human existence. The humor of these puns and other word games was grounded in the fact that in expressions such as "femme molle à la fesse, femme folle à la messe" (woman soft in the ass, mad woman at mass) the resemblance of the letters *f* and *m* change only the morphology of the words. Thighs and church masses do not all of a sudden become synonymous because of linguistic resemblance. The common sense that recognizes this truth is the basis of understanding in the *Quart Livre,* in which resemblance is reduced to the nominal likeness of the word games in *Gargantua* and *Pantagruel.* Only Antiphysie can really believe that her children resemble the creator of the universe, and when words melt in the "Parolles gelées" episode, they do not reveal a higher meaning, they simply make noises.

The conflict of like and unlike in the works of the three authors studied in this book produces some of the most extraordinary images in the French Renaissance. Molinet's comparison of the Virgin Mary and Mary of Burgundy and Rabelais's Antiphysie stand out as remarkable examples. All these works were written in a period when human understanding of the world was undergoing rapid change. What was known and how it was known were questions that continuously demanded new answers. Between the "waning of the Middle Ages" and the dawn of the modern age, writers such as Molinet, Lemaire, and Rabelais produced some of the most troubling images of French literature. Impossible to understand under the aegis of either resemblance or difference, they stand as monuments to a time when human perception of the heavens and earth was in full evolution. Sometimes bizarre, sometimes ghastly, the literature of the sixteenth century was anchored in an ever-changing perception of the world.

Conclusion

❧   ❧   ❧

Michel de Montaigne's last essay, *De l'expérience*, explains in few words everything this book has tried to explain in many. Montaigne, rejecting knowledge based on authority, turns to experience as a source of "connoissance," which is, he reminds us, the most natural of desires.[1] Knowledge from authority, Montaigne explains, has only produced interminable debates: "infinis arrests, et . . . autant d'interpretations" (infinite decrees, and . . . as many interpretations) (1067–68). Personal experience taught Montaigne that the entire corpus of Western thought was nothing but a pile of contradictory interpretations and that, finally, there were more books about other books than about any other subject. As he says, "nous ne faisons que nous entregloser" (we do nothing but gloss one another) (1069).

Montaigne's rejection of commentaries, glosses, and other forms of secondhand knowledge leaves him in a predicament. If the desire to know is the most natural desire, what are we to do with ourselves if we are not to learn from others' books? With the entire system of analogical knowledge in ruins but with no scientific means of capitalizing on the emergent subjective viewpoint, how was the individual in the late sixteenth century to understand his or her universe? Montaigne, as always, explains the problem with wit and style:

> Ingenieux meslange de nature. Si nos faces n'estoient semblables, on ne sçauroit discerner l'homme de la beste; si elles n'estoient dissemblables, on ne sçauroit discerner l'homme de l'homme. Toutes choses se tiennent par quelque similitude, tout exemple cloche, et la relation qui se tire de l'experience est tousjours defaillante et imparfaicte; on joinct toutesfois les comparaisons par quelque coin. Ainsi servent les loix, et s'assortissent ainsin à chacun de nos affaires, par quelque interpretation destournée, contrainte et biaise. (1070)

[Ingenious mix of nature. If our faces were not alike, man could not be distinguished from beast. If they were not unlike, man could not be distinguished from man. All things are held together by some likeness, there is a hitch in every example, and relations drawn from experience are always faltering and imperfect. Comparisons are yet joined by some patch. Thus laws are used and matched to each of our affairs, diverted, cramped, and skewed by some interpretation.]

The world is a problematic *bricolage* (patching together) of comparisons of like and unlike. Human beings resemble each other enough to constitute a species distinct from other animals, and yet within our species we are dissimilar enough to recognize each other. Knowledge is an odd mix of resemblance and difference, and neither *le même* nor *l'autre* can fully constitute the basis of late sixteenth-century epistemology. With Descartes's development of a subjective *je*, which can analyze the world from a singular vantage point, and with the development of a scientific discourse capable of exploiting this subjectivity, knowledge eventually becomes dominated by the "analytico-referentiality" that Timothy Reiss uses to characterize modernity.[2] Within the confines of the sixteenth century, however, the unique mixture of like and unlike provides the epistemological background necessary for the production of the literary images found in Molinet, Lemaire, and Rabelais.

It would be impossible to say for sure whether Montaigne's Pyrrhonism was due to the influence of Roman skepticism or to a historical confrontation of resemblance and difference.[3] However, Montaigne's essays seem to exhibit the same sort of tension between a desire for knowledge based on the general and immutable and a practical dependence on the kind of individual experience found in Rabelais's novels. Nor is this tension limited to Montaigne and Rabelais; it is also found in Du Bellay's poetics, in which the general knowledge of the Ideal in *L'Olive* (1549) gives way to individual and quotidian knowledge of *Contre les pétrarquistes* (1558).[4] Ronsard's poetics exhibit the same sort of movement from the poetic fury of the *Ode à Michel de l'Hospital* (1550) to the decidedly nonidealist love of the *Sonnets sur la mort de Marie* (1578).[5]

In all of these works, there is an increasingly preponderant dependence on the role of the individual in understanding the world. Galileo, Newton, and Kepler had yet to establish the scientific basis of modern understanding, and Descartes still had to establish the individual consciousness as the starting point of human knowledge. Yet in the literature of the sixteenth century, individual consciousness is increasingly manifest, as the old hierarchy that had governed human beings' understanding, which had objectified human existence, fell apart. The individual as subject is increasingly present, as the system that presented him or her as object becomes simply another artifact in the archeological closet of human history.

The old system does not simply disappear as the new system makes itself felt. It continues to dominate the cultural imaginary, making it difficult if not impossible to envisage the new world that the emergent epistemology was creating. The most bizarre and fractured images of sixteenth-century French literature are found in the works of those writers who were the most divided between epistemology and imaginary. Writers such as Lemaire and Scève, whose epistemology was congruent with their symbology, might have produced beautiful and even elaborate images, but they never produced the monstrous and provocative ones found in Rabelais or Molinet. Lemaire and Scève's epistemology was based on resemblance that was akin to that described by Foucault in *Les Mots et les choses*. Rabelais and Molinet, however, are "modern" in their understanding of the world, being skeptical about the ability of the human mind to understand the transcendant design of the universe. The imagery they used to talk about that universe, however, was often at loggerheads with their skeptical understanding. Like storm clouds between cold and warm fronts, Rabelais's Quaresmeprenant and Gaster and Molinet's images from the *Chappellet des dames* rise as two opposing tendencies come head to come.

The trajectory of analogical thought traced in this study provides a possible resolution to the debate between Michel Foucault and Jean Paris referred to at various times in this study. As already mentioned, where Foucault saw the *même* as the dominant force epistemologically in the sixteenth century, Paris established the modernity of Rabelais in relation to his break with a medieval past that mistook the contingent for the absolute. Rabelais would not have been one of those fools who repeated the error of the Middle Ages, who considered the particular and the contingent as a universal, who elevated a gratuitous relation to the level of the absolute.[6] The writers studied in this book show how the "other" and the "same" are in constant dialogue with each other throughout the fifteenth and sixteenth centuries. The futurity or modernity of Rabelais, as identified by Paris, is closer to the nominalism of Ockham than it is to the Neoplatonism of Ficino.[7] The future is in the past, so to speak.

Neither purely nominal nor purely realist or Neoplatonic, the writings of Molinet, Lemaire, and Rabelais show how the sixteenth century was marked by an epistemological dialectic that finally is resolved in the Pyrrhonian skepticism of Montaigne's later essays and in a Cartesian self that regards the universe with a doubting but independent and analytical eye. The conflict between resemblance and difference that produces such bizarre images as Quaresmeprenant and Gaster is part of a historical development from analogical past to analytical future. The past and the future are mixed in a confusing amalgam throughout the sixteenth century and only work themselves out with the evolution of a "self" or an "I" that can begin to comprehend the universe with the analytical instruments necessary for such an observation.[8]

Although Ockham's theory of singularity made such a self epistemologically possible, the lack of an adequate scientific discourse made this concept of selfhood highly problematic. This problematic self is evident in Molinet's portraits of Burgundian nobility, who exist as independent and autonomous agents but whose singularity is expressed with the discursive means of realism. These means, such as allegory and analogy, obscure that singularity by constantly establishing the individual's identity by reference to a higher and more perfect being. The emergent self witnessed in Molinet's portraits is lost in the overwhelming symbolic image used to represent it; the more the self disappears in the portrait's analogical detail, the more exuberant the image becomes. Finally, the image remains floating between two possible referents: as object of an analogical or allegorical portrait and as subject of a encomiastic portrait, which uses the techniques of allegory and analogy as decoration. The genius of Molinet's poetics is, perhaps, never to resolve this tension.

The tension between like and unlike is not unknown in our own postmodern world, where the subjective presence that brought the analogical age to an end is once again called into question. The problem of resemblance and difference is far from being resolved in the literary criticism and the philosophy of the last half century.[9] The modern debunking of nineteenth-century positivism and twentieth-century phenomonology is not so unlike the late medieval deconstruction of realism, and metaphysical presence is today as much a bogeyman for many modern critics as metaphysical universals were for Ockham.

Umberto Eco's recent works on the limits of interpretation contend that modern criticism sins in seeing too much likeness where, in fact, there is none.[10] Rather, one might say that modern criticism sometimes sins in seeing nothing but difference.[11] It is debatable whether there is any substantive difference between complete difference and absolute resemblance, but it is important to recognize the danger of either extreme. Montaigne's *ingenieux meslange* provides a good description of human existence at the end of the sixteenth century as well as at the end of the twentieth.

The play of resemblance and difference in the sixteenth century can help explain how to recognize both what demarcates the individual and the other and what makes the particular a part of the whole. The example of the sixteenth century underlines how the difference of each text needs to be recognized but also how that text is one with its context and how that context, in turn, is both different and the same as the reader's. On a more general level, the questions of like and unlike in the sixteenth century illustrate how each individual has a discrete identity but also how that individual relates to the community and how that community, in turn, relates to the individual.

While the postmodern world cannot be modeled on the premodern one, since the historical differences are so great, the resemblances are strong enough to posit a connection that would allow us to learn from Rabelais and company. The culture of dead, white European males can be incorporated into the emergent world of cultural diversity that is ours. The sixteenth century's confrontation with new peoples and ideas, as bloody and unfortunate as it often was, can help us understand our own predicament, if only by negative example. The study of the "other" of the violent and revolutionary sixteenth century can be used to understand the troubled and fractured "self" of the present.

Notes

❖   ❖   ❖

Introduction

1. Foucault, *Les Mots et les choses*, 32–59.

2. Paris, *Rabelais au futur*.

3. For biographical information on these writers, see Dupire, *Jean Molinet;* Jodogne, *Jean Lemaire de Belges;* Screech, *Rabelais.* The works of Rabelais have been studied in relation to *rhétoriqueur* poets in the past. See Plattard, *L'Etat présent des études rabelaisiennes*, 27–28; Sainéan, *La Langue de Rabelais;* Lebègue, "Rabelais et les grands rhétoriqueurs"; Droz, "Rabelais versificateur"; Rigolot, "Rabelais rhétoriqueur?"

4. See Guy, *Histoire de la poésie française;* Zumthor, *Le Masque et la lumière.*

5. Zumthor, *Le Masque et la lumière*, 9; Zumthor, *L'Anthologie des grands rhétoriqueurs*, 7.

6. Molinet's "building" undergoes the same development described by Focillon in architecture: "Dans un édifice du XIIIe siècle tout est logique. . . . L'architecture du XVe siècle, au contraire, témoigne d'une grande confusion. . . . La structure perd son sens et acquiert une valeur de décor." See Focillon, *L'Art d'occident,* 288.

7. Panofsky, *Gothic Architecture and Scholasticism*, 14.

8. See chaps. 1 and 2 for a discussion of this development.

9. On Aquinas's metaphysics, see Ozment, *Age of Reform, 1250–1550*, 54.

10. Ibid., 115.

11. Ibid.

12. Oberman, *Harvest of Medieval Theology*, 360.

13. See Ficino, *Commentary on Plato's "Symposium,"* and *Teologia platonica,* 1:154–56. For the influence of Ficino's Neoplatonism, see Festugière, *La Philosophie de l'amour de Marsile Ficin;* Chastel, *Marsile Ficin et l'art,* 46–47. Festugière does not see Lemaire as being greatly influenced by Ficino; see ibid., 77. For Agrippa, see *Three Books of Occult Philosophy.*

14. See Tuve, *Allegorical Imagery,* 237.

15. Thomas Aquinas, *Christian Theology,* in *Summa theologiae,* 1:36–41; see also Dupire, *Jean Molinet,* 79–89.

16. Dante, *Dantis alagherii epistolae,* letter 10, 173. Also see Auerbach, "Figura," in his *Scenes from the Drama of European Literature,* 67–76; Hollander, *Allegory in Dante's Commedia,* for an analysis of Dante's allegory.

17. See Thomas Aquinas, *Existence and Nature of God*, in *Summa theologiae*, 2:54–59; Thomas de Vio, *Analogy of Names and the Concept of Being*.

18. See Isidore of Seville, *Isidori Hispalensis Episcopi etymologiarum sive originum, libri xx*, 1:19–20.

19. Masters, *Rabelaisian Dialectic and the Platonic-Hermetic Tradition;* Krailsheimer, *Rabelais and the Franciscans*.

20. Langer, *Divine and Poetic Freedom in the Renaissance;* Compagnon, *Nous, Michel de Montaigne*.

21. Cornilliat, "*Or ne mens.*" See also Cornilliat, "Equivoques moralisées," one of the best short treatises on tension between real and fictive resemblance.

22. Demonet, *Les Voix du signe,* 11.

23. See, for example, Zumthor, *L'Anthologie des grands rhétoriqueurs, Langue, texte, et énigme,* and *Le Masque et la lumière;* Jodogne, *Jean Lemaire de Belges;* Thiry, "Au carrefour des deux rhétoriques"; Thiry, "Rhétorique et genres littéraires au XVe siècle"; Brown, "Rise of Literary Consciousness in Late Medieval France; and "L'Eveil d'une nouvelle conscience littéraire en France à la grande époque de transition technique." See also Gordon, "La Ressource du petit peuple (1481)"; Sutch, "Allegory and Praise in the Works of the Grands Rhétoriquers."

24. See Screech, *L'Evangélisme de Rabelais;* Duval, "Interpretation and the 'Doctrine Absconce'"; Defaux, *Pantagruel et les sophistes.* See also Larmat, *Le Moyen Age dans le Gargantua de Rabelais.*

25. See Cave, *Cornucopian Text;* Rigolot, "Cratylisme et Pantagruélisme"; Jeanneret, "Du mystère à la mystification."

26. Conley, "Image and Code," and *Graphic Unconscious.*

1. The Flamboyant Allegory of Jean Molinet's *Roman de la Rose moralisé*

1. Panofsky, *Gothic Architecture,* 9–20.

2. Ibid., 43.

3. Ockham, *Ockham,* 35, explains that "everything is either one thing and not many, or it is many things." See also Vignaux, *Philosophie au moyen âge,* 199–200: "Comparant Socrate et Platon à Socrate et l'âne, les réalistes déduisent: 'Il y a entre ces êtres une plus grande convenance . . . , donc ils conviennent en quelque *nature*' (est major convenientia . . . , ergo conveniunt in aliqua natura). Occam, au contraire: 'Il y a plus grande convenance entre Socrate et Platon qu'entre Socrate et cet âne; ce n'est pas en raison de quelque chose qui se distingue d'eux en quelque manière que ces êtres conviennent, mais par eux-mêmes ils conviennent davantage' (est major convenientia inter Socratem et Platonem quam inter Socratem et istum asinum; non propter aliquid aliquo modo distinctum, sed seipsis plus conveniunt). Le réaliste fait de la convenance des êtres une communauté de nature, la participation à une même essence, pensable à part; le nominaliste laisse les individus parfaitement indivisés: la ressemblance qu'exprime le concept va de tout l'un à tout l'autre."

4. See Ockham, *Ockham,* 103: "Furthermore, everything known in itself is known either intuitively or abstractively. Therefore, if the divine essence is known

in itself, we know it either intuitively or abstractively. It is clear that it is not intuitively known; for such cognition is beatific, which it is not possible for us to have by purely natural means. Nor is such a cognition abstractive; because as has been declared in the prologue [of the Commentary on the Sentences], we can know nothing abstractively in itself by purely natural means without first knowing it intuitively."

5. See Ozment, *Age of Reform*, 61.

6. See Duby, *Age of the Cathedrals*, 212; "It [Ockhamist doctrine] gave free rein to the deep current of mysticism which had irrigated Latin Christendom since Saint Augustine but had been stemmed by the success of scholasticism and thrust back into the cloister, into Franciscan convents and the small communities of ascetic penitents."

7. Pseudo-Dionysius, *The Divine Names*, in *Works of Dionysius the Areopagite*, 22, emphasizes the unknowableness of the divine: "Further also, the most conspicuous fact of all theology—the God-formation of Jesus amongst us—is both unutterable by every expression and unknown to every mind, even to the very foremost of the most reverent angels." See also Roques, *L'Univers dionysien;* Hathaway, *Hierarchy and the Definition of Order.*

8. Gerson, *De mystica theologia*, 8: "Theologia mistica innititur ad sui doctrinam experientiis habitis ad intra in cordibus animorum devotorum."

9. Panofsky, *Gothic Architecture*, 14.

10. See Delaruelle, Labande, and Ourliac, *L'Eglise au temps du grand schisme*, 2:837: "Il est donc permis de parler, avec les cinquante premières années du XVe siècle, d'un siècle de Gerson. L'influence de Gerson d'ailleurs continuera de se faire sentir dans la deuxième moitié du siècle et plus tard encore." See also Burrows, "Jean Gerson after Constance," 467. For the most recent and one of the most perceptive analyses of Gerson, see Brown, *Pastor and Laity.*

11. For *Querelle de la Rose,* see Gerson, *Contre le roman de la rose,* in *Œuvres complètes*, 7:301–17. See also Hicks, *Le Débat sur le Roman de la Rose;* Baird and Kane, *La Querelle de la Rose;* Hill, *Medieval Debate*, 105–41.

12. Gerson, *Contre le roman de la Rose,* in *Œuvres complètes*, 7:309: "Au feu, bonnes gens, au feu. Pour Dieu ostez, fuies vous tost, sauvez vous et vous en gardez saigement, vous et vos enfans; c'est le remede, meilleur n'y a. Qui ne fuit le peril il y trebuchera et y sera pris comme le rat au lardon et le loup en la louviere ou la papillon au feu de la chandeille pour sa clarté, ou les fols ou les enfans aux espées cleres ou aux chardons vifs pour leur beauté, qui ne les oste de fait."

13. Renaudet, *La Préréforme et l'humanisme à Paris*, 61–68. See also Zumthor, *Le Masque et la lumière*, 27; Courtenay, "Nominalism and Late Medieval Religion," 34–35. The question of Gerson's nominalism has been the subject of much debate. See Ozment, "Mysticism, Nominalism, and Dissent." Brown, *Pastor and Laity,* 80, underlines the complex and often confusing nature of both Gerson's theology and its reception by modern scholars, saying, for example, that "although he has most often been referred to as a nominalist, in both the old and newer senses, Gerson has also been called anti-Occamist, realist, voluntarist, Bonaventurian, Augustinian, Thomistically inclined, and eclectic, while his mysticism has

been labelled as Gersonism by one commentator." See also ibid., 79–115 and 171–208.

Combes identifies a development in Gerson's mystical theology from an early period under the influence of Pierre D'Ailly to a later period in which Gerson became decidedly more realist in tone. See Combes, *La Théologie mystique de Gerson, Jean Gerson, commentateur dionysien, Essai sur la critique de Ruysbroeck par Gerson,* and *Jean de Montreuil et Jean Gerson.* See also Schmiel, *Via Propria and Via Mystica,* 49–50.

Gilson, *La Philosophie au moyen âge,* 713, sees Gerson as adhering to nominalism to counter the excesses of the heretical tendencies of a "certain" realism: "Peut-être faut-il pourtant ajouter que Gerson n'a jamais adhéré au nominalisme que contre un certain réalisme ou, si l'on préfère contre ce qui, dans le réalisme, risquait de conduire à celui de Scot Erigène, de Wiclif, de Jérôme de Prague, de Jean Hus." Connolly, *John Gerson,* 47, also sees Gerson as representing a mixture of nominalist epistemology and realist theology, explaining that "if Gerson was Nominalistic in his philosophy he was certainly Realistic in his Theology." See also Rapp, *L'Eglise et la vie religieuse,* 113; Pourrat, *Christian Spirituality,* 2:271–84; Caiger, "Doctrine and Discipline." See also Ozment, ed., *Jean Gerson;* Kaluza, *Les Querelles doctrinales à Paris.*

14. Massaut, *Josse Clichtove,* 1:255. See also Moody, *Logic of William of Ockham;* Biard, introduction to Ockham, *Somme de logique.*

15. See note 4.

16. Dress, quoted in Ozment, ed., *Jean Gerson,* 3. As mentioned, Gersonian scholars such as André Combes see a renunciation of all nominalist ideas in Gerson in the later part of his career. This study is basically concerned with Gerson's *De mystica theologia,* especially the first part, written in 1402–3, when Gerson's mystical theology, as Oberman explains in *Harvest of Medieval Theology,* could still be considered a "mystical marriage" of nominalism and affective theology.

17. Gerson, *De sensu litterali sacrae scripturae,* in *Œuvres complètes,* 3:338.

18. Ibid., 340.

19. "Quae singularitas, doctorum et doctrinarum, quantum fenestram aperiat ad errores in fide, ad schismata et contentiones in christiana religione, videt qui videt; per eam fit ut affectio depravet intellectum speculativum, quemadmodum per eam intellectus practicus quotidie perturbatur: utrobique enim par est ratio nisi quod in illo vana gloria malum subtilissimum et efficacissimum regnat, in isto brutalis cujusdam dilectionis appetitus magis ad errorem operatur. Hanc subversionis viam notat et removet textus noster, conjungens poenitentiam humilem cum credulitate: Poenitemini, ait, et credite Evangelio." See Gerson, *Contra curiositatem studentium,* in *Œuvres complètes,* 3:239.

20. Gerson, *De mystica theologia,* 1. The *De mystica theologia* of 1408 is actually the combination of two essays, *De mystica theologia speculativa* (1402–3) and *De mystica theologia practica* (1407).

21. Gerson, *De mystica theologia,* 3.

22. Ibid., 73–74.

23. Gerson, *La Montaigne de contemplation,* in *Œuvres complètes* 7:29.

24. "Considerons a cest exemple que l'amour de Dieu fust telle en une personne

qu'elle li feist tant mesprisier le monde comme l'amour mondaine fait oublier Dieu; fust si forte, si ardant et si enracinée dedens le cuer de la personne qu'elle ne peust ou sceust penser ailleurs volentiers et de son gré, qu'elle ne tinst conte de blasme ne de villennye, de persecutions ne mesmement de la mort, pour ceste amour et que tout ce qu'elle verroit ou oroit de ce monde luy samblast uns songe et une fable et un neant au regart de Dieu et de sa gloire." See ibid., 7:29–30.

25. Gerson, *De mystica theologia,* 24.

26. This paragraph is deeply indebted to Ozment, *Homo Spiritualis,* 59–82.

27. "Thus, while both Tauler and Gerson *mutatis mutandis,* conceive the union with God as the point of maximum similitude and intimacy with God, Gerson cautiously removes language which would suggest a substantive union." See ibid., 83. See also Ozment, "Mysticism, Nominalism, and Dissent," 74n.

28. "Dicunt ergo quod talis anima perdit se et esse suum et accipit verum esse divinum. . . . Hanc etiam visus est renovare auctor illius tractatus, cuius titulus est de ornatu spiritualium nuptiarum, cuius initium est: 'Ecce sponsus venit, exite obviam ei.' 'Contra hunc errorem scripsi dudum quamdam epistolam,' licet in aliis scriptis eius hunc errorem correxisse videatur, ponendo quod anima talis semper remanet in esse suo proprio, quod habet in suo genere, sed dicitur tantummodo similitudinarie transformari, sicut amatorum dicimus esse 'cor unum et animam unam': 'quod utique concedimus.'" See Gerson, *De mystica theologia,* 105–6. See also John of Ruysbroeck, *Adornment of the Spiritual Marriage;* Pascoe, *Jean Gerson,* 189. As Combes shows, after 1425 Gerson would change his opinion regarding essentialist mystical union. "Il serait impossible de concevoir rupture plus profonde, discontinuité plus radicale, contradiction plus consciente et plus formelle. Tout ce qu'a vécu et enseigné en ce qui touche à l'essence de la théologie mystique, le Gerson de 1402 à 1425, le Gerson de 1425 à 1429 le condamne et renie. Tout ce que condamnait, comme excessif, dangereux, incompatible avec la saine doctrine, le Chancelier réformateur, le prédicateur de Constance, l'exilé de Melk, le contemplatif lyonnais, le converti de 1425 en découvre soudain le sens exact et s'en rapproche avec une complaisance qui peut aller jusqu'à l'accord complet." See Combes, *La Théologie mystique de Gerson,* 2:671–72.

29. "Dixerunt enim quod anima sic unitur Deo et in ipsum transformatur quemadmodum si gutta aque mittatur in dolium fortis vini: illa namque gutta tunc perdit esse proprium convertiturque totaliter in alienum." See Gerson, *De mystica theologia,* 107. It is noteworthy that many of the analogies that Gerson criticizes are used by Saint Bernard, a mystic whom Gerson quotes extensively. See Ozment, *Jean Gerson,* 87n. See also Bernard of Clairvaux, *St. Bernard on the Song of Songs.*

30. "Huius rei exemplum accipere possumus ex consideratione eorum, que sepe in ipsa sensuali virtute fiunt, in qua videmus tam in nobis quam in brutis, quod quandoque ipsa sensualitas in suis actibus cognitivis permanet sine affectu illorum, que vel audit vel intuetur; sepe tamen ad auditum vel aspectum quorumdam obiectorum ipsa tanto completur affectu, ut iam quasi saliat extra se et tota gestiat, velut si 'equus' potitur 'campo' 'liber' 'aperto.' 'Hoc modo sensualitas aliquando' se 'quasi' non capiens et se deserens, tota nititur in rem desideratam se effundere, se transferre, se unire, ymmo illam penitus quasi introrsus penetrare.

. . . Transferamus hoc exemplum ad vim intelligentie superiorem, considerando qualitatem eius, dum sine affectu in sola cognitione iacet et dum transit in affectum talium qualia contemplatur." See Gerson, *De mystica theologia,* 75.

31. Compare Gerson's mystical union with John of Ruysbroeck's, in which God and human become one. See, for example, John of Ruysbroeck, *Adornment of the Spiritual Marriage,* 122–23: "This makes the lovers melt into each other"; or (ibid., 130): "Now all holiness and all blessedness lie in this: that the spirit is led upwards, through likeness and by means of grace or glory, to rest in the essential unity. For the grace of God is the way by which we must always go, if we would enter into the naked essence in which God gives himself with all His riches."

32. "Introduit, hic et nunc, dans la vie mystique . . . elle réalise la 'theologia' . . . qui est la contemplation de Dieu. En langage moderne, l'une est spéculative, l'autre contemplative." See Henri de Lubac, *L'Exégèse médiévale,* 1:624–25.

33. Gerson, *De mystica theologia,* 72: "Theologia mystica est motio anagogica, hoc est sursum ductiva in Deum, per amorem fervidum et purum."

34. Ibid., 89–93. For another interpretation of anagogy, more typical of Gerson's later views, see Gerson, *Anagogicum de verbo et hymno gloriae* (1428), in *Œuvres complètes,* 8:540–65; and Gerson, *Super cantica canticorum* (1429), in *Œuvres complètes,* 8:565–639. See esp. 576–77 and 581, where Gerson talks about the problem of depicting the "kiss" in the *Song of Songs.* See also 628–39 where Gerson talks about tropology and allegory as opposed to anagogy. See also Katz, "Mystical Speech and Mystical Meaning"; Philips, "Mystic Analogizing and the 'Peculiarly Mystic'"; Cousins, "Bonaventure's Mysticism of Language." See also Harbison, "Visions and Meditations in Early Flemish Painting."

35. Gerson, *De mystica theologia,* 54–55, 208–16.

36. Ibid.

37. Lubac, *L'Exégèse médiévale,* 1:624–25.

38. "Subtilitas metaphysicantium si quaerit reperire in rebus ipsis secundum suum esse reale tale esse quale habent in suo esse objectali, jam non est subtilitas sed stoliditas et vera insania. Quid enim est insania nisi judicare res prout sunt in sola phantasia quod ita sint ad extra, qualiter est in furiosis, phantasticis atque reverisantibus, qui scilicet somniant vigilando dum similitudines rerum pro rebus accipiunt." See Gerson, *De modis significandi,* in *Œuvres complètes,* 9:635.

39. Dupire dates this manuscript (128 C5) after 1498. See Dupire, *Jean Molinet,* 76. All citations from this work are from Molinet, *Roman de la Rose moralisé.* A 1948 dissertation presents the *Roman de la Rose moralisé* in what is called a "critical edition." It does not, however, present a detailed critical apparatus. See Andes, *Le Roman de la Rose moralisé.*

40. The term *moralité* should not mislead the modern reader since, as Jung explains, the term *moralisation,* which became common in the fifteenth century, had the same meaning as the Old French term *allégorie,* which almost always signified *sens chrétien* or *explication chrétienne.* See Jung, *Etudes sur le poème allégorique,* 12.

41. Badel, *Le Roman de la rose,* 162; Tuve, *Allegorical Imagery,* 237. See also Angeli, "Il 'Rude Engin' di Molinet," 22, who claims that extracting the *substantificque moelle* from a profane text is Molinet's aim. See also Joukovsky-Micha,

"La Mythologie," 296; Zumthor, *Le Masque et la lumière*, 85; Huizinga, *Waning of the Middle Ages*, 119; Bourdillon, *Early Editions of the Roman de la Rose*, 162; Dupire, *Jean Molinet*, 79–89; Huot, *Romance of the Rose*, 331n, 315.

42. Molinet, *Roman de la Rose moralisé*, f. 5v: "Il a pleu a vostre treshaulte et noble seigneurie moy commander de reduyre le romant de la rose de rethoricque en prose."

43. See ibid.: "Si puis bien dire avec Ovide: 'Bella mihi video.' Car je me sens desja bersaude de plusieurs menaces/ et apparcoys les engins des mesdisans affutez ensemble les langues serpentines affilees pour dilapider mes ouvrages et debriser les volans de vostre treshumble et poure moulinet se par vostre chevalereux bras et en la splendeur de vostre reflamboyant espee je ne suis secouru et deffendu." The *Ovide moralisé* did provide, however, an obvious precedent. See De Boer, ed., "*Ovide moralisé.*" See also Van 'T Sant, *Le Commentaire de Copenhague.*

44. Molinet, *Roman de la Rose moralisé*, f. 4r. The late fifteenth-century manuscript at the Royal Library in the Hague (128 C5) contains the following *avant-prologue* before the table of contents, a part missing in the 1503 Balsarin edition: "Au tresnoble commandement et pour accomplir le bon plaisir de illustre prince et mon redoubté seigneur. Monseigneur Philippe de Cleves. seigneur de Ravestain fut ce romant de la rose moralisé et translaté de rime en prose. ou sont comprins le prologue. cent et vij chapitres reduis par sens moral de fole amour vicieuse a divine amour vertueuse." I thank Jelle Koopmans for this indication. See Dupire, *Jean Molinet*, 72; Brown, "L'Eveil d'une nouvelle conscience littéraire," 15–35.

45. Angeli, "Il 'Rude Engin' de Molinet," 21, says that "per essere uomo completo, debba giostrare in ben differenti tornei e diventare 'champion des dames,' enseivant le tres plaisant guidon de Venus. Il mezzo fornito dal compiacente rifacitore sarà questa volta la moralizzazione della Rose."

46. Molinet, *Roman de la Rose moralisé*, f. 5v.

47. See ibid., ff. 7r., 10v., 11r., 18r.

48. Ibid., f. 151r.: "Verité est que maistre jehan jarson fort auctorisé en theologie et de tresclere renommée a la requeste faveur daucunes notables dames composa ung petit livre intitulé la reprobacion du romant de la Rose/ mais en ce faisant il sarresta sur le sens litteral sans destouiller la fusée. Et fit ainsi que le petit enfant auquel on donne une grosse noix verde de geauge/ Si tost quil la tient dedans sa main il la porte en sa bouche cuydant que ce soit une pomme et quant il la sent si amere il la rue a ses piedz. Mais se il avait ladvisement de la mettre et oster hors de lescorce et de la coquille et puis la peler il trouveroit le cerneau moult bon et for friant. Le venerable docteur maistre jehan jarson qui nestoit pas enfant/ mais lung des plus grans clercz de tout le monde sarresta seulement a redarguer la verdure de ce romant/ Cest amour folle qui pou dure en detestant paillardise pour lamertume qui se treuve en fin/ et ayma mieulx applicquer la subtillité de son engin en matieres ardues et de plus haulte speculacion que chercher fruit for doulx et savoureux en escaille dure et amere."

49. Gerson also admits that astrology might at one time have been an admirable science but that it has been sullied by impious and erroneous predictions. For Gerson, once again, faith and doctrine are superior to vain speculation. See Gerson, *Trilogium astrologiae theologizatae*, in *Œuvres complètes*, 10:90. See

also Préaud, *Les Astrologues,* 31; Tester, *History of Western Astrology,* 198; Gerson, *Contra Astronomos,* 802.

50. Molinet, *Roman de la Rose moralisé,* ff. 109v.–110r.

51. Nicholas Oresme: "Et samblablement sont faulses les regles speciaux qui sont escriptes pour ceste partie (meterology—'des mutacions de l'air'). Et par ce veons nous communement que de telles mutacions scevent mieulx jugier les mariniers ou les laboureurs des champs que ne font les astronomiciens," in Coopland, *Nicole Oresme and the Astrologers,* 56. See also ibid., 50; "Mon entencion à l'aide de Dieu est moustrer en ce livret, par experience, par auctoritez, par raison humaine, que fole chose, mauvaise, et perilleuse temporelement, est mettre son entente a vouloir savoir ou deviner les aventures et les fortunes avenir, ou les choses occultes, par astrologie, par gromance, par nigromance, ou par quelxconques tielx ars, se on les doit appeller ars, mesmement telle chose est plus perilleuse a personnes d'estat comme sont princes et seigneurs auxquels appartient le gouvernement publique."

52. Oberman's explanation of the notion of contingency is very helpful here: "Contingency is perhaps the best one-word summary of the nominalist program." He goes on to explain how this contingency relates to a hierarchical ontology: "The point is that in the vertical dimension our reality is not the lowest emanation and level in a hierarchy of being which ascends in ever more real steps to the highest reality, God." See Oberman, "Shape of Late Medieval Thought," 13.

53. Molinet, *Roman de la Rose moralisé,* f. 116v.

54. This passage could be interpreted as referring to nominalist soteriology. See Ockham, liber 1, dist. 17, qu. ii, in *Scriptum in librum primum sententiarum,* 3:469–70. This text was cited by the magistrates in Avignon when Ockham was tried for Pelagianism. For modern studies of Ockhamist soteriology, see Courtenay, "Nominalism and Late-Medieval Religion"; Oberman, *Harvest of Medieval Theology*; Ozment, *Age of Reform,* 41–42; Adams, *William of Ockham,* 2:1279–97. For Gerson's soteriology, see Brown, *Pastor and Laity,* 79–115.

55. Molinet, *Roman de la Rose moralisé,* f. 117r. For a discussion of erotic mystical imagery, see McGinn, "Language of Love," 225–26.

56. For a discussion of nature in this debate in Jean de Meung's text, see John Fleming, *Reason and the Lover.*

57. Molinet, *Roman de la Rose moralisé,* f. 27r.

58. Panofsky, *Gothic Architecture.*

2. Molinet's Reversed Analogies

1. The material treated in this chapter is also discussed by Cornilliat in "*Or ne mens.*" Cornilliat treats the figuration of the House of Burgundy in Molinet's *Les Chroniques* and in Molinet's *Chappellet des dames* as a problem of allegorization using Saint Thomas Aquinas as his theoretical model and also concentrates on the "Paradis terrestre" chapter of the *Chroniques.* This study treats this figuration as a problem of analogy and uses Cardinal Cajetan's and Ockham's texts (see *Analogy of Names* and *Ockham,* respectively) as theoretical models and concentrates on Molinet's *Chappellet des dames* rather than the "Paradis terrestre." It is hoped

that these two approaches complement each other and buttress each other's arguments, which are finally somewhat different. See Cornilliat, *"Or ne mens,"* 567–618.

2. Reiss, *Discourse of Modernism,* 140–67.

3. Mondin, *Principle of Analogy;* Anderson, *Bond of Being,* 104–18.

4. Secretan, *L'Analogie,* 7.

5. Ibid., 22. See Plato, *Republic,* 240–45.

6. Secretan, *L'Analogie,* 25. See Aristotle, *Histoire des animaux,* 1:2: "Il existe aussi des animaux dont les parties ne sont pas de même forme et ne diffèrent pas par excès ou par défaut, mais présentent des analogies: c'est le cas si l'on compare l'os à l'arête, l'ongle au sabot, la main à la pince, l'écaille à la plume: car ce que la plume est à l'oiseau, l'écaille l'est au poisson."

7. Cited in Secretan, *L'Analogie,* 31. See also Gilson, *La Philosophie au moyen âge,* 580–91.

8. See Geiger, *La Participation,* 224; Gilson, *La Philosophie,* 525–35; Mondin, *La Filosofia,* 227–29.

9. See Geiger, *La Participation,* 223–26.

10. See ibid., 11, 223–37, 238–58.

11. Gerald B. Phelan, foreword to Anderson, *Bond of Being,* ix; Klubertanz, *St. Thomas Aquinas on Analogy,* 3. See also Mtega, *Analogy and Theological Language in the Summa Contra Gentiles.*

12. Thomas Aquinas, *Summa theologiae,* 2:1a, qu. iv, art. 3, 54–59; see also Anderson, *Bond of Being,* 93–103.

13. See Klubertanz, *St. Thomas Aquinas on Analogy,* 11–12; Secretan, *L'Analogie,* 45–46; Anderson, *Bond of Being,* 104–18.

14. Cajetan, *Analogy of Names,* 9–29; Thomas Aquinas, *Summa contra gentiles,* 78. See Mondin, "Theological Use of Analogy," 466–68; Pinchard, *Métaphysique et sémantique.*

15. Cajetan, *Analogy of Names,* 12–13; Anderson, *Reflections on the Analogy of Being,* 13.

16. *Intrinsic* and *extrinsic* are defined by Cajetan (*Analogy of Names,* 16n) in his commentary to *Summa theologiae,* 1:6, 4 (III–VIII), where he says: "Denomination is twofold. One is intrinsic and the other extrinsic. A denomination is called intrinsic when the form of the denominative [perfection] is in that which is denominated, say, white, quantified, etc.; whereas a denomination is extrinsic if the form of the denominative [perfection] is not in the denominated thing; e.g. located, measured and the like."

17. Cajetan, *Analogy of Names,* 23; Anderson, *Reflections on the Analogy of Being,* 29.

18. Cajetan, *Analogy of Names,* 29.

19. Ibid.; Anderson, *Reflections on the Analogy of Being,* 52.

20. Cajetan, *Analogy of Names,* 57; Anderson, *Reflections on the Analogy of Being,* 52; Klubertanz, *St. Thomas Aquinas on Analogy,* 64–69.

21. Thomas Aquinas, *Summa contra gentiles,* 72; see also Mondin, *St. Thomas Aquinas's Philosophy,* 58–74; Klubertanz, *St. Thomas Aquinas on Analogy,* 51.

22. See Menges, *Concept of Univocity,* 122.

23. See note 4, chap. 1.

24. Leff, *William of Ockham*, 159.

25. Ockham, *Ordinatio*, dist. 11, qu. ix, in *Ockham*, 106–8. See Ghisalberti, *Introduzione a Ockham*, 26–27.

26. Ockham, *Ordinatio*, dist. 11, qu. ix, in *Ockham*, 107.

27. Ghisalberti, *Introduzione a Ockham*, 26–27.

28. Ockham, *Reportatio*, 3, qu. viii, in *Ockham*, 112.

29. See note 6, introduction.

30. Molinet, *Les Faictz et dictz*, 1:101.

31. The terms "Vierge" and "continente" can obviously be understood as resembling each other. Molinet is not making a theological argument, and not every element in his poem can fit into a single theory concerning resemblance and difference. The general gist of this passage does, however, tend toward an emphasis on the difference of the terms of the comparison rather than an emphasis on their likeness. It is also unlikely that Molinet was referring to a Dionysian "dissimilar similitude" in this passage, since its immediate context is one of likeness: the earthly Mary is supposed to be the "propre et vive imaige de la roÿne supernelle." The Pseudo-Dionysian "dissimilar similitude" would accentuate how the two terms were completely unlike. See Pseudo-Dionysius, *On the Heavenly Hierarchy* and *On Mystic Theology*, in *Works of Dionysius the Areopagite*.

32. Molinet, *Les Faictz et Dictz*, 1:123.

33. Molinet, *Les Chroniques (1474–1488)*, 1:529–39. See also Dupire, *Jean Molinet*, 38–60; Huizinga, *Waning of the Middle Ages*, 158; Devaux, "La Fin du Téméraire."

34. See Zumthor, *Le Masque et la lumière*, 213.

35. Molinet, *Chroniques*, 529. See Rothstein, "When Fiction Is Fact," 362. In Biel's 1501 collection of William of Ockham's commentary on the *Sentences*, this sort of comparison between the Holy Trinity and an earthly creature is expressly prohibited: "Secunda conclusio proprie loquendo nulla creatura est vestigium trinitatis." See Biel, *Epitome et collectorium ex Occamo*, bk. 1, dist. 3, qu. ix.

36. Molinet, *Chroniques*, 533.

37. Ibid., 539. Langer, "Jean Molinet," 44, notes: "Les juxtapositions opérées par les textes de Molinet, textes allégoriques, historiques, et poétiques, mènent au rejet d'un ordre du texte qui serait le pur reflet d'un ordre, d'un sens extérieur. Le texte ne réfère pas non plus à un ordre détruit du monde extérieur, il refuse tout simplement la possibilité de voir en lui un reflet quelconque d'un sens, détruit ou non, de l'extérieur."

38. Molinet, *Chroniques*, 533.

3. "Etymologies tant ineptes"

1. Bloch, *Etymologies and Genealogies*, 54.

2. Isidore of Seville, "Etymologia est origo vocabulorum, cum vis verbi vel nominis per interpretationem colligitur," in his *Isidori Hispalensis Episcopi*, 1:19–20. See also Curtius, *European Literature*, 495–500; Zumthor, *Langue, texte, et*

énigme, 144–60; Guiette, "L'Invention étymologique"; Guiraud, "Etymologie et ethymologia."

3. Thomas Aquinas, "Dicendum quod nomina debent proprietatibus rerum respondere," in *Summa theologiae,* 52:146.

4. Philip of Thaon, "Li lunsdis par raisun / Sulunc m'entunciun / Signifiet lumiere," in *Der Computus des Philipp Von Thaün,* 18.

5. "Non autem omnia nomina a veteribus secundum naturam imposita sunt, sed quaedam et secundum placitum, sicut et nos servis et possessionibus interdum secundum quod placet nostrae voluntati nomina damus." See Isidore of Seville, *Isidori Hispalensis Episcopi,* 1:19–20.

6. Aquinas distinguishes between a vocal sound, which is a natural thing, and a name, which is instituted by human beings. Thomas Aquinas, *Aristotle,* 38.

7. "E cumpoz pur cunter / E pur bien esguarder / Les termes et les cles / E les festes anuels." See Philip of Thaon, *Der Computus des Philipp Von Thaün,* 2.

8. Ockham, *Ockham,* 48: "A concept or mental impression signifies naturally whatever it does signify; a spoken or written term, on the other hand, does not signify anything except by free convention."

9. "Ce rappel de l'arbitraire du signe linguistique nous semble aller de soi. Historiquement, il marque pourtant la fin d'une longue tradition, celle du cratylisme médiéval, des preuves par l'étymologie dont on entendait encore des échos au XIIIe siècle et qui est définitivement enterrée par Ockham." Alféri, *Guillaume d'Ockham,* 275.

10. Gerson, *De modis significandi,* in *Œuvres complètes,* 9:633.

11. See Reiss, *Discourse of Modernism,* 41–42.

12. See Foucault, *Les Mots et les choses,* 39.

13. Molinet, *Les Faictz et dictz,* 1:100–126. For different analyses of the *Chappellet des dames,* see Guy, *Histoire de la poésie française;* Rigolot, *Poétique et onomastique,* 27–53.

14. Molinet, *Les Faictz et dictz,* 1:107.

15. Ibid.

16. Foucault, *Les Mots et les choses,* 32–59.

17. For a discussion of attribution of floral virtues in poetry of the late Middle Ages, see Jourdan, "Le Langage amoureux."

18. Molinet, *Les Faictz et dictz,* 1:107–8.

19. See Paracelsus the Great, *Hermetic and Alchemical Writings,* 1:171–94; Ficino, *Three Books on Life,* 249–50.

20. "Four humours corresponding to the four elements (earth, air, fire and water) of Empedocles and Aristotle, determined by their proportions the state of the human organism, its health or its disease: the yellow bile, hot and dry, corresponded to fire; the blood, hot and dry, corresponded to earth; phlegm, cold and wet, corresponded to water. All living beings contained these four humours. The excess of one or another caused ailments." See Opsomer, *Livre des simples médecines,* 17.

21. "There is, therefore, a wonderful virtue and operation in every Herb and Stone, but greater in a Star, beyond which, even from the governing Intelligences every thing receiveth and obtains many things for itself, especially from the Su-

preme Cause, with whom all things do mutually and exactly correspond, agreeing harmonious consent." Agrippa, *Three Books of Occult Philosophy,* 67–69.

22. Ibid., 57.

23. Larkey, ed., *An Herball,* 23.

24. Opsomer, *Livre des simples médecines,* 134.

25. Gerard, *Leaves from Gerard's Herball,* 14–15.

26. For the values attributed to these herbs, see De Vriend, *Old English Herbarium,* 111 (ancollye), 195 (jennette), 215 (englentier); Apuleius Barbarus, *Herbarium,* 15–16, 63 (ancollye).

27. See Rufinus, *Herbal of Rufinus,* 270–273.

28. Bernardino de' Busti, *Mariale* (1493).

29. Ibid., pt. 3, sermon 1, I:ii–v. See Charland, *Artes praedicandi.* The rhetorical, as opposed to epistemological nature of etymology is noted as early as Evrard L'Allemand's *Laborintus,* in which *interpretatio* is described as "aliquando fit per litteras, aliquando per syllabas, aliquando per dictiones. In litteris exemplum: 'Mors rapuit Heinricum'; prolongamus: 'Meta omnium rerum sensibilium rapuit Heinricum,'" in Faral, *Les Arts poétiques,* 65.

30. Bernardino de' Busti, *Mariale,* sermon 1, I:ii: "Nomen virginis Maria. Luce i."

31. He begins "Licet propria nomina ponantur et mutentur pro libito proprie voluntatis" but very quickly passes on to the other side of the question: "Tamen alibi dicitur quam expressio proprii nominis multum operatur." Ibid.

32. "Pro cuius declaratione est sciendum quam ut inquit beatus Thomas in .iii. parte summe qu. xxxvii. art. ii. nomina debent proprietatibus rerum correspondere"; and "Item solet dici quam magnum est privilegium vocari bono nomine." Ibid.

33. The values that Bernardino assigns to his stones are close to those found in medieval lapidaries. He differs from Molinet, who changes the values traditionally associated with flowers in medieval and Renaissance herbals.

34. "Mihi autem videtur quo nimis sunt arctati, qui se nesciunt aliter dilatare. Iste autem modus neque fundatur super ethymologiam, nec super derivationem aut compositionem nominis, aut aliquid [rationis] habet pro fundamento."See Waleys, *De modo componendi sermones,* in Charland, *Artes praedicandi,* 396.

35. Mombaer, *Rosetum exercitiorum spiritualium et sacrarum* (1494); see also Debongnie, *Jean Mombaer de Bruxelles;* Hyma, *Christian Renaissance.*

36. Mombaer, *Rosetum exercitiorum spiritualium* (1510). For a more understandable version of the *Rosetum,* see Mombaer, *Rosetum exercitiorum spiritualium* (1620).

37. "Et in mariali suo Bernardinus de Busto, varias huius tanti nominis etymologizationes litterales ponit. Primo secundum proprietates quinque lapidum pretiosorum quorum nomina incipiunt a litteris, unde contexitur Mariae nomen." Mombaer, *Rosetum exercitiorum spiritualium* (1620), 647.

38. Ibid., 644.

39. This etymology is common throughout the Middle Ages and dates back, at least, to the Church Fathers. See *Dictionnaire de la Bible,* 4:774–75; Isidore of Seville, *Isidori Hispalensis Episcopi,* bk. 7, x.

40. "Nam (ut scribit doctissi. ille Laurentius de Valla, in Correctorio suo novi testamenti) sibi videtur nomen Matris Domini atque aliarum, quae Maria nuncupantur, esse diversum. Caeterarum enim in 'a,' semper exiit in Graeca veritate, ut Maria Magdelenae, Maria Jacobi, etc. At Matris Domini in 'am,' terminatur, termino finali differens, et etiam accentu, qui acuto in fine, caeterarum in penultima: Dicitur enim Mariam etiam in nominativo. Unde Lucas 'nomen Virginis Mariam.' Item, dixit autem Mariam, Ecce ancilla, etc. Unde facile (ait) colligitur, non nihil fuisse differens nomen Matris Domini, atque aliarum in originali, licet in latino nostro (ut pluria alia) confundantur." Mombaer, *Rosetum exercitiorum spiritualium* (1620), 644. See also *Dictionnaire de la Bible*, 4:774, for a discussion of the Greek spelling of Mary's name in the New Testament.

41. "Quomodo autem nec in litteris ipsis mysterio caret, qui scire volet Io. Dominicum, et Dominum Antonium, qui eum allegat, videat. Aiunt enim quod in litteris Haebraicis, quibus nomen ipsum in Evangelio Matthaei, et aliis passibus conscribitur, secretum mysterium designatur, quia per 'mem clausum' in principio, conscribitur, quod nusquam reperitur, quoniam 'mem clausum' nusquam in principio sed in fine semper ponitur dictionis, iuxta Hebreorum grammaticam." Mombaer, *Rosetum exercitiorum spiritualium* (1620), 644. Thanks to Moshe Sluhovsky and Ora Avni for their help in deciphering this passage.

42. Ibid.

43. "Sunt etenim litterae eorum quemadmodum, et Graecorum, numerales. Et longa differentia est numeri signati per 'Mem apertum,' et 'mem clausum;' 'mem' etenim apertum, signat in numero quadraginta: 'mem' vero clausum notat sexcenta." Ibid., 645.

44. Ibid.

45. "Sat sit gravium virorum dicta allegasse nobis, et materiam inquirendae veritatis reliquisse studiosis. Clarum et certum est, nomen istud praegnare mirandis, et abditis mysteriis: Ita, ut ei dici potest, admirabile est nomen tuum et stupendium nimis." Ibid.

46. Rabelais, *Gargantua*, 293.

47. Ibid, 67.

4. Jean Lemaire de Belges

1. Guy's analysis of Lemaire is, as usual, exceptional in its vociferousness and sense of *parti-pris*. He says of Lemaire that "voici, à n'en pas douter, le plus grand des rhétoriqueurs, le seul grand, le seul presque en qui l'on trouve une nature d'artiste, une forte personnalité. Il a, du vrai poète, les dévorantes et fécondes inquiétudes. Tandis que ses confrères ne discutent de rien, et végètent placidement parmi les dogmes qu'ils croient intangibles, il n'accepte pas, lui, tout le 'credo' du moyen âge." Guy, *Histoire de la poésie française*, 174–75. For an analysis of how Lemaire's position as *indiciaire* affected his poetics, see Kritzman, "Rhetoric of Dissimulation."

2. See Jodogne, *Jean Lemaire de Belges*, 75–78; Frappier, introduction to Lemaire, *La Concorde des deux langages*, 7. Thibaut says Lemaire was Molinet's nephew but distinguishes Lemaire from other Rhétoriqueurs: "Tandis que les

autres poètes français étaient de plus en plus entraînés vers les grands 'Rhétoric-queurs,' il se détacha au contraire chaque jour davantage de l'école bourguignonne. Il renonça à ces puérilités laborieuses et pédantesques, et à ces combinaisons de syllabes qui n'assuraient à leurs auteurs que le frivole mérite de la difficulté vaincue." See Thibaut, *Marguerite d'Autriche,* 236.

3. Jodogne, *Jean Lemaire de Belges,* 76–77.

4. Lemaire, *Œuvres de Jean Lemaire de Belges,* 3:172.

5. See Munn, *Contribution to the Study of Jean Lemaire de Belges,* 5–7; Berrong, "Jean Lemaire de Belges."

6. Rabelais, *Pantagruel,* 164.

7. Lemaire, *Œuvres de Jean Lemaire de Belges,* 3:231–359, 361–409. See Britnell, "Jean Lemaire de Belges and Prophecy."

8. Rabelais, *Le Tiers Livre.* The editor, Michael Screech, notes: "Aucuns veulent y voir une allusion à Guillaume Crétin; d'autres dont Lefranc, à Jean Lemaire de Belges" (385).

9. See Marichal, "*Quart Livre*: commentaires," 185–86; Cave, "Reading Rabelais." Munn, *Contribution to the Study of Jean Lemaire de Belges,* 18, remarks on the relation of Lemaire and Rabelais: "The distinctive mark of Lemaire's literary gift is the intensity of sensation. Herein he differs markedly from two near contemporaries, Marot and Rabelais, in whose work the five senses play an essential rôle. Marot's voluptuousness was urbane, dilettante, entirely painless. . . . Rabelais's sensuousness, on the contrary, was no by-play of the intellect. He yielded himself bodily and without reserve to the process of expression, with positive relish for the totality of experience. . . . Lemaire, in contrast to both these men, was a Romantic." See also, for influence of the *Concorde* on Ronsard, Joukovsky-Micha, "Ronsard et 'La Concorde des deux langages.'"

10. Frappier sees Lemaire as being unaware of any difference between Middle Ages and Renaissance: "Jean Lemaire . . . ne semble pas avoir senti de rupture entre ce que nous appelons le Moyen Age et ce que nous appelons la Renaissance." See Frappier, "L'Humanisme de Jean Lemaire de Belges," 290.

11. Zumthor, *Le Masque et la lumière,* 213.

12. Panofsky, *Early Netherlandish Painting,* 8.

13. "Mais est-ce bien tout ce qu'il doit à l'Italie? N'en a-t-il pas subi 'l'influence secrète,' ce genre d'action qu'on n'aperçoit pas directement dans des lignes écrites. Les conjectures sur ce point sont évidemment permises." Doutrepont, *Jean Lemaire de Belges,* 296. Doutrepont also says that Lemaire "n'est pas un descendant du Moyen Age parce qu'il en recueille la succession" (185).

14. Jodogne, *Jean Lemaire de Belges,* ix–xi, 60; see Frappier's introduction to Lemaire, *La Concorde des deux langages,* xxiii; and Becker, *Jean Lemaire,* 11. It is, perhaps, of some importance that Lemaire spent so little time in Malines in the North and seemed to prefer the amenities of the Lyonnais. See Lemaire, *Concorde des deux langages,* xvii; and Rigolot, *Poétique et onomastique,* 47–50, on Lyons and Lemaire. See Festugière, *La Philosophie de l'amour de Marsile Ficin,* for an analysis of Ficino's influence in France. Festugière does not see Lemaire as being greatly influenced by Ficino: "Mais, si Lemaire de Belges a lu, parmi les auteurs italiens de la Renaissance, quelques écrivains platoniciens, dont Ficin et Cristo-

foro Landino, il en a peu subi l'influence, sauf dans le sens très général de l'exaltation de la beauté et de l'amour" (77).

15. For analysis of Lemaire's use of magic and the occult, see Kem, "Magic and Prophecy"; see also Griffin, "Jean Lemaire's Epic Contraption."

16. Regnault, *Le Petit Livret sommaire*. See also Jodogne, *Jean Lemaire de Belges*, 146–58; Bergweiler, *Die Allegorie im Werk von Jean Lemaire de Belges*, 107–17; Jodogne, "Un recueil poétique de Jean Lemaire de Belges," 179–210.

17. Jodogne, "Un recueil poétique de Jean Lemaire de Belges," 181. See Hornik's critical edition of Lemaire, *Le Temple d'honneur et de vertus*, 7–40, for more on this poem; and Brown, *Les Grands Rhétoriqueurs*, 103–23, esp. 117–23; as well as Brown, "Confrontation between Printer and Author in Early Sixteenth-Century France."

18. "Rappelons d'autre part que le Cantique était à l'époque l'une des principales sources de méditation des mystiques français et flamands. Lemaire aurait-il lui-même été touché par le courant de mysticisme qui pénétra dans les milieux intellectuels à la fin du XVe siècle?" Jodogne, *Jean Lemaire de Belges*, 152.

19. Jodogne, "Un recueil poétique de Jean Lemaire de Belges," 205.

20. For an analysis of these Marian poems, see Rigolot, "La Figure de la lettre," 55–59.

21. Jodogne, *Jean Lemaire de Belges*, 152.

22. Guy, *Histoire de la poésie française*, 177. See also Doutrepont, *Jean Lemaire de Belges et la Renaissance*, 277: "On est certainement en droit de penser que Lemaire avait appris à connaître l'Italie et à l'apprécier, dès son premier séjour à Lyon." See also Frappier, "La Cour de Malines," 143; and Marlier, *Erasme et la peinture flamande*, 53–61.

23. See Frappier, "L'Humanisme de Jean Lemaire de Belges," 274.

24. *Couronne*, 42, 45. See Lemaire, *Œuvres de Jean Lemaire de Belges*, vol. 4. See also Jodogne, *Jean Lemaire de Belges*, 222: "Par cette matérialisation du symbole . . . il renverse la conception de l'œuvre poétique." I also examined the 1549 edition of Lemaire, *Œuvres*, for variations. This poem was never published during Lemaire's lifetime; see Dora Yabsley, introduction to Lemaire, *La Plainte du désiré*.

25. For an analysis of the word *italique* in Lemaire, see Wolf, "Un Problème de première datation"; also see Humpers, *Etude sur la langue de Jean Lemaire de Belges*, 131.

26. As Frappier notes (introduction to Lemaire, *La Concorde des deux langages*, xii–xiii), little is actually said of Philibert, and the poet quickly turns to the allegorical glorification of Margaret.

27. See Kem, "Allegorical Images in the Cardinal Virtue Prudence," 19–31.

28. See Griffin, "Lemaire's 'Couronne Margaritique,'" 288.

29. *Couronne*, 57. See Lemaire, *Œuvres de Jean Lemaire de Belges*, vol. 4.

30. "Prima: nomen circuli mutabile est: potest enim usu linguae variato aliter appellari. Si est ita, descriptio quoque mutabilis est, quae componitur ex nominibus. Idolum quoque mutabile: potest enim ligneus circulus destrui, et qui pictus autem aboleri. Formula quoque ex eo mutabilis, quod ex potentia sive habitu migrat in actum deque actu rursus in habitum. Illud autem quod per scientiam cir-

culi comprehenditur, est penitus immutabile, quoniam et universale est, et non potest aliter se habere. Quapropter idea immutabili opus est ad rationem circuli immutabilem comprehendendam." See Ficino, *Teologia platonica,* 2:156. Collins, *Secular Is Sacred,* 49, describes the Ficinian understanding of the essential nature of forms: "Being, then, belongs to a thing because of its form; but it belongs to the form in virtue of itself as rotundity belongs to the circle. A circle by its very nature is round. No condition outside the circle itself is necessary to establish its rotundity. Wood, on the other hand, is round not because it is wood, but because an artisan has imposed upon it a circular figure, and rotundity necessarily belongs to such a figure." See also Bergweiler, *Die Allegorie im Werk von Jean Lemaire de Belges,* 182–83.

31. See Koenigsberger, *Renaissance Man and Creative Thinking,* 227: "By contrast the religious and Platonic currents that conveyed the analogy between the whole and the parts of nature to Renaissance men were, at least potentially, man-glorifying currents. For, in this line of thought, man was esteemed as one who—even in his base terrestrial condition—shared a part of the qualities of divine mind and spirit."

32. Lemaire also writes frequently about etymology in the *Illustrations de Gaule et singularitéz de Troye.* See Lemaire, *Œuvres de Jean Lemaire de Belges,* 1:133, 272, 281, 287.

33. *Couronne,* 58. See Lemaire, *Œuvres de Jean Lemaire de Belges,* vol. 4.

34. See Copenhaver, *Symphorien Champier,* 34, for a discussion of the "cognitive validity" of occultism in sixteenth-century France: "The occultist tradition was still intellectually respectable; it possessed what the sociologists of knowledge call 'cognitive validity.' In fact, it seems that the validity and authority of occultism grew stronger in the Renaissance, thanks to the attention which Marsilio Ficino and Pico della Mirandola gave to astrology, Cabala, the 'Hermetica,' magic and other species of occultism."

35. *Couronne,* 63. See Lemaire, *Œuvres de Jean Lemaire de Belges,* vol. 4.

36. Ibid., 58.

37. Ibid., 66.

38. "Contra debilitatem et syncopim ex medicina vel fluxu ventris vel sanguinis et contra cardiacam passionem in febribus detur pulvis margaritarum cum zucaro rosaceo." See Rufinus, *Herbal of Rufinus,* 181.

39. Evans and Serjeantson, *English Mediaeval Lapidaries,* 108.

40. Agrippa, *Three Books of Occult Philosophy,* 70.

41. *Couronne,* 76. See Lemaire, *Œuvres de Jean Lemaire de Belges,* vol. 4.

42. *Couronne,* 79. See ibid.

43. See Jenkins, *Artful Eloquence,* 37. See also Faral, *Les Arts poétiques,* 61–66.

44. *Couronne,* 159–60. See Lemaire, *Œuvres de Jean Lemaire de Belges,* vol. 4.

45. "In speciei naturalis, ceu pulchritudinis, cognitione, primo quidem descriptionem pulchritudinis aliquam singulis rebus pulchris communem excogitamus. Addimus statim proprietates aliquas pulchritudinis a descriptione deductas. Has notiones forsitan concedemus posse per formulam pulchritudinis menti innatam

excogitari. Sed quando in hac ipsa consideratione diutius immoramur, invenimus eam naturam pulchritudinis quam definivimus, quia mera sit, esse infinitam, et quia infinita sit, esse Deum." See Ficino, *Teologia platonica,* 2:158–60.

46. "Là où il est d'usage de souligner l'infirmité des comparaisons, Ficin, fidèle aux croyances hermétiques, insiste au contraire sur la valeur singulière. Même quand elle n'a pas cette saveur quasi magique, l'image semble toujours pour Ficin plus qu'un ornement." Chastel, *Marsile Ficin et l'art,* 46–47.

47. Lemaire was put in charge of the construction of the Church of Brou by Margaret. His choice of alabaster for this tomb was responsible for his leaving the court of Burgundy. See "Letter from Lemaire to Margaret," Nov. 20, 1510, in Lemaire, *Œuvres de Jean Lemaire de Belges,* 4:396–413; see also Lemaire, *Jean Lemaire de Belges, indiciaire de Marguerite d'Autriche et Jean Perreal,* 6.

48. "Les tombeaux de Brou et les deux cents statues qui peuplent l'église elle-même représentent donc une période de transition . . . c'est la période comprise entre le vieux style gothique et le style de l'âge nouveau." Thibaut, *Marguerite d'Autriche,* 80–81.

49. The relationship between the *Couronne* and this tomb gave rise in 1941 in Belgium to two rather curious articles. The first, by Lemoine, "Autour du tombeau de Philibert le Beau à Brou," sees the *Couronne* as a literal description of Philibert's tomb: "Résumons notre point de vue: Dans la *Couronne Margaritique* nous sommes en présence d'un texte analysant un projet si minutieusement que nous ne pourrons plus désormais avoir une minute d'hésitation sur ses éléments: ce sont ceux même du tombeau de Philibert" (44). The second article, a response by Boom, "A propos du tombeau de Philibert de Savoie," notes: "Si donc, je me rallie pleinement à la première partie de la conclusion de M. Lemoine: 'Lemaire a simplement pris la plume, pour traduire à sa manière, la pensée de la princesse' je ne puis que rejeter la seconde partie de la phrase 'et la réalisation plastique de Perréal'" (227).

50. See Frappier, introduction to Lemaire, *La Concorde des deux langages,* ix; and Guy, *Histoire de la poésie française,* 177.

51. See Françoise Charpentier, preface to Scève, *Délie,* 14–15: "La langue et la poétique de Scève reflètent encore une autre tradition, moins ouvertement présente dans la culture lyonnaise, et dont il fera un usage très personnel: c'est la Grande Rhétorique encore toute proche. Dans son lexique notamment, mais aussi dans certains procédés, jeux verbaux, figures, allégories, on retrouve sans peine la trace de cette tradition; quand Scève veut archaïser, il se contente souvent de donner à un mot toujours en usage une acception en voie de disparition, qu'il a lue chez Gringore ou Jean Lemaire—Jean Lemaire de Belges, lui surtout, à la frontière exacte de la Rhétorique et de la toute jeune Renaissance, probablement l'une de ses influences importantes, peut-être insuffisamment signalée."

52. See Calin, "Jean Lemaire de Belges."

53. Lemaire, *La Concorde du genre humain,* 81n.

54. Ibid., 52.

55. Ficino, *Commentary,* 184. See also, Fletcher, *Allegory,* 25–69.

56. Lemaire, *La Concorde du genre humain,* 63.

57. Ficino's explanation of the "heavenly and clear wrap" applies to souls be-

fore they become human. As such, it does not apply to daemons. The image, both in Ficino and in Lemaire, does indicate a more pure form of being than that of human imperfection. It is also intertwined in Ficino's explanation of daemonic descent to human existence. See Ficino, *Commentary*, 186.

58. Brown remarks on the strong tie that existed between politics and poetic creation in Lemaire's poem. See her "Rise of Literary Consciousness," 64.

59. Frappier, introduction to Lemaire, *La Concorde des deux langages,* xxiv, lxiv. See also Bergweiler, *Die Allegorie im Werk von Jean Lemaire de Belges*, 199–229; Becker, *Jean Lemaire,* 174–94; Jodogne, *Jean Lemaire de Belges,* 443–462; Lemaire, *Jean Lemaire de Belges (um 1473–1515) Dichtungen,* 77–110.

60. Jodogne, *Jean Lemaire de Belges,* 443; Frappier, introduction to Lemaire, *La Concorde des deux langages,* xxxvi; Bergweiler, *Die Allegorie im Werk von Jean Lemaire de Belges,* 200; Brown, "Jean Lemaire's *La Concorde des deux langages.*"

61. Frappier, introduction to Lemaire, *La Concorde des deux langages,* xxv; see also Fenoaltea, "Doing It with Mirrors."

62. See Jodogne, *Jean Lemaire de Belges,* 112.

63. See Griffin, "*La Concorde des deux langages*"; Griffin, "Cosmic Metaphor in *La Concorde des deux langages.*"

64. During the years 1509–11, Lemaire's correspondence with Margaret, when he was in charge of the construction of the church she was building at Brou in Bourg-en-Bresse, offers proof of the increasing disfavor in which the administrators at court in Malines viewed him. See Lemaire, *Œuvres de Jean Lemaire de Belges,* 4:396–426.

65. See Jodogne, "L'Orientation culturelle de Jean Lemaire de Belges," esp. 101–2. Champier also wrote his *Le Triumphe du tres chrestien roy de France Loys XII* in Latin, French, and Italian. Giovanna Trisolini, the editor of that book, says "Le but polémique est ici évident: en opposant la tradition théologale française à l'éloquence et à la rhétorique des Italiens, en insistant sur la persistance de cette tradition, l'auteur ne fait que souligner la suprématie culturelle nationale en opposition aux prétentions des humanistes italiens." See foreword to Champier, *Le Triumphe,* 9. See also Jenkins, *Artful Eloquence,* 48.

66. Ficino, *Commentary,* 130.

67. For a discussion of this and other temples in Lemaire's poetry, see Richter, "Image of the Temple."

68. Lemaire, *La Concorde des deux langages,* 23.

69. Ficino, *Commentary,* 128.

70. Ibid., 155.

71. Lemaire, *La Concorde des deux langages,* 34.

72. As explained first by Marichal, "*Quart Livre:* commentaires," 185.

73. Lemaire, *La Concorde des deux langages,* 37.

74. Montaigne, *De l'institution des enfants,* in *Essais,* 1:161.

75. Lemaire, *La Concorde des deux langages,* 12.

76. See Frappier, introduction to ibid., xxxi. Marcel Françon believes the Temple of Venus is modeled after the Cathedral of Saint John in Lyons. See Françon's introduction to Lemaire, *La Concorde des deux langages et les Epîtres de l'amant*

vert. See also Bergweiler, *Die Allegorie im Werk von Jean Lemaire de Belges,* 205.

77. Lemaire, *La Concorde des deux langages,* 39.

78. Ibid., 44. Whether one is to understand "contemplation" or "endormiz" as governing the nature of Labeur Historien's apparition is, perhaps, not essential, as both contemplation and dreams in a Ficinian context effect the same liberation from the bonds of the body. See Festugière, *La Philosophie de l'amour de Marsile Ficin,* 23: "Ficin croyait à la théorie platonicienne du songe, à savoir que l'esprit, libéré par le sommeil des chaînes corporelles, peut voir, comme le dit Cicéron, 'ea, quae permixtus cum corpore videre non potest.' (*De Div.* I, 129); le *Songe* enfin, parce que le sentiment de la vanité des choses terrestres et l'aspiration vers la Vérité, vers la Béatitude célestes qui font la marque de cet ouvrage, correspondaient merveilleusement au tempérament mélancolique de Ficin, et à son désir ardent d'atteindre à une vie plus belle."

79. Lemaire, *La Concorde des deux langages,* 44–45.

80. Ibid., 45–46; see Kem, "Allegorical Images," 177–85.

81. Lemaire, *La Concorde des deux langages,* 45–46.

82. Simone sees a direct relationship between Lemaire's superiority as a poet vis-à-vis the other *rhétoriqueurs* and his search for inspiration: "In quella poesia mancata [the *rhéthoriqueurs'*] ultimo raffinamento scolastico e pedantesco di una versificatoria alla ricerca dell'ispirazione, un poeta poteva ritrovare se stesso, cioè il suo cuore e la sua fantasia. Il poeta atteso fu Jean Lemaire de Belges." See Simone, *Umanesimo, Rinascimento, Barocco in Francia,* 192.

83. If Lemaire was indeed influenced by Ficino it is not unusual for his poetry to reflect a more Thomistic ontology. The relationship between Ficino and Aquinas is complex and well documented. See Kristeller, *Le Thomisme et la pensée italienne de la renaissance;* Collins, *Secular Is Sacred;* Gilson, "Marsile Ficin et le Contra Gentiles."

5. From *ius gentium* to *Gaster*

1. See Langer, "Friendship and the Adversarial Rhetoric."

2. For a discussion of "presence" in the writing of the French Renaissance, see Defaux, *Marot, Rabelais, Montaigne.*

3. Saulnier, *Rabelais II,* 13.

4. See Defaux, *Pantagruel et les sophistes,* 156–64.

5. Rabelais, *Pantagruel,* 59.

6 Defaux, *Pantagruel et les sophistes,* 95–96.

7. See ibid.: "Le savoir s'embesogne tant après les 'mots' qu'il en oublie les 'choses.' L'univers verbal acquiert ainsi sa propre autonomie, interposant ses miroitements trompeurs et ses cliquetis de mots vides entre l'esprit et l'univers réel." See also Berrong, "Non est solum Sophista quis loquitur."

8. Defaux, *Pantagruel et les sophistes,* 97: "La vérité devient simple affaire de technique, de maîtrise d'un art de l'illusion: elle se réduit à son apparence." See also Demerson, *Rabelais,* 71; Duval, *Design of Rabelais's Pantagruel,* 53–62.

9. Rabelais, *Pantagruel,* 31–35.

10. Ibid., 72.

11. Thaumaste wants to debate "par signes seulement, sans parler: car les 'materies' sont tant ardues, que les parolles humaines ne seroient suffisantes à les explicquer à mon plaisir." See ibid., 104.

12. Defaux, *Pantagruel et les sophistes*, 152.

13. Rabelais, *Pantagruel*, 111.

14. See Gilson, *Les Idées et les lettres*, 215: "On comprend dès lors ce qui faisait rire les lecteurs de Rabelais: cette Chimère qui bourdonne dans le vide ne se nourrit que d'abstractions d'abstractions; elle ne mange ni les choses, ni même leurs idées, mais des idées des idées."

15. Defaux, *Pantagruel et les sophistes*, 95–96.

16. Beaujour, *Le Jeu de Rabelais*, 160, like many critics, sees these chapters as attacking a medieval belief in natural language: "Les chapitres consacrés aux couleurs et livrées de Gargantua visent, à travers les signes, le système médiéval de la loi naturelle, et toute la méthode scolastique. Critique radicale des façons de signifier périmées. Tout le Moyen Age est en cause." Screech, "Emblems and Colours," on the other hand, shows how Rabelais, in fact, defends that natural language. See Defaux, "Rabelais et son masque comique." See also Conley, *Graphic Unconscious*, 41–69.

17. Rabelais, *Gargantua*, 66, 67.

18. Ibid., 67.

19. See Agrippa, *Three Books of Occult Philosophy*.

20. Rabelais, *Gargantua*, 71.

21. Ibid., 58, 59. See Defaux, *Pantagruel et les sophistes*, 149: "Par ce discours polémique, Pantagruel devient définitivement le porte-parole de l'Humanisme et l'adversaire des Sophistes, 'l'invincible champion de la Vérité.'"

22. See Plattard, *L'Etat présent des études rabelaisiennes*, 19: "Le langage technique de cette philosophie se glissait en son livre. Les cadres et les méthodes de cette discipline s'imposeront à son esprit. C'est à la tradition scolastique, qui faisait de l'argumentation l'exercice scolaire par excellence et l'épreuve décisive du savoir, qu'il devra la virtuosité de sa dialectique, peut-être son goût du paradoxe et sa joie malicieuse à humilier la raison ou le bon sens par le raisonnement."

23. Rabelais, *Pantagruel*, 65, 93.

24. Rabelais, *Gargantua*, 293.

25. Rigolot, "Cratylisme et Pantagruélisme," 132: "En condamnant l'emploi fortuit du rébus dans tout emblème, dans tout texte sacré, Rabelais proscrit l'autonomie du signe, source de mensonge et de tromperie; il affirme, en bon Pantagruéliste, son 'mespris des choses fortuites.' Mais en recourant aux jeux de mots circonstanciés, dans les *passages insignes* du texte, il nous invite à participer à une vision poétique du monde, folle et sage à la fois, où l'alliance contingente des mots (consonnance) cautionne l'alliance nécessaire, parce qu'universellement admise, des choses (concordance)."

26. Screech, *L'Evangélisme de Rabelais*, 18.

27. Ozment, *Age of Reform*, 235.

28. Undoubtedly, Rabelais, like most humanists, overstates the Pelagianism of the scholastics. The vehemence of Rabelais' attack on the voluntarism of the *caphards* should be understood as part of the polemic between the early humanists

and the scholastics, who represented ignorance of the Gothic shadows. In fact, as will shortly be seen, these differences regarding the question of free will between evangelical humanists and the scholastics was not always so great. See Langer, *Divine and Poetic Freedom*, 53–56, 71–83, esp. 126–53; see also Adams, *William of Ockham*, 2:1279–97.

29. Rabelais, *Pantagruel*, 145–46. See Demerson, *Rabelais*, 83: "Comme les Luthériens, les Géants enseignent à l'homme qu'il ne doit pas avoir la présomption de se confier en ses propres forces et s'appuyer sur ses mérites pour son salut, mais s'en remettre à Dieu seul; c'est le message solennel que Pantagruel confie à son prisonnier: 'mets tout ton espoir.'"

30. See Rapp and Watson, *Luther and Erasmus*, 141.

31. "Tellement que nul peché ne leur est imputé. Laquelle foy povons obtenir par seul don de dieu: Par grace (dit sainct Paul) estes sauvez par foy, et non de vous. Car c'est ung don de dieu, non des œuvres, affin que nul ne se glorifie." See "Breve instruction pour deuement lire l'escripture saincte," in Lefèvre d'Etaples, *The Prefatory Epistles*, 510–11. See also Greene, *Rabelais*, 54: "On the supreme doctrinal issue—justification by faith alone or by works—he never took a clear stand. But he admired the Evangelicals chiefly for the enterprise revealed in their very name."

32. See Ozment, *Age of Reform*, 234.

33. See Telle, "A propos de la lettre de Gargantua," 217–18: "Le médecin fit sienne cette philosophie qui découvrait son energie dynamique dans cette constatation pessimiste commune à tous les réformateurs, au départ: l'homme demeure toujours dans l'impossibilité d'atteindre la perfection, parce qu'il n'est pas fait pour l'atteindre. Il ne doit pas imiter le Christ, mais l'admirer en suivant son exemple; il ne vise pas au Christ, il tend vers Lui."

34. Rabelais, *Pantagruel*, 153.

35. Erasmus, *Praise of Folly*, 90.

36. See O'Rourke-Boyle, *Christening Pagan Mysteries*, 17–18: "There is no real tolerance in Erasmus's evangelical humanism for the learning of even the best scholastics, for, although they too would understand theology as 'sacra pagina,' they interpret the text by philosophical method, which he judges superseded."

37. See Ozment, *Age of Reform*, 295: "The confrontation with Luther brought about a shift in Erasmus's theology from a traditional Augustinian-Thomist position, which gave God's grace clear priority in salvation, to the semi-Pelagianism of late medieval Ockhamism, which applied free will directly to man's salvation."

38. Erasmus, *On the Freedom of the Will*, in Rapp and Watson, *Luther and Erasmus*, 96.

39. Rabelais, *Quart Livre*, 152. See also Frame, *François Rabelais*, 66–67.

40. Calvin, *Traité des scandales*, 140–41; see also Marichal, introduction to Rabelais, *Quart Livre*, xiv. Febvre analyzes and refutes Calvin's charge of atheism in his *Le problème de l'incroyance*.

41. Cited in introduction to Rabelais, *Quart Livre*, xiii–xiv.

42. See Marichal, "L'Attitude de Rabelais," 186: "Rabelais semble donc, en 1546, brûler ce qu'il avait adoré en 1525."

43. Rabelais, *Quart Livre*, 141.

44. Ibid., 27.

45. Krailsheimer, *Rabelais and the Franciscans*, 216, would disagree: "knowledge in the last analysis is for Rabelais a question of authority more than of experience." See also Cave, *Cornucopian Text*, 204: "If the tautology embodied by Panurge (his 'philautia') was made evident in his dialogue with topical manifestations of 'doctrina,' the fourth book breaks out of the 'circle of learning' and proposes an open-ended confrontation with 'experientia.'"

46. Rabelais, *Quart Livre*, 128.

47. See Glauser, *Rabelais créateur*, 239: "Ce voyage est fait d'étapes dans les îles qui sont chaque fois le lieu d'une manie, le refuge de personnages rendus ridicules par une idée qui détermine les traits de leur corps, de leur costume, de leurs discours. Les îles sont une série d'huis-clos; elles abritent et encouragent un défaut; îles mentales qui croient toutes se suffire à elles-mêmes et c'est ce qui les empêche d'être vraiment vivantes."

48. See Screech, *L'Evangélisme de Rabelais*, 42.

49. Rabelais, *Pantagruel*, 153; Rabelais, *Le Quart Livre*, 122.

50. See Screech, *L'Evangélisme de Rabelais*, 45: "La Tempête du *Quart Livre*, en se moquant du culte des saints, des pèlerinages et des mots pieux qu'on exploite au moment du danger, comme des charmes magiques, s'oppose ouvertement aux 'superstitions papistes'; mais les 'mathéologiens' qu'elle attaque en 1552 comprennent aussi les partisans de Calvin,—non pas que Calvin se fût facilement reconnu sous ce nom, qui s'appliquait normalement aux suppôts de la Sorbonne."

51. See Chappell, *The Enigma of Rabelais*, 147: "There is a subtly conveyed impression that the travellers wholly fail to sympathize with the two main creeds; their fellowship with the old Macrobe is indeed far closer."

52. See Weinberg, "Comic and Religious Elements," 133: "The nine ships of monks are sailing to the council of 'Chesil' (and consensus has it that Chesil meant Trent); 'chesil' in Hebrew means 'fool,' or 'the baleful storm,' yet another evil omen."

53. Rabelais, *Quart Livre*, 104.

54. See Lebègue, *Rabelais*, 6: "Il ne lui suffit, comme à tant d'autres humanistes, de mettre en centons Virgile et Cicéron et de mener une vie paisible aux dépens de quelque Mécène. Il ne lui suffit de lire les oeuvres des Anciens et les compilations. Il s'applique, au cours de ses voyages, à recueillir l'expérience la plus riche et la plus variée."

55. Rabelais, *Quart Livre*, 106.

56. Rigolot, *Les Langages de Rabelais*, 45.

57. Rabelais, *Quart Livre*, 106.

58. Ibid.

59. Ibid., 107.

60. Ibid., 122. See Lebègue, *Rabelais*, 8: "Rabelais a confiance dans la volonté humaine. Il n'admettra jamais la prédestination calvinienne, et il croit au libre-arbitre. Comme Erasme, comme les Jésuites et Corneille, il affirme—en citant S. Paul—que l'homme peut et doit coopérer à son salut (IV, 23)."

61. Screech, *L'Evangélisme de Rabelais*, 46, 50.

62. Krailsheimer, *Rabelais and the Franciscans*, 235–36, disagrees, saying that

there is "no trace of the exaggerated voluntarism of the Nominalists, with whose doctrines Rabelais would have been acquainted in his Franciscan days."

63. See Perrat, "Sur 'Un tas de prognostications'"; Screech, "Some Aspects of Rabelais's Almanachs"; Antonioli, "Rabelais et la médecine," 67–70, 113–22.

64. For Molinet's prognostications, see Molinet, *Les Faictz et dictz,* 2:888–914. For a discussion of Molinet's use of astrology within the context of late medieval folklore, see Sautman, "Des Vessies pour des lanternes."

65. Molinet, *Les Faictz et dictz,* 2:907.

66. Rabelais, *Pantagrueline Prognostication,* 11.

67. See Perrat, "Sur 'Un tas de prognostications,'" 69.

68. Rabelais, *Pantagrueline Prognostication,* 7–8.

69. Ibid., 10.

70. Rabelais, *Quart Livre,* 133. See also Cave, "Death of Guillaume Du Bellay."

71. Rabelais, *Quart Livre,* 133.

72. Ibid., 134. See also Krailsheimer, *Rabelais and the Franciscans,* 244–45.

73. Rabelais, *Quart Livre,* 134.

74. Lefèvre d'Etaples, Preface to *Astronomicon,* written in 1503, in *Prefatory Epistles,* 112–13: "Quare post tantorum virorum commendata studia, res mihi visa non est astrorum cognitio non magni pendi digna." Like Pico della Mirandola, Lefèvre had earlier been much more indulgent toward astrological claims before adopting a much more skeptical position. In 1494, Lefèvre had written a treatise on *Natural Magic* but did not publish it, showing perhaps that he had become leery of astrological correspondences by the time he finished the treatise.

75. Ibid., 114: "Id enim quis dubitat ex immortalis naturae cognatione illi obtingere."

76. Ibid.: "Absit igitur ut ex huiusmodi sidereorum corporum contemplationibus aliud tandem meditemur quam divinae sapientiae et bonitatis laudes gratiarumque actiones."

77. Ibid.: "Erraret enim plurimum qui in horoscopi observatione et aliorum locorum erectione harum speculationum finem statueret." Some humanists are even more skeptical; for example, see Gaguin, *Epistole et orationes,* 2:22–39.

78. Montaigne, "L'Apologie de Raimond Sebond," in *Essais,* 2:470.

6. Fractured Resemblance in the *Quart Livre*

1. Erasmus died in 1536 and Luther died in 1546. I am speaking, in a broad sense, of the debate between evangelical moderates and the leaders of the Reformation.

2. See Foucault, *Les Mots et les choses,* 44: "La ressemblance dans le savoir du xvie siècle est ce qu'il y a de plus universel; à la fois ce qu'il y a de plus visible mais qu'on doit cependant chercher à decouvrir, car c'est le plus caché."

3. See Paris, *Rabelais au futur,* 112: "Ne demeurent valables qu'à condition d'en exempter premièrement Rabelais."

4. Ibid., 120: "Ces niais" qui "répètent ainsi l'erreur dont a vécu le Moyen Age:

ils affirment le particulier, le contingent comme universel; ils élèvent à l'absolu une relation fortuite."

5. Rabelais, *Gargantua*, 71.

6. Ibid., 67.

7. Screech, "Emblems and Colours," 69, 71.

8. Paris, *Rabelais au futur*, 116: "L'univers, à l'évidence de la foi, se répartissait en qualités concrètes, mais soutenues, articulées par des structures invisibles, échelonnées, de plus en plus lointaines, jusqu'à la source de leur cohérence: le divin."

9. Ibid., 121: "Une conception substantialiste du langage."

10. Rigolot, "Cratylisme et Pantagruélisme," 132.

11. Demerson, "Rabelais et l'analogie," 40–41.

12. Ibid., 24: "Quand Bakhtine prétend expliquer la pensée globale de Rabelais, il en cherche les fondements dans la culture du moyen âge; or c'est la notion centrale d'analogie qui unifie le système du théoricien russe: il fait apparaître une similitude de fonctions, de structures qui, à l'intérieur de la conscience populaire, relierait le corps au cosmos, la biologie à l'histoire, le langage à la prise de conscience révolutionnaire." See Bakhtin, *Rabelais and His World*. See Berrong, *Rabelais and Bakhtin*, for an insightful analysis of Bakhtin's understanding of popular culture in Rabelais. See also Cornilliat, "Equivoques moralisées," 286–87.

13. Bakhtin, *Rabelais and His World*, 7.

14. Ibid., 19–20.

15. Spitzer ("Rabelais et les 'rabelaisants,'" 422) remarks on the constructed nature of Rabelais's novels: "Si Rabelais décrit du concret 'réel,' ce n'est pas pour copier le monde extérieur, à la façon d'un Balzac ou d'un Zola (en somme ce que Auerbach appelle 'mimesis,' mais pour donner une réalité au mythe à l'irréel: 'pace' Lefranc, chez Rabelais le réel ne transparaît pas autant dans le mythe que le mythe ne transforme le réel dont il a besoin pour s'incarner." (Also in Spitzer, *Linguistics and Literary History*, 24.) See also Koopmans and Verhuyck, "Quelques Sources," 178–79.

16. Rabelais, *Quart Livre*, 142, 143.

17. Ibid., 150; see also Eskin, "Physie and Antiphysie."

18. Rabelais, *Quart Livre*, 150–51.

19. Ibid., 152.

20. Ibid. The name *Putherbe* refers to Gabriel de Puy-Herbault, a doctor at the Sorbonne who accused Rabelais "de se damner, chaque jour ne faire que se souler, goinfrer, vivre à la grecque, flairer les odeurs des cuisines, imiter le singe à longue queue." See Marichal, introduction to Rabelais, *Quart Livre*, xiii.

21. Rabelais, *Quart Livre*, 141.

22. Ibid., 165.

23. Rigolot, "Cratylisme et Pantagruélisme," 129. See also Kritzman, "La Quête de la parole," 199: "si les noms de ces personnages déterminent leurs actions dans le récit, c'est que le nom accomode la chose en même temps qu'il la génère; en d'autres termes, au lieu de masquer les choses, les mots les révèlent et les deviennent."

24. Rabelais, *Quart Livre*, 223.

25. Ibid.

26. Jeanneret, to the contrary ("Les Paroles dégelées," 16) sees Homenaz as a nominalist: "Homenaz est un nominaliste, il ne connaît d'autre réalité que celle désignée préalablement par un signe: sa saisie est circonscrite aux phénomènes nommés clairement par les mots. La position de Pantagruel est inverse. Il façonne le signe à sa volonté et transforme la donnée évidente—la poire-poire en une espèce insolite—la poire de bon chrétien." Also see Saulnier, "Le Silence de Rabelais."

27. Rabelais, *Quart Livre,* 224.

28. Ibid., 226. See Pouilloux, "Notes sur deux chapitres du 'Quart Livre' LV–LVI"; Nash, "Interpreting 'Parolles degelées.'"

29. Masters, *Rabelaisian Dialectic,* 18.

30. "L'impuissance des mots, le danger des mots. Prétendre faire passer en formules verbales, orales ou écrites, l'intégralité d'une pensée: l'étrange entreprise." Saulnier, "Le Silence de Rabelais," 241.

31. Rabelais, *Quart Livre,* 228.

32. Ibid., 229.

33. Ibid. According to Gray, *Rabelais et l'écriture,* 207: "L'écrivain médiéval était avant tout l'interprète d'une réalité transcendante, un lecteur du Livre dont Dieu était l'auteur. Rabelais s'efforce de mettre l'écriture en liberté, de lui donner les moyens de se déployer en se référant à elle-même. En se débarrassant d'un système d'interprétation pléonastique, elle retrouve son dynamisme non plus dans la convergence de mondes disparates, mais dans la divergence de lectures possibles. L'altérité à laquelle elle se réfère étant introuvable, l'écriture regagne par là l'intégrité que l'exégèse lui niait : au jeu de l'analogie succède définitivement celui de l'ambiguïté. Mais l'ambiguïté rabelaisienne procède d'intentions ludiques plutôt que sémantiques; elle sert à créer une texture linguistique suffisamment épaisse pour que l'écriture puisse y fonder sa dynamique essentielle."

34. "Une chose semble acquise: c'est que le signifiant cesse ici de participer du signifié, qu'entre eux le lien est désormais tranché." Paris, *Rabelais au futur,* 126.

35. "Le rejet des symboles comme des 'temps tenebreux' accompagne celui de leur commune transcendance: elle ouvre l'ère d'une connaissance rationnelle où signes et langage changent du tout au tout." Ibid., 130–31.

36. "Puis, par curieuse leczon et meditation frequente, rompre l'os et sugcer la substantificque mouelle—c'est à dire, ce que j'entends par ces symboles Pythagoricques—avecques espoir certain d'estre faictz escors et preux à ladicte lecture. Car en icelle bien aultre goust trouverez et doctrine plus absconce, que vous revelera de tresaultz sacremens et mysteres horrificques, tant en ce que concerne notre religion que aussi l'estat politicq et vie oeconomicque." Rabelais, *Gargantua,* 14.

37. Ibid., 15–16: "Croiez vous en vostre foy qu'oncques Homere, escrivent l'*Iliade* et *Odyssée,* pensast es allegories lesquelles de luy ont beluté Plutarche, Heraclides Ponticq, Eustatie et Phornute, et ce que d'iceulx Politian a desrobé? Si le croiez, vous n'aprochez ne de pieds ny de mains à mon opinion, qui decrete icelles aussi peu avoir esté songéez d'Homere que d'Ovide en ses *Metamorphoses* les sacremens de l'Evangile, lesquelz un Frere Lubin, vray croquelardon, s'est efforcé demonstrer, si d'adventure il rencontroit gens aussi folz que luy, et (come dict le proverbe) couvercle digne du chaudron." See also Jeanneret, "Commentary on Fiction."

38. See Chappell, *Enigma of Rabelais;* Grève, "Les Contemporains de Rabelais"; Jeanneret, "Du mystère à la mystification"; Rigolot, "'Enigme' et 'Prophétie'"; Screech, "Sense of Rabelais's 'Enigme en Prophétie.'" For the debate on the presence of allegory in Rabelais's novels, especially as it pertains to the prologue of *Gargantua,* please see Duval, "Interpretation and the 'Doctrine Absconce'"; Defaux, "D'un problème l'autre," and "Sur la prétendue pluralité"; Cave, Jeanneret, and Rigolot, "Sur la prétendue transparence de Rabelais." Although this fascinating and very learned debate orients itself around the notion of an *absconce* doctrine, or allegorical reality in *Gargantua,* it also is concerned with the question of the transparency of language in Rabelais.

39. Even as early as *Gargantua,* allegorical meaning is problematic. The "Enigme en prophetie" that Gargantua and Frere Jan find in the foundations of the Abbey of Thélème, for example, poses the question of human interpretation. On the issue of allegory, see Telle, "Thélème et le paulisme matrimonial érasmien"; Screech, "Sense of Rabelais's 'Enigme en Prophétie'"; Rigolot, "'Enigme' et 'Prophétie'"; Plattard, "Rabelais et Mellin de Saint-Gelais"; Bowen, *Age of Bluff.*

40. *Sacrosancti et œcumenici concilii tridentini,* 22–23. See also Midali, *Rivelazione, chiesa, scrittura e tradizione,* 97–110; Dejob, *De L'Influence du concile de Trente.*

41. Gerson, *De sensu litterali sacrae scripturae,* in *Œuvres complètes,* 3:334.

42. See *Sacrosancti et œcumenici concilii tridentini,* 22: "Præterea; ad coercenda petulantia ingenia; decernit, ut nemo, suæ prudentiæ innixus, in rebus fidei, et morum, ad ædificationem doctrinæ Christianæ pertinentium, sacram Scripturam ad suos sensos contorquens, contra eum sensum, quem tenuit et tenet sancta Mater Ecclesia, cujus est judicare de vero sensu et interpretatione Scripturarum sanctarum, aut etiam contra unanimem consensum Patrum, ipsam Scripturam sacram interpretari audeat; etiamsi hujusmodi interpretationes nullo umquam tempore in lucem edendæ forent. Qui contravenerint, per Ordinarios declarentur, et pœnis a jure statutis puniantur."

43. Calvin, *Commentaries,* 135. See also Calvin, *Institutes of the Christian Religion,* 1:304.

44. Calvin, *Commentaries,* 136–37.

45. Luther, "Answer to the Hyperchristian, Hyperspiritual, and Hyperlearned Book by Goat Emser in Leipzig—Including Some Thoughts Regarding His Companion, the Fool Murner," in *Martin Luther's Basic Theological Writings,* 80.

46. Massaut, *Josse Clichtove,* 2:272. See also Lefèvre d'Etaples, *Prefatory Epistles,* 389.

47. Massaut, *Josse Clichtove,* 2:281.

48. Ozment, *Age of Reform,* 69.

49. Ibid. See Lefèvre d'Etaples: "Quapropter duplicem crediderim sensum litteralem, hunc improprium caecutientium et non videntium qui divina solum carnaliter passibiliterque intelligunt; illum vero proprium videntium et illuminatorum; hunc humano sensu fictum, illum divino spiritu infusum; hunc deprimentem, illum vero mentem sursum attollentem," in Bedouelle, *Le Quincuplex Psalterium,* 23–24. See also Bedouelle, *Lefèvre d'Etaples;* Graf, *Essai sur la vie et les écrits de Jacques Lefèvre d'Etaples;* Massaut, *Critique et tradition.*

50. Bedouelle, *Lefèvre d'Etaples*, 184.

51. "Ergo non confundamus haec, sed iis quae requirant literam, literam tribuamus; quae allegoriam, allegoriam; quae utrumque, tribuamus utrumque, ut historia Abraae et filiorum ejus utrumque habet, hic enim spiritus et historiam intendit et allegoriam; et quae sunt per anagogen expressa, illis solum tribuamus anagogicam intelligentiam." Quoted in ibid., 183.

52. "Sunt, qui fastidiant omnes allegorias tamquam rem arbitrariam somniique simillimam. A quibus ut vehementer dissentio, cum videam absque his plerosque sensus aut absurdos esse aut perniciosos aut futtiles, leves ac frigidos, cumque constet Christum allegoriis usum et Paulum aliquot veteris instrumenti locos per allegoriam interpretari, ita non possum non improbare quorundam ineptum allegorismum, qui fingunt ipsi, quod explicent allegoria: Viator fessus insedit tergo ingentis draconis arboris truncum esse ratus, is excitatus devoravit miserum. Viator est homo, draco mundus, qui sibi innitentes perdit. Aliaque his magis frivola iustis voluminibus prodita sunt a quibusdam miroque studio leguntur a nonnulis. Satis est ea, quae reperiuntur in sacris litteris, ad allegoriam accomodare, si res ita postulet, *ut ipsi nihil affingamus.*" See Erasmus, *Ausgewählte Schriften*, 3:422. See also Erasmus, *Enarratio Allegorica in primum psalmum beatus vir*, in *Opera omnia*, 2:31–80. Also see Margolin, "Erasme et le verbe," 86–110.

53. See Cave, *Cornucopian Text*, 86–87.

54. Erasmus, *Paraclesis*, in Olin, *Christian Humanism*, 103.

55. Cave, *Cornucopian Text*, 91.

56. Gerson, *De sensu litterali sacrae scripturae* in *Œuvres complètes*, 3:336.

57. Rabelais, *Quart Livre*, 206.

58. Ibid., 218.

59. This is not, of course, the only way to understand the Gaster episode. Greene, *Rabelais*, 95, takes a much more optimistic approach to Gaster: "Messer Gaster himself is a powerful, stern, and implacable monarch, but his influence is really beneficial, just as the access to his country is arduous but, once attained, its climate is salubrious and delightful."

60. Marichal, "L'Attitude de Rabelais," 208, says that "visant plus haut, déjà, au *Tiers Livre*, dans la louange des *Debteurs*, il s'était moqué du rôle donné à l'Amour par Ficin dans la conduite de l'Univers, dans sa description du manoir de Messere Gaster il y revient plus sérieusement; en face de l'idéalisme et de l'optimisme ficiniens il semble se complaire à développer, avec une certaine âpreté, une conception matérialiste de l'Histoire."

61. Rabelais, *Quart Livre*, 230–31.

62. Lemaire, *La Concorde des deux langages*, 39. See also Marichal, "*Quart Livre*: commentaires," 185–88.

63. Marichal, "*Quart Livre*: commentaires," 186, 198. See also Cave, "Reading Rabelais," 80: "The Rock of Virtue retains its antithetical character initially (rebarbative slopes, idyllic summit) but proves to be very much a latter-day Eden: if it is the place described by Hesiod, it is no longer as Hesiod described it, since the 'Manoir de Arete' has been usurped by Gaster, who has also, it seems, displaced Porus, god of spiritual abundance, as the spouse of Penia."

64. Lemaire, *La Concorde des deux langages*, 45–46.

65. Rabelais, *Quart Livre*, 231–32.

66. Ibid., 232. See also Masters, *Rabelaisian Dialectic*, 27.

67. Rabelais, *Quart Livre*, 232.

68. Ibid., 249: "La pouldre consommée, advenoit que pour eviter vacuité (laquelle n'est tolerée en Nature; plus toust seroit la machine de l'Univers, Ciel, Air, Terre, Mer reduicte en l'antique Chaos, qu'il advint vacuité en lieu du monde) la ballote et dragées estoient impetueusement hors jectez par la gueule du faulconneau, afin que l'air penetrast en la chambre d'icelluy, laquelle aultrement restoit en vacuité, estant la pouldre par le feu tant soubdain consommée."

69. For references to Pliny's *Natural History*, see Marichal's notes to Rabelais, *Quart Livre*, 250–51.

70. Rabelais, *Quart Livre*, 251.

71. Jeanneret, "Les paroles dégelées," 22, on the other hand, sees Gaster as representing the dangers of literal interpretation: "Le leitmotiv resurgit: comme avec les Papimanes et les Paroles gelées, la fixation littérale est associée à des actes brutaux et des conduites fanatiques."

72. Lemaire, *La Concorde des deux langages*, 40, 42.

73. Rabelais, *Quart Livre*, 231.

74. Montaigne would become an adept of Pyrrhonian skepticism, especially in his later *Essays*. See following chapter for a short discussion of Montaigne's *De l'expérience*.

Conclusion

1. Montaigne, *Essais*, 3:1065: "Il n'est desir plus naturel que le desir de connoissance. Nous essayons tous les moyens qui nous y peuvent mener. Quand la raison nous faut, nous y employons l'experience."

2. Reiss, *Discourse of Modernism*, 29–40.

3. See Popkin, *History of Skepticism*, 42–86.

4. Compare, for example, the second stanza of the "Sonnet a tresillustre Princesse Madame Marguerite seur unique du roy luy presentant ce livre," the introductory poem to *L'Olive* (1549): "Là elevé au cercle radieux / Par un Demon heureux, qui me conforte, / Celle fureur tant doulce j'en rapporte, / Dont vostre nom j'egalle aux plus haulx Dieux." See Du Bellay, *L'Olive*, 41. Compare with *Contre les pétrarquistes* (1558): "Quelque autre encor' la terre dedaignant / Va du tiers ciel les secrets enseignant, / Et de l'Amour, où il se va baignant, / Tire une quinte essence: / Mais quant à moy, qui plus terrestre suis, / Et n'ayme rien, que ce qu'aymer je puis, / Le plus subtil, qu'en amour je poursuis, / S'appelle jouissance," in Du Bellay, *Œuvres poétiques*, 5:74. This stanza appeared earlier in "A Une Dame" (1553); see ibid., 4:210–11. See also Bellenger, "Les poètes français."

5. Compare stanza 15 of *Ode à Michel de l'Hospital* (1550): "Ceulx là que je feindray Poëtes / Par la grace de ma bonté / Seront nommez les Interpretes / Des Dieux, & de leur volunté," in Ronsard, *Œuvres complètes*, 3:145–46, with the first sonnet of *Les Amours sur la mort de Marie* (1578): "Amour est donc sujet à nostre humaine loy, / Il a perdu son regne, et le meilleur de soy, / Puis que par une mort sa puissance est perie," in Ronsard, *Ronsard: Les Amours*, 233.

6. Paris, *Rabelais au futur,* 120.

7. Demonet, *Les Voix du signe,* 11, explains that "au XVIe siècle, on retrouve les principaux courants de la pensée linguistique médievale, bien que Scot et Ockham soient rarement revendiqués, et même si les néoplatoniciens rebaptisent 'Idées' les 'espèces' de la scolastique; très utilisées aussi sont les analyses linguistiques d'Augustin sur le signe détaché de son référant, analyses nullement incompatibles avec une forme de nominalisme."

8. See Cassirer's analysis of Nicholas of Cusa in *Individual and the Cosmos,* which remains one of the fundamental texts for students of the Renaissance. For a recent reappraisal of Cassirer's thesis, see also Kerrigan and Braden, *Idea of the Renaissance.*

9. See Descombes, *Le Même et l'autre.*

10. Eco, *Les Limites de l'interprétation;* Eco, et al., *Interpretation and Overinterpretation.*

11. See Rorty, *Contingency, Irony, and Solidarity;* Goodheart, *Skeptic Disposition.*

References

Adams, Marilyn McCord. *William of Ockham*. Vol. 2. Notre Dame, Ind.: Univ. of Notre Dame Press, 1987.

Agrippa, Henry Cornelius. *Three Books of Occult Philosophy, Book One—Natural Magic*. Ed. W. F. Whitehead; trans. J. F. New York: Samuel Weiser, 1971.

Alféri, Pierre. *Guillaume d'Ockham: Le Singulier*. Paris: Les Editions de Minuit, 1989.

Anderson, James F. *The Bond of Being: An Essay on Analogy and Existence*. St. Louis: Herder, 1949.

———. *Reflections on the Analogy of Being*. The Hague: Martinus Nijhoff, 1967.

Andes, Raymond N. "Le Roman de la Rose moralisé." Ph.D. diss., Univ. of North Carolina at Chapel Hill, 1948.

Angeli, Giovanna. "Il 'Rude Engin' di Molinet." *Paragone* 327 (1977): 21–47.

Antonioli, Roland. "Rabelais et la médicine." *Etudes Rabelaisiennes* 12 (1976): 1–394.

Apuleius Barbarus. *Herbarium apulei (1481), Herbolario volgare (1522)*. Intro. Erminio Caprotti (with an essay by William T. Stearn). Milan: Polifilio, 1979.

Aristotle. *Histoire des animaux*. Vol. 1, bks. 1–4. Ed. and trans. Pierre Louis. Paris: Belles Lettres, 1964.

Auerbach, Erich. *Scenes from the Drama of European Literature*. New York: Meridian, 1959.

Badel, Pierre Yves. *Le Roman de la rose au XIVe siècle: Etude de la réception de l'œuvre*. Geneva: Droz, 1980.

Baird, Joseph L., and John R. Kane. *La Querelle de la Rose: Letters and Documents*. Chapel Hill: North Carolina Studies in the Romance Languages and Literatures, 1978.

Bakhtin, Mikhail. *Rabelais and His World*. Trans. Hélène Iswolsky. Bloomington: Indiana Univ. Press, 1984.

Beaujour, Michel. *Le Jeu de Rabelais*. Paris: L'Herne, 1969.

Becker, Philipp August. *Jean Lemaire: Der Erste Humanistische Dichter Frankreichs*. Strasbourg: Karl J. Trübner, 1893.

Bedouelle, Guy. *Lefèvre d'Etaples et l'intelligence des écritures*. Geneva: Droz, 1976.

————. *Le Quincuplex Psalterium de Lefèvre d'Etaples: un guide de lecture.* Geneva: Droz, 1979.

Bellenger, Yvonne. "Les poètes français et la peinture: la ressemblance comme critère esthétique au XVIe siècle." In *Mélanges à la mémoire de Franco Simone: France et Italie dans la culture européenne I: Moyen Age et Renaissance.* Geneva: Slatkine, 1980.

Bergweiler, Ulrike. *Die Allegorie im Werk von Jean Lemaire de Belges.* Geneva: Droz, 1976.

Bernard of Clairvaux. *St. Bernard on the Song of Songs.* Ed. and trans. by a Religious of C.S.M.V. London: A. R. Mowbray, 1952.

Bernardino de' Busti. *Mariale.* 1493.

Berrong, Richard M. "Jean Lemaire de Belges, Dictys of Crete, and Giovanni Boccaccio: Possible Sources for *Gargantua*, Chap. 1." *Etudes Rabelaisiennes* 17 (1983): 89–92.

————. "'Non est solum Sophista quis loquitur': Further Thoughts on Rabelais's Presentation of Linguistic Mastery in Gargantua." *Etudes Rabelaisiennes* 22 (1988): 27–42.

————. *Rabelais and Bakhtin: Popular Culture in Gargantua and Pantagruel.* Lincoln: Univ. of Nebraska Press, 1986.

Biel, Gabriel. *Epitome et collectorium ex Occamo circa quatuour sententiarum libros.* Frankfurt am Main: Minerva, 1965 (originally published in Tubingen, 1501).

Bloch, R. Howard. *Etymologies and Genealogies: A Literary Anthropology of the French Middle Ages.* Chicago: Univ. of Chicago Press, 1983.

Boom, Ghislaine de. "A propos du tombeau de Philibert de Savoie, érigé par Marguerite d'Autriche." *Revue Belge d'Archéologie et d'Histoire de l'Art* 11.4 (1941): 219–27.

Bourdillon, Francis William. *The Early Editions of the Roman de la Rose.* London: Biographical Society at the Chiswick Press, 1906.

Bowen, Barbara C. *The Age of Bluff: Paradox and Ambiguity in Rabelais and Montaigne.* Urbana: Univ. of Illinois Press, 1972.

Britnell, Jennifer. "Jean Lemaire de Belges and Prophecy." *Journal of the Warburg and Courtauld Institutes* 42 (1979): 144–66.

Brown, Catherine D. *Pastor and Laity in the Theology of Jean Gerson.* Cambridge: Cambridge Univ. Press, 1987.

Brown, Cynthia J. "The Confrontation between Printer and Author in early Sixteenth-Century France: Another Example of Michel Le Noir's Unethical Printing Practices." *Bibliothèque d'Humanisme et Renaissance* 53.1 (1991): 105–18.

————. "L'Eveil d'une nouvelle conscience littéraire en France à la grande époque de transition technique: Jean Molinet et son moulin poétique." In *Du manuscrit à l'imprimé,* ed. Giuseppe Di Stefano and Rose M. Bidler. Montreal: CERES, 1989.

————. "Jean Lemaire's *La Concorde des deux langages*: The Merging of Politics, Language, and Poetry." *Fifteenth-Century Studies* 3 (1980): 29–39.

————. " Du manuscrit à l'imprimé en France: le cas des Grands Rhétoriquers."

In *Les Grands Rhétoriqueurs: Actes du Ve Colloque International sur le moyen français*. Milan: Università Cattolica del Sacro Cuore, 1985.

———. "The Rise of Literary Consciousness in Late Medieval France: Jean Lemaire and the Rhétoriqueur Tradition." *Journal of Medieval and Renaissance Studies* 13.1 (1983): 51–74.

Burrows, Mark S. "Jean Gerson after Constance: 'Via Media et Regia' as a Revision of the Ockhamist Covenant." *Church History* 59.4 (1990): 467–81.

Buttrick, G. A., ed. *The Interpreter's Dictionary of the Bible*. Vol. 4. New York: Abingdon, 1962.

Caiger, B. J. "Doctrine and Discipline in the Church of Jean Gerson." *Journal of Ecclesiastical History* 41.3 (1990): 389–407.

Cajetan, Thomas de Vio. *The Analogy of Names and the Concept of Being*. Trans. Edward A. Bushinski, with Henry J. Koren. Pittsburgh: Duquesne Univ. Press, 1953.

Calin, William. "Jean Lemaire de Belges: Courtly Narrative at the Close of the Middle Ages." In *The Nature of Medieval Narrative*, ed. Minnette Grunman-Gaudet and Robin F. Jones. Lexington, Ky.: French Forum, 1980.

Calvin, John. *Commentaries on the Epistles of Paul to the Galatians and Ephesians*. Trans. William Pringle. Grand Rapids, Mich.: Eerdmans, 1948.

———. *Institutes of the Christian Religion*. Vol. 1. Ed. and trans. J. Allen. Philadelphia: Presbyterian Board of Publishers, 1844.

———. *Traité des scandales*. Ed. O. Fatio. Geneva: Droz, 1984.

Cassirer, Ernst. *The Individual and the Cosmos in Renaissance Thought*. Trans. Mario Domandi. Philadelphia: Univ. of Pennsylvania Press, 1972.

Cave, Terence. *Cornucopian Text: Problems of Writing in the French Renaissance*. Oxford: Clarendon, 1979.

———. "The Death of Guillaume Du Bellay: Rabelais' Biographical Representation." In *Writing the Renaissance: Essays on Sixteenth-Century French Literature in Honor of Floyd Gray*, ed. Raymond C. La Charité. Lexington, Ky.: French Forum, 1992.

———. "Reading Rabelais: Variations on a Rock of Virtue." In *Literary Theory/Renaissance Texts*, ed. Patricia Parker and David Quint. Baltimore: Johns Hopkins Univ. Press, 1986.

Cave, Terence, Michel Jeanneret, and François Rigolot. "Sur la prétendue transparence de Rabelais." *Revue d'Histoire Littéraire de la France* 4 (June–July 1986): 709–16.

Champier, Symphorien. *Le Triumphe du tres chrestien roy de France Loys XII*. Ed. Giovanna Trisolini. Rome: Ateneo and Bizzarri, 1977.

Chappell, A. F. *The Enigma of Rabelais: An Essay in Interpretation*. Cambridge: Cambridge Univ. Press, 1924.

Charland, Th.-M. *Artes praedicandi: contribution à l'histoire de la rhétorique au moyen âge*. Paris: Vrin, 1936.

Chastel, André. "Art et religion dans la renaissance." *Bibliothèque d'Humanisme et Renaissance* 7 (1945): 7–61.

———. *Marsile Ficin et l'art*. Geneva: Droz, 1975.

Collins, Ardis B. *The Secular Is Sacred: Platonism and Thomism in Marsilio Ficino's "Platonic Theology."* The Hague: Martinus Nijhoff, 1974.

Combes, André. *Essai sur la critique de Ruysbroeck par Gerson.* Paris: Vrin, 1945.

———. *Jean de Montreuil et Jean Gerson: Contribution à l'histoire de l'humanisme et de la théologie en France au début du XVe siècle.* Paris: Vrin, 1942.

———. *Jean Gerson, commentateur dionysien: les notulae super quaedam verba dionysii de caelesti hierarchia.* Paris: Vrin, 1940.

———. *La Théologie mystique de Gerson: profil de son évolution.* Vols. 1, 2. Rome: Pontifical University of the Lateran and Desclée, 1964.

Compagnon, Antoine. *Nous, Michel de Montaigne.* Paris: Seuil, 1980.

Conley, Tom. *The Graphic Unconscious in Early Modern French Writing.* Cambridge: Cambridge Univ. Press, 1992.

———. "Image and Code: On Some Figural Problems of Flamboyant Architecture (1480–1520)." In *Image and Code*, ed. Wendy Steiner. Ann Arbor: Univ. of Michigan Press, 1981.

Connolly, James L. *John Gerson: Reformer and Mystic.* Louvain: Librairie Universitaire, 1928.

Coopland, G. W. *Nicole Oresme and the Astrologers: A Study of His "Livre de divinacions."* Cambridge: Harvard Univ. Press, 1952.

Copenhaver, Brian. *Symphorien Champier and the Reception of the Occultist Tradition in Renaissance France.* The Hague: Mouton, 1978.

Cornilliat, François. "Equivoques moralisées: Guillaume Alexis." *Poétique* 83 (Sept. 1990): 281–304.

———. *"Or ne mens": couleurs de l'éloge et du blâme chez les "grands rhétoriqueurs."* Paris: Champion, 1994.

Courtenay, William J. "Nominalism and Late Medieval Religion." In *The Pursuit of Holiness in Late Medieval and Renaissance Religion: Papers from the University of Michigan Conference,* ed. Charles Trinkaus, with Heiko A. Oberman. Leiden: Brill, 1974.

Cousins, Ewert H. "Bonaventure's Mysticism of Language." In *Mysticism and Language,* ed. Steven T. Katz. Oxford: Oxford Univ. Press, 1992.

Curtius, Ernst Robert. *European Literature and the Latin Middle Ages.* Princeton: Princeton Univ. Press, 1955.

Dante Alighieri. *Dantis alagherii epistolae: The Letters of Dante.* Trans. Paget Toynbee. Oxford: Clarendon, 1966.

———. *La Divina commedia.* Turin: Einaudi, 1975.

De Boer, C., ed. *"Ovide moralisé": poème du commencement du quatorzième siècle.* Amsterdam: North Holland, 1954.

Debongnie, Pierre. *Jean Mombaer de Bruxelles, Abbé de Livry, ses écrits et ses réformes.* Louvain: Librairie Universitaire, 1927.

Defaux, Gérard. "D'un problème l'autre: herméneutique de l' 'altior sensus' et 'captatio lectoris' dans le Prologue de *Gargantua.*" *Revue d'Histoire Littéraire de la France* 4 (Mar.–Apr. 1985): 195–216.

———. *Marot, Rabelais, Montaigne: l'écriture comme présence.* Geneva: Slatkine, 1987.

————. *Pantagruel et les sophistes: contribution à l'histoire de l'humanisme chrétien*. The Hague: Martinus Nijhoff, 1973.

————. "Rabelais et son masque comique: sophista loquitur." *Etudes rabelaisiennes* 11 (1974): 89–135.

————. "Sur la prétendue pluralité du Prologue de *Gargantua*." *Revue d'Histoire Littéraire de la France* 4 (June–July 1986): 716–22.

Dejob, Charles. *De L'Influence du concile de Trente sur la littérature et les beaux-arts chez les peuples catholiques: essai d'introduction à l'histoire littéraire du siècle de Louis XIV*. Geneva: Slatkine Reprints, 1969.

Delaruelle, Etienne, E.-R. Labande, and Paul Ourliac. *L'Eglise au temps du grand schisme et de la crise conciliaire (1378–1449)*. Vol. 2. Paris: Bloud and Gay, 1964.

Demerson, Guy. *Rabelais*. Paris: Ballard, 1986.

————. "Rabelais et l'analogie." *Etudes Rabelaisiennes* 14 (1977): 23–41.

Demonet, Marie-Luce. *Les Voix du signe: nature et origine du langage à la renaissance (1480–1580)*. Paris: Champion, 1992.

Descombes, Vincent. *Le Même et l'autre: quarante-cinq ans de philosophie française (1933–1978)*. Paris: Les Editions de Minuit, 1979.

Devaux, Jean. "La Fin du Téméraire . . . ou la mémoire d'un prince ternie par l'un des siens." *Le Moyen Age: Revue d'Histoire et de Philologie* 1 (1989): 105–28.

De Vriend, Hubert Jan, ed. *The Old English Herbarium and Medicina de quadrupedibus*. Oxford: Oxford Univ. Press, 1984.

Dictionnaire de la Bible. Vol. 4. Paris: Letouzey et Ané, 1908.

Doutrepont, Georges. *Jean Lemaire de Belges et la renaissance*. Brussels: Marcel Hayez, 1934.

Droz, E. "Rabelais versificateur." *Bibliothèque d'Humanisme et Renaissance* 3 (1936): 203–6.

Du Bellay, Joachim. *Œuvres poétiques*. Vols. 4, 5. Ed. H. Chamard. Paris: Nizet, 1983.

————. *L'Olive*. Ed. E. Caldarini. Geneva: Droz, 1974.

Duby, Georges. *The Age of the Cathedrals: Art and Society, 980–1420*. Trans. Eleanor Levieux and Barbara Thompson. Chicago: Univ. of Chicago Press, 1981.

Dupire, Noël. *Jean Molinet: la vie et les œuvres*. Paris: Droz, 1932.

Duval, Edwin M. *The Design of Rabelais's Pantagruel*. New Haven: Yale Univ. Press, 1991.

————. "Interpretation and the 'Doctrine Absconce' of Rabelais's Prologue to *Gargantua*." *Etudes Rabelaisiennes* 18 (1985): 2–17.

Eco, Umberto. *Les Limites de l'interprétation*. Paris: Grasset, 1990.

Eco, Umberto, with Richard Rorty, Jonathan Culler, and Christine Brooke-Rose. *Interpretation and Overinterpretation*. Ed. Stefan Collini. Cambridge: Cambridge Univ. Press, 1992.

Erasmus, Desiderius. *Ausgewählte Schriften*. Vol. 3. Darmstadt: Wissenschaftliche Buchgesellschaft, 1967.

————. *Opera omnia, desiderii Erasmi Roterdami.* Pt. 5, vol. 2. Amsterdam: North Holland, 1985.

————. *The Praise of Folly.* Trans. Clarence H. Miller. New Haven: Yale Univ. Press, 1979.

Eskin, Stanley G. "Physie and Antiphysie: The Idea of Nature in Rabelais and Calcagnini." *Comparative Literature* 14.2 (1962): 167–73.

Evans, Joan, and Mary S. Serjeantson. *English Mediaeval Lapidaries.* London: Early English Text Society, 1933.

Faral, Edmond. *Les Arts poétiques du XIIe et du XIIIe siècles: Recherches et documents sur la technique du moyen âge.* Paris: Honoré Champion, 1958.

Febvre, Lucien. *Le problème de l'incroyance au 16e siècle: la religion de Rabelais.* Paris: Albin Michel, 1968.

Fenoaltea, Doranne. "Doing It with Mirrors: Architecture and Textual Construction in Jean Lemaire's *La Concorde des deux langages.*" In *Lapidary Inscriptions: Renaissance Essays for Donald A. Stone,* ed. Barbara C. Bowen and Jerry C. Nash. Lexington, Ky.: French Forum, 1991.

Festugière, Jean. *La Philosophie de l'amour de Marsile Ficin et son influence sur la littérature française au XVIe siècle.* Paris: Vrin, 1941.

Ficino, Marsilio. *Commentary on Plato's "Symposium."* Ed. and trans. Sears Reynolds Jayne. Columbia: Univ. of Missouri Press, 1944.

————. *Teologia platonica.* Ed. Michele Schiavone. Vols. 1, 2. Bologna: Zanichelli, 1965.

————. *Three Books of Life.* Ed. and trans. Carol V. Kaske and John R. Clark. Binghamton, N.Y.: Medieval and Renaissance Texts and Studies, 1989.

Fleming, John. *Reason and the Lover.* Princeton: Princeton Univ. Press, 1984.

Fletcher, Angus. *Allegory: The Theory of a Symbolic Mode.* Ithaca: Cornell Univ. Press, 1964.

Focillon, Henri. *L'Art d'occident: le moyen âge gothique.* Vol. 2. Paris: Armand Colin, 1938.

————. *La Vie des formes.* Paris: Ernest Leroux, 1934.

Foucault, Michel. *Les Mots et les choses: une archéologie des sciences humaines.* Paris: Gallimard, 1966.

Frame, Donald. *François Rabelais: A Study.* New York: Harcourt Brace Jovanovich, 1977.

Frappier, Jean. "La Cour de Malines et Jean Lemaire de Belges." In *Histoire illustrée des lettres françaises de belgique,* ed. Joseph Hanse and Gustav Charlier. Brussels: La Renaissance du Livre, 1958.

————. "L'Humanisme dans la poésie de Jean Lemaire de Belges." *Romance Philology* 17.2 (1963): 272–84.

————. "L'Humanisme de Jean Lemaire de Belges." *Bibliothèque d'Humanisme et Renaissance* 25 (1963): 289–306.

Gaguin, Robert. *Roberti Gaguini Epistole et orationes.* Ed. E. Bouillon. Vol. 2. Paris: Louis Thuasne, 1903.

Geiger, L. B. *La Participation dans la philosophie de S. Thomas d'Aquin.* Paris: Vrin, 1953.

Gerard, John. *Leaves from Gerard's Herball*. Arranged by Marcus Woodward. London: Gerald Howe, 1931.

Gerson, Jean. *Contra Astronomos*. In *Joannis Gersonii doctoris theologi et cancellarii Pariensis opera omnia*. Antwerp: Ellies du Pin, 1706.

———. *De mystica theologia*. Ed. André Combes. Padua: Thesaurus Mundi, 1959.

———. *Œuvres complètes*. 10 vols. Ed. P. Glorieux. Paris: Desclée, 1962–73.

Ghisalberti, Alessandro. *Introduzione a Ockham*. Rome: Laterza, 1976.

Gilson, Etienne. *Les Idées et les lettres*. Paris: Vrin, 1955.

———. "Marsile Ficin et le *Contra Gentiles*." *Archives d'Histoire Doctrinale et Littéraire du Moyen Age* 24 (1957): 101–13.

———. *La Philosophie au moyen âge: des origines patristiques à la fin du XIVe siècle*. Paris: Payot, 1986.

Glauser, Alfred. *Le Faux Rabelais ou de l'inauthenticité du Cinquième Livre*. Paris: Nizet, 1975.

———. *Rabelais créateur*. Paris: Nizet, 1966.

Goodheart, Eugene. *The Skeptic Disposition: Deconstruction, Ideology, and Other Matters*. Princeton: Princeton Univ. Press, 1991.

Gordon, Alex L. "La Ressource du petit peuple (1481): essai de pleine rhétorique." *Travaux et littérature* 2 (1989): 55–67.

Graf, Charles-Henri. *Essai sur la vie et les écrits de Jacques Lefèvre d'Etaples*. Geneva: Slatkine Reprints, 1970.

Gray, Floyd. *Rabelais et l'écriture*. Paris: Nizet, 1974.

Greene, Thomas. *Rabelais: A Study in Comic Courage*. Englewood Cliffs: Prentice Hall, 1970.

Grève, Marcel de. "Les contemporains de Rabelais, découvrirent-ils la substantifique mouelle." In *François Rabelais: ouvrage publié pour le quatrième centenaire de sa mort, 1553–1953*. Geneva: Droz, 1953.

Griffin, Robert. "*La Concorde des deux langages*: Discordia concors." In *Literature and the Arts in the Reign of Francis I: Essays Presented to C. A. Mayer*, ed. Pauline M. Smith and I. D. McFarlane. Lexington, Ky.: French Forum, 1985.

———. "Cosmic Metaphor in 'La Concorde des deux langages.'" In *Pre-Pléiade Poetry*, ed. Jerry Nash. Lexington, Ky.: French Forum, 1985.

———. "Jean Lemaire's Epic Contraption." *Modern Language Review* 83.1 (1988): 16–29.

———. "Lemaire's 'Couronne Margaritique' and the Life of Allegory." *Journal of Medieval and Renaissance Studies* 19.2 (1989): 243–96.

Guiette, Robert. "L'Invention étymologique dans les lettres françaises au moyen âge." *Cahiers de l'Association Internationale des Etudes Françaises* 11 (1959): 273–85.

Guiraud, Pierre. "Etymologie et ethymologia (Motivation et retromotivation)." *Poétique* 11 (1972): 405–13.

Guy, Henry. *Histoire de la poésie française au XVIe siècle: l'ecole des rhétoriqueurs*. Vol. 1. Paris: Champion, 1968.

Hanse, Joseph, and Gustave Charlier, eds. *Histoire illustrée des lettres françaises de Belgique.* Brussels: La Renaissance du Livre, 1958.

Harbison, Craig. "Visions and Meditations in Early Flemish Painting." *Simiolus* 15.2 (1985): 87–118.

Hathaway, Ronald F. *Hierarchy and the Definition of Order in the Letters of Pseudo-Dionysius: A Study in the Form and Meaning of the Pseudo-Dionysian Writings.* The Hague: Martinus Nijhoff, 1969.

Hicks, Eric. *Le Débat sur le Roman de la Rose.* Paris: Champion, 1977.

Hill, Jillian M. L. *The Medieval Debate on Jean de Meung's Roman de la Rose: Morality versus Art.* Lewiston, N.Y.: Mellen, 1991.

Hollander, John. *Allegory in Dante's Commedia.* Princeton: Princeton Univ. Press, 1969.

Huizinga, J. *The Waning of the Middle Ages.* New York: Doubleday Anchor, 1954.

Humpers, Alfred. *Etude sur la langue de Jean Lemaire de Belges.* Liège: Vaillant-Carmanne, 1921.

Huot, Sylvia. *The Romance of the Rose and Its Medieval Readers: Interpretation, Reception, Manuscript Transmission.* Cambridge: Cambridge Univ. Press, 1993.

Hyma, Albert. *The Christian Renaissance: A History of the Devotio Moderna.* Grand Rapids: Reformed Press, 1924.

Isidore of Seville. *Isidori Hispalensis Episcopi etymologiarum sive originum libre xx.* Vol. 1. Ed. W. M. Lindsay. Oxford: Oxford Univ. Press, 1911.

Jeanneret, Michel. "Commentary on Fiction, Fiction as Commentary." *South Atlantic Quarterly* 91.4 (1992) 909–28.

———."Du mystère à la mystification: le sens caché à la Renaissance et dans Rabelais." *Versants, Revue Suisse des Littératures Romanes* 11 (winter 1981): 31–52.

———. "Les Paroles dégelées." *Littérature* 17 (Feb. 1975): 14–30.

Jenkins, Michael F. O. *Artful Eloquence: Jean Lemaire de Belges and the Rhetorical Tradition.* Chapel Hill: North Carolina Studies in the Romance Languages and Literatures, 1980.

Jodogne, Pierre. *Jean Lemaire de Belges, écrivain franco-bourguignon.* Brussels: Palais des Académies, 1972.

———. "L'Orientation culturelle de Jean Lemaire de Belges." *Cahiers de l'Association Internationale des Etudes Françaises* 23 (May 1971): 85–103.

———. "Pour la fortune d'Ermalao Barbaro en France: un texte de Jean Lemaire de Belges." *Studi Francese* 26 (May–Aug. 1965): 260–61.

———. "Un recueil poétique de Jean Lemaire de Belges en 1498 (le ms. de la Bibl. Nat. de Paris, Nouv. Acq. fr. no. 4061)." In *Miscellanea di studi e ricerche sul Quattrocento francese,* ed. Franco Simone. Turin: Giappichelli, 1967.

John of Ruysbroeck. *The Adornment of the Spiritual Marriage, the Sparkling Stone, the Book of Supreme Truth.* Ed. Evelyn Underhill, trans. C. A. Wynschenk. London: Dent and Sons, 1916.

Joukovsky-Micha, Françoise. "La Mythologie dans les poèmes de Jean Molinet." *Romance Philology* 21.3 (1968): 286–302.

———. "Ronsard et 'La Concorde des deux langages.'" *Revue d'histoire littéraire de la France* 3 (Sept.–Oct. 1975): 791–93.

Jourdan, J. P. "Le Langage amoureux dans le combat de chevalerie à la fin du Moyen Age (France, Bourgogne, Anjou)." *Le Moyen Age: Revue d'Histoire et de Philologie* 1 (1993): 83–106.

Jung, Marc-René. *Etudes sur le poème allégorique en France au moyen âge.* Berne: Francke, 1971.

Kaluza, Zénon. *Les Querelles doctrinales à Paris: nominalistes et réalistes aux confins du XIVe et du XVe siècles.* Bergamo: Pierluigi Lubrina, 1988.

Katz, Steven T. "Mystical Speech and Mystical Meaning." In *Mysticism and Language,* ed. Steven T. Katz. Oxford: Oxford Univ. Press, 1992.

Kem, Judy Kay. "Allegorical Images in the Cardinal Virtue Prudence in the Works of the Rhétoriqueurs." *Romance Notes* 28.3 (1988): 177–85.

———. "Magic and Prophecy in the Works of Jean Lemaire de Belges." Ph.D. diss., Univ. of North Carolina at Chapel Hill, 1985.

Kerrigan, William, and Gordon Braden. *The Idea of the Renaissance.* Baltimore: Johns Hopkins Univ. Press, 1989.

Klubertanz, George P. *St. Thomas Aquinas on Analogy: A Textual Analysis and Systematic Synthesis.* Chicago: Loyola Univ. Press, 1960.

Koenigsberger, Dorothy. *Renaissance Man and Creative Thinking: A History of Concepts of Harmony, 1400–1700.* Hassocks, Sussex: Harvester, 1979.

Koopmans, Jelle, and Paul Verhuyck. "Quelques Sources et parallèles des sermons joyeux français des XVe and XVIe siècles." *Neophilologus* 70 (1986): 168–84.

Krailsheimer, A . J. *Rabelais and the Franciscans.* Oxford: Clarendon, 1963.

Kristeller, Paul Oskar. *Le Thomisme et la pensée italienne de la renaissance.* Montreal: Institut d'études médiévales, and Paris: Vrin, 1967.

Kritzman, Lawrence D. "La Quête de la parole dans le QL de Rabelais." *French Forum* 2.3 (1977): 195–204.

———. "The Rhetoric of Dissimulation in 'La Premiere Epistre de l'amant vert.'" *Journal of Medieval and Renaissance Studies* 10.1 (1980) 23–39.

Langer, Ullrich. *Divine and Poetic Freedom in the Renaissance: Nominalist Theology and Literature in France and Italy.* Princeton: Princeton Univ. Press, 1990.

———. "Friendship and the Adversarial Rhetoric of Humanism." *Common Knowledge* 3.1 (1994): 40–53.

———. "Jean Molinet: allégorie et textualité." *Bulletin de l'association d'étude sur l'humanisme, la réforme et la renaissance* 9 (June 1979): 37–46.

Larkey, Sanford V., ed. *An Herbal* (1525). New York: Scholars' Facsimiles and Reprints, 1941.

Larmat, Jean. *Le Moyen Age dans le Gargantua de Rabelais.* Nice: Belles Lettres, 1973.

Lebègue, Raymond. *Rabelais.* Tubingen: Max Niemeyer, 1952.

———. "Rabelais et les grands rhétoriqueurs." *Les Lettres Romanes* 12 (1957): 5–18.

Lefèvre d'Etaples, Jacques. *The Prefatory Epistles of Lefèvre d'Etaples and Related Texts*. Ed. Eugene Rice. New York: Columbia Univ. Press, 1972.

Leff, Gordon. *William of Ockham: The Metamorphosis of Scholastic Discourse*. Manchester: Manchester Univ. Press, 1975.

Lemaire de Belges, Jean. *La Concorde des deux langages*. Ed. Jean Frappier. Paris: Droz, 1947.

———. *La Concorde des deux langages et les Epîtres de l'amant vert*. Ed. Marcel Françon. Cambridge, Mass.: Schoenhof, 1964.

———. *La Concorde du genre humain*. Ed. Pierre Jodogne. Brussels: Palais des Académies, 1964.

———. *Jean Lemaire de Belges (um 1473–1515) Dichtungen*. Ed. Erhard Lommatzsch and Max Leopold Wagner. Berlin: Weidmannsche, 1924.

———. *Jean Lemaire de Belges, indiciaire de Marguerite d'Autriche et Jean Perreal, pourtraicteur de l'Eglise de Brou: Documents inédits*. Ed. Etienne Charavay. Paris: Lemerre, 1876.

———. *Œuvres de Jean Lemaire de Belges*. Vols. 1–4. Ed. J. Stecher. Geneva: Slatkine Reprint, 1969. Also see the 1549 edition: Item L2K2548, Bibliothèque Nationale, Paris.

———. *La Plainte du désiré*. Ed. Dora Yabsley. Paris: Droz, 1932.

———. *Le Temple d'honneur et de vertus*. Ed. Henry Hornik. Geneva: Droz, 1957.

Lemoine, J. G. "Autour du tombeau de Philibert le Beau à Brou: une description du projet Perreal-Colombe par Jean Lemaire de Belges." *Revue Belge d'Archéologie et d'Histoire de l'Art* 11.1 (1941): 35–52.

Lubac, Henri de. *L'Exégèse médiévale: les quatre sens de l'écriture, première partie*. Vol. 1. Paris: Aubier, 1959.

Luther, Martin. *Martin Luther's Basic Theological Writings*. Ed. Timothy F. Lull. Minneapolis: Fortress Press, 1989.

McGinn, Bernard. "The Language of Love in Christian and Jewish Mysticism." In *Mysticism and Language*, ed. Steven T. Katz. Oxford: Oxford Univ. Press, 1992.

Margolin, Jean-Claude. "Erasme et le verbe," in *Erasme, l'Alsace et son temps*. Strasbourg: Palais de l'Université, 1971: 87–110.

Marichal, Robert. "L'Attitude de Rabelais devant le néoplatonisme et l'italianisme (*Quart Livre*, ch. IX–XI)." In *François Rabelais: ouvrage publié pour le quatrième centenaire de sa mort, 1553–1953*. Geneva: Droz, 1953.

———. "*Quart Livre*: commentaires." *Etudes Rabelaisiennes* 1 (1956): 151–202.

Marlier, Georges. *Erasme et la peinture flamande de son temps*. Damme, Belgium: Van Maerlant, 1954.

Massaut, Jean-Pierre. *Critique et tradition à la veille de la réforme en France*. Paris: Vrin, 1974.

———. *Josse Clichtove, l'humanisme et la réforme du clergé*. Vols. 1, 2. Paris: Belles Lettres, 1968.

Masters, George Mallary. *Rabelaisian Dialectic and the Platonic-Hermetic Tradition*. Albany: State Univ. of New York Press, 1969.

Menges, Matthew C. *The Concept of Univocity Regarding the Predication of God and Creature According to William of Ockham*. Louvain, Belgium: Nauwelaerts, 1952.

Midali, Mario. *Rivelazione, chiesa, scrittura e tradizione alla iv sessione del concilio di Trento*. Rome: Università Pontificia Salesiana, 1973.

Molinet, Jean. *Cest le romant de la Rose moralisé cler et net translaté de rime en prose par vostre humble Molinet*. Lyon: Guillaume Balsarin, 1503.

―――. *Les Chroniques (1474–1488)*. Vol. 1. Ed. Georges Doutrepont and Omer Jodogne. Brussels: Palais des Académies, 1935.

―――. *Les Faictz et dictz de Jean Molinet*. Ed. Noël Dupire. 2 vols. Paris: Société des Anciens Textes Français, 1936.

Mombaer, Jean. *Rosetum exercitiorum spiritualium et sacrarum*. Zwolle (?), 1494. Paris: Jean Petit, 1510. Douay: Belleri, 1620.

Mondin, Battista. *La Filosofia dell'essere di s. Tommaso d'Aquino*. Rome: Herder, 1964.

―――. *The Principle of Analogy in Protestant and Catholic Theology*. The Hague: Martinus Nijhoff, 1968.

―――. *St. Thomas Aquinas's Philosophy in the Commentary to the Sentences*. The Hague: Martinus Nijhoff, 1975.

―――. "The Theological Use of Analogy." *New Catholic Encyclopedia*. Vol. 1. New York: McGraw-Hill, 1967.

Montaigne, Michel de. *Essais*. Vols. 1–3. Ed. Pierre Villey. Paris: Quadrige/PUF, 1988.

Moody, Ernest A. *The Logic of William of Ockham*. New York: Russell and Russell, 1965.

Munn, Kathleen. *A Contribution to the Study of Jean Lemaire de Belges: A Critical Study of Bio-bibliographical Data, Including a Transcript of Various Unpublished Works*. Geneva: Slatkine, 1975.

Nash, Jerry. "Interpreting 'Parolles degelées': The Humanist Perspective of Rabelais and His Critics." *L'Esprit Créateur* 21.1 (1981): 5–11.

Oberman, Heiko. *The Harvest of Medieval Theology: Gabriel Biel and Late Medieval Nominalism*. Grand Rapids, Mich.: Eerdmans, 1963.

―――. "The Shape of Medieval Thought: The Birthpangs of the Modern Era." In *The Pursuit of Holiness in Late Medieval and Renaissance Religion: Papers from the University of Michigan Conference,* ed. Charles Trinkaus, with Heiko A. Oberman. Leiden: Brill, 1974.

Ockham, William of. *Ockham: Philosophical Writings*. Ed. and trans. Philotheus Boehner. Edinburgh: Nelson, 1957.

―――. *Scriptum in librum primum sententiarum: ordinatio (distinctiones IV–XVIII)*. Vol. 3, *Opera Theologica*. Ed. Girardus I. Etzkorn. Saint Bonaventure, N.Y.: Franciscan Institute Editions, 1977.

―――. *Somme de logique*. Pt. 1. Trans. Joël Biard. Mauvezin, France: Trans-Europ-Repress, 1988.

Olin, John C., ed. *Christian Humanism and the Reformation: Selected Writings.* New York: Harper and Row, 1965.

Opsomer, Carmelia, adapter. *Livre des simples médecines: codex Bruxellensis IV. 1024: A 15th-Century French Herbal.* Trans. Enid Roberts and William T. Stearn. Antwerp: De Schutter, 1984.

O'Rourke-Boyle, M. *Christening Pagan Mysteries: Erasmus in Pursuit of Wisdom.* Toronto: Univ. of Toronto Press, 1981.

Ozment, Steven. *The Age of Reform, 1250–1550: An Intellectual and Religious History of Late Medieval and Reformation Europe.* New Haven: Yale Univ. Press, 1980.

————. *Homo spiritualis: A Comparative Study of the Anthropology of Johannes Tauler, Jean Gerson, and Martin Luther (1509–16) in the Context of Their Theological Thought.* Leiden: Brill, 1969.

————. "Mysticism, Nominalism, and Dissent." In *The Pursuit of Holiness in Late Medieval and Renaissance Religion: Papers from the University of Michigan Conference,* ed. Charles Trinkaus, with Heiko A. Oberman. Leiden: Brill, 1974.

————, ed. *Jean Gerson: Selections from "A Deo exivit," "Contra curiositatem studentium," and "De mystica theologia speculativa."* Leiden: Brill, 1969.

Panofsky, E. *Early Netherlandish Painting: Its Origins and Character.* Cambridge: Harvard Univ. Press, 1953.

————. *Gothic Architecture and Scholasticism.* New York: Meridian, 1985.

Paracelsus the Great. *The Hermetic and Alchemical Writings of Aureolus Philippus Theophrastus Bombast, of Hohenheim, called Paracelsus the Great.* Vol. 1. Ed. Arthur Edward Waite. London: James Elliot, 1894.

Paris, Jean. *Rabelais au futur.* Paris: Seuil, 1970.

Pascoe, Louis B. *Jean Gerson: Principle of Church Reform.* Leiden: Brill, 1973.

Perrat, Charles. "Sur 'Un tas de prognostications de Lovain.'" In *François Rabelais: ouvrage publié pour le quatrième centenaire de sa mort, 1553–1953.* Geneva: Droz, 1953.

Philip of Thaon. *Der Computus des Philipp von Thaün mit einer einleitung über die sprache des autors.* Ed. Eduard Mall. Strasbourg: Trübner, 1873.

Phillips, Stephen H. "Mystic Analogizing and the 'Peculiar Mystic.'" In *Mysticism and Language,* ed. Steven T. Katz. Oxford: Oxford Univ. Press, 1992.

Pinchard, Bruno. *Métaphysique et sémantique: la signification analogique des termes dans les principes métaphysiques suivi de L'Analogie des noms.* Paris: Vrin, 1987.

Plato. *Republic.* Trans. Robin Waterfield. Oxford: Oxford Univ. Press, 1993.

Plattard, Jean. *L'Etat présent des études rabelaisiennes.* Paris: Belles Lettres, 1927.

————. "Rabelais et Mellin de Saint-Gelais." *Revue des Etudes Rabelaisiennes* 9 (1911): 90–108.

————. "Rabelais réputé poète par quelques poètes de son temps." *Revue des Etudes Rabelaisiennes* 10 (1912): 291–304.

Popkin, Richard H. *The History of Skepticism from Erasmus to Spinoza.* Berkeley: Univ. of California Press, 1979.

Pouilloux, Jean-Yves. "Notes sur deux chapitres du 'Quart Livre,' LV–LVI." *Littérature* 5 (1972): 88–94.

Pourrat, Pierre. *Christian Spirituality in the Middle Ages.* Vol. 2. Trans. S. P. Jacques. Westminster, Md.: Newman, 1953.

Préaud, Maxime. *Les Astrologues à la fin du moyen âge.* Paris: Lattes, 1984.

Pseudo-Dionysius, the Areopagite. *The Works of Dionysius the Areopagite.* Pt. 1, *The Divine Names, Mystic Theology, Letters, Etc.* Trans. John Parker. Merrick, N.Y.: Richwood, 1976.

Rabelais, François. *Gargantua.* Ed. Ruth Calder. Geneva: Droz, 1970.

———. *Pantagruel.* Ed. V. L. Saulnier. Geneva: Droz, 1965.

———. *Pantagrueline Prognostication pour l'an 1533.* Ed. Michael Screech. Geneva: Droz, 1974.

———. *Le Quart Livre.* Ed. R. Marichal. Geneva: Droz, 1947.

———. *Le Tiers Livre.* Ed. Michael Screech. Geneva: Droz, 1964.

Rapp, Ernest Gordon, with A. N. Marlow, and Philip Saville Watson with B. Drewery, trans. and eds. *Luther and Erasmus: Free Will and Salvation.* Philadelphia: Westminster, 1969.

Rapp, Francis. *L'Eglise et la vie religieuse en occident à la fin du moyen âge.* Paris: Presses Universitaires Françaises, 1971.

Regnault, Maître, comp. *Le Petit Livret sommaire.* Bibliothèque Nationale de Paris, Nouvelle Acquisitions Françaises 4061. Paris: Regnault, 1498.

Reiss, Timothy. *The Discourse of Modernism.* Ithaca: Cornell Univ. Press, 1982.

Renaudet, Augustin. *La Préréforme et l'humanisme à Paris pendant les premières guerres d'Italie (1494–1517).* Paris: Champion, 1916.

Richter, Bodo L. "The Image of the Temple in the Works of Jean Lemaire de Belges." *Medievalia* 12 (1989): 305–38.

Rigolot, François. "Cratylisme et Pantagruélisme: Rabelais et le statut du signe." *Etudes Rabelaisiennes* 13 (1976): 115–32.

———. "'Enigme' et 'Prophétie': les langages de l'hermétisme chez Rabelais." *Œuvres et Critiques* 11.1 (1986): 37–47.

———. "La Figure de la lettre." *Revue des sciences humaines* 179 (July–Sept. 1980): 47–59.

———. *Les Langages de Rabelais.* Geneva: Droz, 1972.

———. *Poétique et onomastique.* Geneva: Droz, 1977.

———. "Rabelais rhétoriqueur?" *Cahiers de l'Association internationale des études françaises* 30 (1978): 87–103.

———. *Le texte à la renaissance.* Geneva: Droz, 1982.

Ronsard, Pierre de. *Œuvres complètes.* Vol. 3. Ed. Paul Laumonier. Paris: Hachette, 1921.

———. *Ronsard: Les Amours (1552–1584).* Ed. Marc Bensimon and James L. Martin. Paris: Garnier-Flammarion, 1981.

Roques, René. *L'Univers dionysien: structure hiérarchique du monde selon le Pseudo-Denys.* Paris: Aubier, 1954.

Rorty, Richard. *Contingency, Irony, and Solidarity.* Cambridge: Cambridge Univ. Press, 1989.

Rothstein, Marian. "When Fiction Is Fact: Perceptions in Sixteenth-Century France." *Studies in Philology* 83.3 (1986): 359–75.

Rufinus. *The Herbal of Rufinus (De virtutibus herbarum)*. Ed. Lynn Thorndike, assisted by Francis S. Benjamin Jr. Chicago: Univ. of Chicago Press, 1964.

Sacrosancti et œcumenici concilii tridentini, paulo iii, julio iii, et pio iv, pontificibus maximis, celebrati canones et decreta; pluribus annexis ad idem concilium spectantibus. Paris: Gauthier Frères, 1823.

Sainéan, Lazare. *La Langue de Rabelais*. Geneva: Slatkine, 1976.

Saulnier, Verdun L. *Rabelais II: Rabelais dans son enquête–etude sur le "Quart" et le "Cinquième Livre."* Paris: SEDES, 1982.

———. "Le Silence de Rabelais et le mythe des paroles gelées." In *François Rabelais: ouvrage publié pour le quatrième centenaire de sa mort, 1553–1953*. Geneva: Droz, 1953.

Sautman, Francesca. "'Des Vessies pour des lanternes': Villon, Molinet, and the Riddles of Folklore." *Neophilologus* 69 (1985): 161–84.

Scève, Maurice. *Délie*. Ed. Françoise Charpentier. Paris: Gallimard, 1984.

Schmiel, David. *Via Propria and Via Mystica in the Theology of Jean le Charlier de Gerson*. St. Louis: Oliver Slave, 1969.

Screech, Michael. "Emblems and Colours: The Controversy over Gargantua's Colours and Devices (*Gargantua* 8, 9, 10)." In *Mélanges d'histoire du XVIe siècle offerts à Henri Meylan*. Geneva: Droz, 1970.

———. *L'Evangélisme de Rabelais: aspects de la satire religieuse au XVIe siècle*. Geneva: Droz, 1959.

———. *Rabelais*. Ithaca: Cornell Univ. Press, 1979.

———. "The Sense of Rabelais's 'Enigme en Prophétie' (*Gargantua* LVII)." *Bibliothèque d'Humanisme et Renaissance* 18 (1956): 392–404.

———. "Some Aspects of Rabelais's *Almanachs* and of the *Pantagrueline Prognostication* (Astrology and Politics)." *Etudes Rabelaisiennes* 11 (1974): 1–7.

Secretan, Philibert. *L'Analogie*. Paris: PUF, 1984.

Simone, Franco. *Umanesimo, Rinascimento, Barocco in Francia*. Milan: Univ. Mursia, 1968.

Spitzer, Leo. *Linguistics and Literary History: Essays in Stylistics*. Princeton: Princeton Univ. Press, 1948.

———. "Rabelais et les 'rabelaisants.'" *Studi Francesi* 12 (Sept.–Dec. 1960): 401–23.

Sutch, Susie Speakman. "Allegory and Praise in the Works of the Grands Rhétoriqueurs." Ph.D. diss., Univ. of California at Berkeley, 1983.

Telle, E. V. "A propos de la lettre de Gargantua à son fils (*Pantagruel*, chapt. VIII)." *Bibliothèque d'Humanisme et Renaissance* 19 (1957): 217–18.

———. "Thélème et le paulisme matrimonial érasmien: le sens de l'énigme en prophétie." In *François Rabelais: ouvrage publié pour le quatrième centenaire de sa mort (1553–1953)*. Geneva: Droz, 1953.

Tester, S. Jim. *A History of Western Astrology*. Woodbridge, Suffolk, U.K.: Boydell, 1987.

Thibaut, Françisque. *Marguerite d'Autriche et Jehan Lemaire de Belges ou de la littérature et des arts aux Pays-Bas sous Marguerite d'Autriche*. Paris: Leroux, 1888.

Thiry, Claude. "Au Carrefour des deux rhétoriques: les prosimètres de Jean Molinet." In *Du Mot au texte: actes du IIIème colloque international sur le moyen français, Düsseldorf, 17–19 septembre 1980*. Tubingen: Narr, 1982.

———. "Rhétorique et genres littéraires au XVe siècle." In *Sémantique lexicale et sémantique grammaticale en moyen français*, ed. Marc Wilet. Brussels: Vrije Universiteit Brussel, 1979.

Thomas Aquinas. *Aristotle: "On Interpretation," Commentary by St. Thomas and Cajetan (Peri Hermeneais)*. Trans. Jean T. Oesterle. Milwaukee: Marquette Univ. Press, 1962.

———. *The Summa contra gentiles*. Trans. English Dominican Fathers. New York: Benziger Brothers, 1924.

———. *Summa theologiae* . Vol. 1. Trans. Thomas Gilby. Vol. 2. Trans. Timothy McDermott. Cambridge: Blackfriars, 1964.

———. *Summa theologiae*. Vol. 52. Trans. Roland Potter. Cambridge: Blackfriars, 1972.

Thomas de Vio, Cardinal Cajetan. *The Analogy of Names and the Concept of Being*. Trans. Edward Bushinski, with Henry Koren. Pittsburgh: Duquesne Univ. Press, 1953.

Tuve, Rosemond. *Allegorical Imagery: Some Medieval Books and Their Posterity*. Princeton: Princeton Univ. Press, 1966.

Van 'T Sant, Jeannette Theodora Marie. *Le Commentaire de Copenhagen de "L'Ovide moralisé" avec l'édition du septième livre*. Amsterdam: H. J. Paris, 1929.

Vignaux, Paul. *Philosophie au moyen âge, précédé d'une introduction nouvelle et suivi de Lire Duns Scot aujourd'hui*. Albeuve, Switzerland: Castella, 1987.

Weinberg, Florence M. "Comic and Religious Elements in Rabelais's 'Tempête en mer.'" *Etudes Rabelaisiennes* 15 (1980): 129–40.

Wolf, Lothar. "Un Problème de première datation 'Lettres Ytallicques' chez Jean Lemaire de Belges." *Le Français Moderne, Revue de Linguistique Française* 2 (Apr. 1973): 182–85.

Zumthor, Paul. *L' Anthologie des grands rhétoriqueurs*. Paris: Seuil, 1978.

———. *Langue, texte, et énigme*. Paris: Seuil, 1975.

———. *Le Masque et la lumière: la poétique des grands rhétoriqueurs*. Paris: Seuil, 1978.

Index

✣   ✣   ✣

Library of Congress Cataloging-in-Publication Data

Randall, Michael, 1953–
    Building resemblance : analogical imagery in the early French
Renaissance / Michael Randall.
        p.   cm.
    Includes bibliographical references and index.
    ISBN 0-8018-5298-6 (alk. paper)
    1. French literature—16th century—History and criticism.
2. French literature—To 1500—History and criticism.   3. Meaning
(Philosophy) in literature.   4. Molinet, Jean, 1435–1507—Criticism
and interpretation.   5. Lemaire de Belges, Jean, b. 1473—Criticism
and interpretation.   6. Rabelais, François, ca. 1490–1553?—
Criticism and interpretation.   I. Title.
PQ235.R36   1996
840.9′384—dc20   96-2251
                                                              CIP